Our Parents' Lives

Also by Ruth Schwartz Cowan

MORE WORK FOR MOTHER: *The Ironies of Household Technology*
from the Open Hearth to the Microwave

To Nurit, with Thanks

Our Parents' Lives

The Americanization of Eastern European Jews

NEIL M. COWAN

RUTH SCHWARTZ COWAN

Neil M. Cowan

Ruth Schwartz Cowan

Basic Books, Inc., Publishers   *New York*

December, 1989

Library of Congress Cataloging-in-Publication Data

Cowan, Neil M.
  Our parents' lives.

  Includes index.
    1. Jews, East European—United States—
Interviews. 2. Jews—United States—Interviews.
3. Jews—United States—Cultural assimilation.
4. Immigrants—United States—Interviews.
5. Oral history. 6. United States—Ethnic
relations. I. Cowan, Ruth Schwartz. II. Title.
E184.J5C79 1989   973'.04924   88–47900
ISBN 0–465–05425–0

To our past with affection

Marcy H. Cowan and Jennie E. T. Cowan (1898–1968)

Louis E. Schwartz and Betty A. Schwartz

To their future with love

Jennifer Rose, May Deborah, and Sarah Kiva Cowan

*A Jewish neighborhood in Philadelphia,
early twentieth century.*

One generation passeth away, and another generation cometh: but the earth abideth forever.

—Ecclesiastes 1:4

Contents

Acknowledgments

Many people have asked us how a marriage can survive a collaboration on a book. We have often wondered ourselves. Since we cannot imagine how couples managed this feat before the invention of the word processor we begin our acknowledgments with gratitude to the SAMNA Corporation, whose superb software (ranging from SAMNA Word to SAMNA Plus IV) helped us handle our transcripts and drafts without murdering one another. (Divorce, never; murder, perhaps!) Thanks also to the unfortunately anonymous folk at the other end of SAMNA's 800-number in Atlanta who answered our hysterical questions without ever once losing their patience.

Being able to rely on exceedingly competent people also helps. Jim Campbell of Superior Fototech in New York provided the photographic reproductions used in this book; his calm good humor was of enormous help when deadlines loomed. Sam Ferrara and Jorge Alban of Tara Audio, also in New York, supplied the audio cassettes used in the interviews; we are especially grateful to Jorge for the technical advice that allowed us to record hundreds of hours of interviews without one breakdown. Staff people at Charles River Computers in New York City cheerfully assisted with technical support and equipment when we needed it.

Scholarship, as all scholars know, depends on good libraries and supportive librarians. Much of the research for this book was done at the New York Public Library on Forty-second Street: the Reference Room on the third floor and the Jewish Division on the first. Our special thanks to the librarians of the Jewish Division—Norman Gechlik, Claire Dienstag, Ruth Yarden, Nadine Wener, Alexander Gewirtz, Judy Fixler—whose commitment to their profession extended to thinking up suggestions for us even during their off hours. Our chapter on Jewish life in Eastern Europe was enriched by research in the library and archives of the YIVO Institute for Jewish Research, New York City, and we thank Dina Abramowicz, head librarian, for her assistance. Similarly, the chapter on health depended on work we did in the library of the New York Academy of Medicine; William Landers, John Balkema, Michael Ellerby, and Tina Cunnane helped us manage the arcane details of the library's general collection, and Alice Weaver, director of the Rare Book Division, and her assistant Jeffrey Gordon did likewise. Our friend Irving Mauss, a fellow of the Academy, extended his privileges to us, which eased our time there, as his friendship has eased so much else in our lives. Kevin Proffitt, of the American Jewish Archives in Cincinnati, came to our aid, expeditiously and accurately, at a crucial moment in our photo research, when we were beginning to lose hope. So did Victoria Williams of the Amalgamated Clothing Workers of America in New York and Martha Hodges of the New York State School of Industrial and Labor Relations, Cornell University, New York City.

We continue to value the collegiality of many librarians on the staff of the Frank Melville Jr. Memorial Library, State University of New York at Stony Brook. We thank all of the people in the reference room who tolerated our endless questions, pointed us in the right directions, and never complained about the noise our children made as they hunted down titles and call numbers. We are most especially grateful to Richard Feinberg and Barbara Brand for their cheerful encouragement and helpful suggestions. Two members of the history department of SUNY-Stony Brook also patiently answered our frequently ill-formed questions about Eastern Europe: Gary Marker and Ruben Weltsch.

As all scholars know the significance of good libraries, so all authors know the significance of good friends. Many of our friends encouraged us when we were overwhelmed by this project and celebrated with us when it was going well; without their support our marriage might have foundered and the book might never have been written. We are especially grateful to our dear friends Michael and Chris Swirnoff for, respectively, never once sounding put upon when asked to help rescue a lost file late at night or early in the morning, and for patiently acquainting us with the aesthetics of book design. Separately they have been excellent instructors; together, wonderful companions. Phoebe

ACKNOWLEDGMENTS

Hoss and Jo Ann Miller, editors *extraordinaires*, corrected our English and—more importantly—kept us from falling off the track, no matter what. Carole Kessner's conversation and hospitality helped us in equal measure, as did her willingness to correct our Yiddish. We are grateful also for extended conversations with Sandra Silverstein regarding the nature of extended *Yiddish* conversations. Friends who commute with us on the Oyster Bay line of the Long Island Railroad listened to stories from and about this book for four long years and must have occasionally wondered whether they would ever see the finished product. We thank them for repeated kindnesses and consistent good temper in the face of such trials.

Our best supporters, in this and all other endeavors, have been our children: Jennifer Rose, May Deborah, and Sarah Kiva. They have tolerated our compulsions with good cheer (well, most of the time), even when frequently excluded from dinner-table conversation by our endless discussions about *the book*. We thank them for never once going out on strike, charging us with child abuse, or hauling us into family court. We take this opportunity to apologize to them publicly for every minute during which they felt either neglected or ignored—and to tell them, also publicly, that we cannot wait to read (and will, by way of penance, happily do the index for) the work of revenge that they are planning—*Our Parents' Lives: The Saga Continues*.

Finally, a note of deep gratitude to our parents, our aunts and uncles, their friends, their friends' friends, and all of the others who welcomed us to their homes and offices and allowed us to conduct our interviews. They have let us into their private lives, and in so doing have provided future generations with a portrait of American Jews that we consider ourselves privileged to record. With our heads and hearts we hope this personal record has been treated justly and we thank them for their trust.

Prologue

ANOTHER
GENERATION
COMETH

THIS BOOK was conceived during a condolence call in 1984. Ruth's uncle had died, and her aunt and cousin were receiving visitors—sitting shiva, the traditional Jewish ritual—when we arrived. In the middle of the small apartment—mirrors and photographs were covered, a Jewish mourning custom—the widow and her daughter were seated. Their faces were tense, not with grief but with frustration; a tape recorder sat on the coffee table before them—by no means customary.

"I decided I wasn't going to wait another minute to record Mom's stories about her youth," Ruth's cousin explained. "I missed my father's and I don't want to miss my Mom's. The trouble is she isn't giving me what I want, she's not answering my questions."

"Maybe you ought to let me try. I have a feeling that I can do it differently," said Neil, who once interviewed people on his own radio program.

Ruth's cousin got up gladly, and Neil began the first interview of what, many interviews later, turned into this book. He began with a simple question: "What do you remember about your home when you were a child?" The widow's face brightened, and she launched into a detailed description of a tenement apartment.

Four hours and four cassettes later, both interviewer and interviewee were talked out. In the process, Ruth's aunt had told dozens of stories about her childhood and youth. On the way home, as Neil retold some of the stories, Ruth, a trained historian, recognized in them many of the prosaic but telling details that social historians savor, details about the past that can seldom be gleaned from published or official documents.

"There's a book in this," one of us—and we have yet to agree on which it was—said to the other, and our project began. Early on, we decided to interview only people who were part of our parents' generation, Eastern European Jews born, either here or abroad, between 1895 and 1915. We could have interviewed German Jewish Americans, descendants of people who had immigrated from Central Europe in the middle of the nineteenth century, but we decided not to because we suspected that their culture and their stories would be quite different.

The people we interviewed were not chosen at random but were literally our parents, and generically our parents as well: relatives, friends of the family, parents of our friends, parents of acquaintances, people we met in a variety of places—museums, parties, trains and planes, retirement communities, nursing homes. They have only two common denominators: they were the sons and daughters of Eastern European Jews and they were willing to share their memories with us.

Beginning with the simple request "Tell me the earliest memory you have of your childhood," each interview crawled or raced off in whatever direction the speaker found most comfortable. We tried to keep our initial questions deliberately mundane: Did you have a bedroom in your home? How many rooms in the apartment? Was there a toilet? Did you have a *bar mitzvah*? Did you do chores around the house? Elsewhere? Do you remember your first period? Your first date? Did your father have to work on *Shabbos*? Did you ever eat nonkosher food? When, and where?

As each interview moved to the personal ("Tell me about your mother. Your father. What were they really like?"), the response would become more animated—a change of expression or a softer tone of voice, a rapid, heated reply, or a syncopated motion of the hand.

And, quite often, tears and pain. Once it was the memory of a baby, a sibling, who had died seventy years earlier; and another time, of a mother's ministrations—a kind word spoken at a difficult moment, a gentle touch in passing. Several women remembered, angrily, parents playing favorites, love being given to a brother: Sol, Max, Moishe, Joe getting the bed or the bathroom or the schooling or the toys—while Sylvia, Rebecca, Esther, Sophie had to wait or make do. Many were stirred by the memory of a long-dead parent, perhaps one who had lovingly braided long hair every morning; or—contrarily—by the memory of one who had been remote and punitive. People born in Europe became agitated when they recalled watching someone being taunted, maimed, or murdered, or when they told of hiding in hay-barns to avoid rampaging mobs.

To encourage people to unburden themselves, we aimed to elicit memories without forcing a direction, and we made a solemn promise of anonymity. We heard astonishing things, secrets deeply buried, no longer worth keeping now that the actors were long dead. We discovered, for example, that many of our grandparents, while able to tell lengthy stories and complex jokes, were actually uncommunicative with their own children, were tight, closed off. We found this difficult to believe, given the stereotypes we had grown up with about warm, enveloping, supportive, and—above all—talkative Jewish families; but it was repeated so frequently, and by so many different people, that we had to take the assertion seriously. There were other surprising assertions we had to take seriously as well—about deep family conflict, about hatred, about premarital sexuality, about abortions, about dozens of things that parents avoid discussing with their children, today as well as yesterday. Several people agreed to talk with us only on the condition that we would *never* tell their own children what they had said. We kept our promise.

The raw material on our tapes, though rich and provocative, did not turn itself automatically into a book, and the text has been through at least four transmutations. At first we tried to create a collective memoir, a series of vignettes, to let the strong voices of our parents dominate and to keep ourselves, as much as possible, in the background. Surely, we thought, it will be easy to assemble a collage out of such rich material. But this first effort failed. "The stories run too long," our editors said, "and the cast of characters is confusing. Find a theme—some thread to follow, some unifying principle."

We had not intended to handle the material in that fashion—too academic, we thought, too argumentative; but we tried. Out came a new box of computer disks, and we reorganized—this time by subject: life in Europe, schooling, sex, health, careers, and so forth. Starting at the beginning, we tried a chapter on life in Europe, and from it emerged a theme—trauma. We felt that those of our parents who had been born in Europe had often been emotionally wounded by the experience of growing up not just as outsiders but as "susceptible" outsiders: that all those fistfights with the *goyim*, all those pogroms ordered by the czar and carried out by the *goyim*, all those dead and wounded relatives, all those hours spent hiding in terror must have left ineradicable psychic scars.

We hastened to the library to read up on childhood trauma, and started a second chapter: housing. But try as we would, that second chapter could not be shaped to fit our theme: housing was not a matter, apparently, that had traumatized the people we interviewed. Some actually remembered with affection the "primitive" dwellings and "horrendous" tenements of their youth: crowded, yes, but miserable, no—and sometimes lots of fun. The theme of this second chapter seemed to be nostalgia. The third topic we broached—schooling—suggested yet another theme: neither trauma nor nostalgia, but myth. Some of the people we interviewed not only hated school but also did not think it had helped them succeed—in fact, it had been positively a hindrance in later life. And so we had another theme: myth versus reality, the much-vaunted people of the book versus those immigrants who had succeeded without benefit of education.

Back to the editors we went. "Too many themes," they said. "This version wanders all over the map. Simplify," they cautioned, "and while you're at it, try to figure out what makes the Jews distinctive, different from other immigrant groups. Nothing you've written so far couldn't also be written about the Italians, the Poles, or the Irish. Aren't the Jews different?" "We're not sociologists," we grumbled to each other as we left the editors' office. "Not likely that we'll solve that particular puzzle." So we ignored their advice and forged ahead, assembling more of the mundane details, each in its appropriate chapter—sex, health, child care, careers—until we reached the chapter on religion.

And there we found our clue. The immigrant Jews—our parents and grandparents, the men and women we interviewed—were different precisely because they were Jews. They assimilated to a culture whose everyday structure was overwhelmingly Christian, a paradoxical situation that did not exist for Irish, Italian, Greek, German, or Swedish immigrants. Judaism is a religion of the mundane (no accident, then, that we started out with questions about mundane matters!), governing every action, as the liturgy says, "from when thou risest up, till when thou liest down." The clothes you wear (long-sleeved dresses, skullcaps, caftans), the food you eat (no clams, no pork, no squid), the order in which your food is consumed (no milk until six hours after meat), the way you dress your hair (*payess* for young men, wigs for married women): these are all subject to the dictates of religious law (*halakha*) or to the equally pervasive dictates of cultural tradition (often, for the Jews of Eastern Europe, called *Yiddishkeit*). A young Jew, growing up in America in the early decades of this century, was continually being reminded—every waking hour of the day, quite literally from head to toe—of his or her Jewishness in a Christian world, of his or her separateness. Learning to eat, let's say, bacon was no problem for most immigrant boys, but for a Jewish boy it was an act of rebellion, leading his parents to believe that he was being delivered over to the Enemy.

In those years, the United States was developing a strongly secular culture: proud and boisterous. At the turn of the twentieth century, the nation was passing out of the first phase of industrialization and into the second. The frontier had closed; land was no longer cheap; farming was being mechanized. The smoke of the steel mills, the speed of the railroads, the hum of millions of sewing machines—they all testified to the nation's exploding productive capacity. The geographic frontier was gone, but an economic frontier remained: a growing population, a mass national market.

Industrialization had brought with it also powerful new ways to create that market, to address all those consumers: cheap daily newspapers with lithographed drawings, glossy magazines illustrated with photographs, movies that cost only a nickel, and, later, radio programs that were entirely free once one had purchased a set. A whole new business had developed since the middle of the nineteenth century—advertising—devoting all of its energy and its considerable financial resources to making people admire and desire consumer goods, indispensable adjuncts to the American way of life.

The people we interviewed, Eastern European Jewish Americans born between 1895 and 1915, were subjected, in their youth, to the first broad effort to create a unified national market. The city where many of the immigrants lived—New York—was the communications capital of the world, but the impact of the new media was felt just as strongly in the other metropolitan centers of the country: Chicago, Boston, Baltimore, Philadelphia, St. Louis. While the authors of advertising copy were trying to sell products—shoe polish and scouring powder, perfume and pipe tobacco—they were also, perhaps inadvertently, selling something else, something immigrant youths were eager to buy into: that is, being an American. The *Ladies' Home Journal* sold like latkes on Delancy Street—and also on Commonwealth Avenue, the Grand Concourse, and Market Street.

To immigrant youths, the newspaper and the magazines, the movies and the radio program were primers, teaching them to become Americans by showing them how to walk and talk and dress and act like Americans: to drink Maxwell House Coffee out of a cup instead of tea out of a glass; to chew gum; to hold a cigarette between two fingers as movie stars did; to apply lipstick as Clara Bow did; to imitate the English pronunciation of radio announcers; to make up a bed not with one but with two sheets, as the advertisements suggested.

In secular and Christian America, factories and retail shops were open on Saturdays and closed on Sundays: How, then, to observe *Shabbos*? Nutritious foods, the kinds with vitamins and minerals, the kinds the doctors recommended, were packed in cans by strangers in faraway places, according to unknown rules: How, then, to observe *kashrut*? A boy had to cut his *payess* in order to apply for a job; a girl, to put on lipstick to work at Macy's. And so on, and so on, ad infinitum, as pieces of the past were irretrievably lost.

As we pored over our interview transcripts, they began to reveal something else: the significance of Yiddish. Yiddish is a blend of Hebrew, medieval German, Polish, Russian, and now English; it is the language spoken uniquely by Ashkenazic Jews, who derive from Eastern and Central Europe; it is also the unique designator of the culture these Jews had developed over the centuries. Yiddish and *Yiddishkeit* distinguish Ashkenazic Jews from the Sephardic descendants of the Jews who lived in Spain, Portugal, and North Africa during the Middle Ages. Most of the people we interviewed slipped out of English and into Yiddish without thinking; even some of those who were born in the United States call Yiddish their *mama-loshen*, their mother tongue. While they will argue with each other about how a word should be pronounced (the Galitzianas—from Galicia—despising the pronunciation of the Litvaks—from Lithuania) or how a phrase should be transliterated into English (there being, grievously, no Yiddish equivalent of *Webster's International* or *Oxford English Dictionary*), all agree that Yiddish expresses something about themselves, *Yiddishkeit*, that cannot be communicated in any other language. How odd, we thought, that people who regard themselves as wholeheartedly American should still feel most comfortable in a language other than English. How strange that people who have repudiated so many other aspects of their past still cling to the rudiments of *Yiddishkeit*.

Yet in America, *Yiddishkeit* has proved useful to the Jews from Eastern Europe; indeed, we have come to believe that it contains part of the secret of their success on these shores. If we think of our parents' generation as one historical river, flowing through time, and American culture as another, then it is possible to say that the tiny stream of Eastern European immigrant Jewish culture met the big river of American culture at an ideal moment for both—at a moment when the river needed, and was willing to accept (if occasionally grudgingly), precisely what the stream had to offer. The river abounded in consumer goods; the stream, in experts—skilled over the centuries—at getting goods to market.

What the United States needed—and could pay for—in the years between the Panic of 1893 and the Depression of 1929, the years in which the immigrants were arriving in record numbers, was not only a good five-cent cigar but also inexpensive, mass-produced ladies' underclothes, electric irons, porcelain-coated cast-iron bathtubs, and machine-made noodles. The kinds of goods that sell in high enough volume to make a small profit on each item for the manufacturer, but do not need a huge capital investment to produce; the kinds of goods that need jobbers and wholesalers and retailers in order to be sold. Just the kinds of goods Jews had been accustomed to making, moving, and selling all over Eastern Europe for dozens of generations. Small wonder that even those among our parents who have chucked all vestiges of religious observances still wish to preserve something of Jewish culture, of *Yiddishkeit*. *Yiddishkeit* in America was, to many Eastern European Jews, of more practical value than Orthodoxy.

What makes our parents' generation unique, we think, is the intense emotional conflict in which many of its members were caught: an unremitting battle between the future and the past, between assimilation and tradition, how to become American while remaining Jewish. Caught in this dilemma, some of our parents ended up ambivalent. While our tape recorder managed to catch that ambivalence, as we have tried to let our text reflect, it caught something else as well. Some of our parents managed to stand up straight and straddle that dilemma: courageously and triumphantly, they asserted and defined themselves, encouraged by the paradox instead of squashed by it. Immigrant Jewish youth managed to create a new, Jewish-American culture—an adventure whose story we have tried to capture in these pages.

Our book contains three voices. The first is ours, providing the introductions and the transitions needed for coherence. The second voice comes from documents of the period. Since memories can be fallible, we have, wherever it proved possible and reasonable to do so, bolstered them with documents—newspaper accounts, advertisements, a reformer's polemics, a physician's advice.

The third and most important voice (actually, many voices, not just one) belongs to the men and women we interviewed, members of a generation swiftly passing from the scene, droplets in the small stream that has profoundly shaped the mighty river it entered some eighty or ninety years ago. These are the people who traveled from the Old World to the New, from tiny villages in Eastern Europe to giant cities, from wood-burning stoves to gas ranges, from *cheders* to public schools, from an established church to religious toleration, from almost official anti-Semitism to almost equal opportunity. They altered that new world, and it altered them. They produced us, and their world produced ours. Hence our effort to convey their voices and their stories.

There are a few groups of this generation with whom we do not deal. Among these are Jews who made their living as writers or could be classified as intellectuals. Much has already been written about the immigration and assimilation experiences of such people, and we believe that other (and larger) segments of the Jewish population deserve attention. We also say little about politics. While the immigrant Jewish generation was active in mainstream party politics, in socialist and communist politics, and in the labor movement, Jewish politics in this period has nonetheless been analyzed by many historians. In any event, most of the people we interviewed were fundamentally apolitical. Finally, we have not considered the impact on this generation of the Depression, the New Deal, and the Second World War, preferring to concentrate on patterns of daily life.

Before we begin, however, we ought properly to say a few words about names and numbers. What lies behind the name *Eastern European*? Wars have been fought over that apparently trivial question, and millions of people have died in their wake. During the period about which we write, all of Eastern Europe was contested territory. Poland had belonged to Russia since early in the nineteenth century (and did not become an independent nation until just after the First World War); yet the Polish Jews we interviewed (even those who emigrated before the war) emphatically referred to themselves as Polish—not Russian—in part, we suppose, because the language they spoke (aside from Yiddish) was Polish. Galicia, which is a region, not a nation, belonged partly to Russian Poland and partly to Austria-Hungary before 1918; but the people we interviewed shortcircuited the whole matter and just called themselves "Galitzianas." The Ukraine, in which many Jews lived, was unquestionably part of Russia—except in the chaotic years between 1917 and perhaps 1921 when the Whites, the Reds, and the Ukrainian nationalists were battling each other for supremacy in the region. In like manner, Rumanian and Bessarabian Jews were caught between contending national forces before the First World War caused the destruction of the conglomerate that was Austria-Hungary. Since making linguistic sense out of this geopolitical chaos is unquestionably difficult, we have throughout this text—since geopolitics is not our main concern—glossed over the difficulties with the general rubric *Eastern Europe*.

Statistics is also not a main concern. It would be nice to know precisely how many Jews emigrated from Eastern Europe between 1880 and 1930, just as it would be to know the real size of the population that our sample of one hundred interviews is intended to represent. We cannot be certain of either number because even those who specialize in such numbers cannot be certain of them. Since the governments of Eastern Europe did not make regular or thorough censuses, we can only estimate the size of the Jewish population that was divided between Russia and Austria-Hungary before the First World War. The government of the United States, for a different reason, cannot tell us precisely how many Jews immigrated. Until the 1890s, immigration was handled by the states, not the federal government; and upon taking over immigration, the federal government became, for constitutional reasons, careful not to inquire into the religious affiliation of immigrants. And since we can know neither how many Jews arrived nor how their birth rate compared with the general population, we cannot know with any precision how many immigrant children grew to adulthood on these shores and how many children the immigrants had after they got here. Suffice it to say that estimates for the number of Jews who arrived between 1881 (when a string of devastating pogroms began) and 1923 (when Congress closed the door by slapping on restrictive quotas) range from three million to five million—tiny compared with the total population of the United States in those days (almost ninety-two million in 1910).

Not many people in the great scheme of things, but they deserve our attention nonetheless. They are our parents, both literally and figuratively. Mothers and fathers to some of us, they are also mothers and fathers of this nation, parents to the society that has nurtured so many of us so well. The lessons they have to teach deserve to be heard by the children to whom they have given so much. The promised land they sought for themselves, and also for us, was worth the trek. This book is meant to be a testament from the past, to the future, of our gratitude to our parents and to this country in which they, and we, have flourished.

A Note on the Text

IN ORDER to protect the anonymity of the people we interviewed, we have changed people's names and various identifying details in their stories. In doing this, we have tried to remain both historically and demographically sensible, transforming an Isaac into an Aaron perhaps, but not into a Jason or a Lance; moving someone from Boston to Philadelphia perhaps, but not from Chicago to Paterson or New London. Further to protect anonymity, but also to assure readability, we have created composite characters: defining types of people and then merging several individual voices into one character who represents the type—a professional who was born in the United States, for example, or a factory worker who was born and lived abroad until her teens.

With one exception, all transcriptions from tape were done by us. Interjections such as *uh* and words that became repetitive were deleted. In adding punctuation, we tried to make it fit the rhythms of a person's speech. Our questions were edited out, along with such phrases as "No, you haven't got it quite right," which were clearly responses to our questions.

A passage chosen for our text was subjected to further editing and refining of punctuation. Since people rarely speak in full sentences, we dropped sentence fragments that seemed diversionary. Most of the people we interviewed were fond of digressing as they spoke; one story might be interrupted midstream by another story or an extended comment that seemed relevant to the speaker. When those digressions seemed relevant to the point we were trying to make, we left them in, but occasionally felt that they had to be deleted in order to preserve the attention (perhaps even the sanity) of readers. We retained unique intonations and special grammatical patterns wherever we could, but English is not Yiddish—and the tapes will inevitably be a more accurate record of Yinglish (as Leo Rosten calls it) than our text.

xxiv

A NOTE ON THE TEXT

One linguistic pattern deserves special attention. In doing the transcriptions, we noticed that the speakers seemed to shift, almost at random, between present and past tenses. We have not "corrected" those shifts, especially because we noticed that they were not, in fact, random; many such shifts occurred when an emotional corner had been turned. Thus, although we cannot provide the facial expressions and the tones of voice we saw and heard during our interviews, we can provide the changes of tense, and we urge our readers to notice them.

A few passages in the first four chapters come not from our interviews but from transcriptions of interviews conducted, in the late 1970s, by our friend Lucille Brown Hershenhart and Stephen Berk, her colleague at Union College (Schenectady, New York). Some of these transcriptions belong to Union College, and some to the American Jewish Committee; we use them with the gracious permission of both institutions and of Lucille Hershenhart. The sources of passages that derive from her transcriptions are provided in the endnotes; here again, in the interest of anonymity, we do not give the real name of the person interviewed. As with our own interview material, Mrs. Hershenhart's has been merged into the composite characters. We are grateful to Lucille Hershenhart for lending us her copies of the transcripts for extended periods; our understanding of life in the shtetls and cities of Eastern Europe would have been much the poorer without her help.

Our Parents' Lives

WE have used pseudonyms for all of the people we have interviewed as well as for the names of the people the interviewees refer to or speak about, whether they be relatives or friends. All public names have been kept. In all but one instance, we have combined more than one interview into a single voice and created composites. The names of the cities where they live have been changed. The gender has remained the same. No other changes have been made that affect the substance of the interviews.

1

"DANGEROUS JUST TO BE": LIFE IN THE OLD COUNTRY

AT THE TURN OF the twentieth century, several million Jews lived in Eastern Europe. Roughly four million lived in Russia, another million or so in Poland (which was then governed by Russia), and perhaps another million in Czechoslovakia, Rumania, and Hungary, parts of the Austro-Hungarian empire. These Jewish communities were very old. Medieval Jewish folktales ascribe the first settlement of Jews in the areas around the Black Sea to the period of the First Exile (*c.* 590 B.C.) when the combined forces of the Babylonians and Assyrians drove the Israelites out of their ancient Middle Eastern homeland. At that time, some Jewish refugees went west (to Egypt); others went east (to what is now Iran and Iraq); others may well have headed north, settling in the Caucasus. Even if the folktales exaggerate, various Greek inscriptions indicate beyond doubt that Jewish communities flourished on the northern shores of the Black Sea as early as the first century of the modern era.

Few areas of the globe have had as troubled a history as these segments of Eastern Europe: tribal invasions, religious strife, geopolitical machinations have all taken their toll on the inhabitants of the area, century after century. Not infrequently, the Jews—being both different and separate—were persecuted, especially when Christians ruled their territory, and especially when times were bad: they were refused the right to do business; evicted from their homes there; murdered by riotous crowds at one time; burned by order of religious or secular authorities at another. Through it all, until the twentieth century, the Jewish communities of Eastern Europe managed not just to survive but also to flourish.

Separated for many centuries from their co-religionists in other parts of Europe, Africa, and the Middle East (the *Sephardim*), these Jews of Eastern Europe (the *Ashkenazim*) created their own vernacular language, Yiddish, a blend of medieval German and Hebrew. Under, over, around, and through this special language, they also developed their own unique culture, *Yiddishkeit*. Ashkenazic Jews do not pronounce Hebrew quite the same way that Sephardic Jews do;* they have their own characteristic liturgy, their own ritualistic practices (the Ashkenazim, for example, refuse to name their children after someone who is still alive, while Sephardim are encouraged to do so), and their own ways of doing things, of expressing emotion: the gestures they make with their hands, the musical keys they prefer to sing in, the way they raise their children.

Aside from their vernacular language and their religion, the Jews of Eastern Europe also shared a similar social location: the middle of the Eastern European socioeconomic scale. As soon as the Christians came to dominate in Eastern Europe, they sought ways to keep Jews (and other "infidels") from owning land, the single most important economic resource in an agricultural society. As a result of this longstanding prohibition, the Jews of Eastern Europe were neither peasants nor aristocrats. Instead, they occupied the commercial rungs in between: acting as agents for large landholders, trading in cattle, keeping inns, lending money, carting grain, tailoring, carpentering, baking. As the long arm of industrialization began to stretch down the Vistula and up the Danube, the Jews also began to work in factories—and to own them.

* The Ashkenazic Jews pronounce as *s* what the Sephardim pronounce as *t*; hence, *Shabbot* becomes *Shabbos*, and *Sukkot, Sukkos.*

4

Yet whatever common history, common culture, and common enemies they may have shared, by the turn of the twentieth century the
Eastern European Jews were in other ways diverse. Some were rich;
others "made do"; and others, probably the majority, were grindingly
poor. Some clung tenaciously to their ancient religious traditions; some
had wandered into apostasy, atheism, and assimilation. Some, especially the women, were functionally illiterate; others were superbly
well educated in the classic texts of Judaism; yet again, others had acquired, although the acquisition had not been easy, extensive secular
and professional education. Most were, like many of their descendants,
apolitical; but some were socialists and even revolutionaries; and perhaps among the wealthiest bankers, there may have even been one or
two monarchists. No easy generalization—beyond *Yiddishkeit*—defines the Jews of Eastern Europe at the beginning of the twentieth
century.

"In the Fireplace": Where They Lived

Nowhere is this diversity better illustrated than in the realm of demog-
raphy. Many American descendants of Eastern European Jews believe
that their ancestors came from tiny rural towns—*shtetls* or, more accurately, *shtetlech*—insular villages that had had nothing but Jewish residents from time immemorial. While it is true that the shtetl may have
been the oldest type of Jewish community, and the one most influential
in defining Yiddish culture, it is not true that the majority of Eastern
European Jews still lived there in the last decades of the nineteenth
century and the early decades of the twentieth. Many Jews, for example, lived in rural towns, large and small, with mixed populations: Jews
in one block of houses, Christians in another—neighbors, trading partners, constantly in contact. Still other Jews—and some authorities now
believe they were the majority—were urban, residents of Warsaw,
Odessa, Lodz, Riga, Vilna, Vienna, even Moscow and St. Petersburg.
Indeed, by the beginning of the twentieth century, the Jewish populations of Eastern European cities had expanded so explosively that they
could no longer be confined to a special, ghettoized neighborhood.
Sadie Rehstock, one such urbanized Jew, was born in Warsaw in 1901:

5

I was born right opposite the Citadel, we called it the Citadel, an armory, for cavalry, as they had horses there. [The Citadel had been built in the nineteenth century; it was also a jail.] As in all the houses then, we had a balcony. My earliest memory: I must have been three years old and I sat on the balcony with my grandmother. When all of a sudden, from one end of the long street I saw a huge mass of people. It seemed to me that they were all dressed in black, marching down toward us, toward this armory, and at the head was a red flag. [Perhaps a demonstration during the Revolution of 1905.] And when they came opposite our house, my grandmother pulled me into the house and closed the shutters. And that was my earliest memory.

The whole area was a slum area. We lived on the ground floor, and the apartment faced the courtyard. It consisted of a little corridor, you open the door into a corridor, a small corridor, and that led to a kitchen on the left-hand side, and opposite the front door was a large room, and then there was a smaller room out of the larger room, a door leading into a smaller bedroom. The kitchen had a stove. It was iron, black, and it used wood and coal, I guess. The first time I saw gas was in America.

The children played in the courtyard. I saw my first Punch and Judy show. When we came to America and they talked about puppets, it was nothing new to me. I saw the performers do that in the courtyard. A huge gate let the performers in. People would come and sell ice cream in the courtyard. The mothers would throw down coins, and the children would run and get the ice cream and take it from the man if they were already playing in the courtyard. Or the children would run down the stairs with coins their mother had given them.

The kitchen floors were washed every Friday for the Sabbath and then white sand would cover the floor. A man would come into the courtyard with a huge bucket, and he would call out in Polish—and I don't remember the [Polish] words—"White sand, white sand," and someone would come with a container to buy the sand.

Gypsies would come into the courtyard.* There was a big rumor about gypsies that they stole everything in sight, including children.

---

* Gypsies were the only nomadic peoples left in Europe in the twentieth century. They had arrived from India in the fourteenth century and were virtually wiped out by the Nazis in the Holocaust. They often camped in courtyards at night, partly to find temporary shelter, partly to peddle their wares.

People would hang out their pots and pans on nails—or brooms, or whatever they wanted to dry quickly. They were also rumored to kidnap children. And the cry was "Tsigayner!" and that meant gypsies. The women would pull in anything that was hanging out the windows, and the children would run inside.

In our apartment there was a very large room, used as a dining room, a bedroom, and a workroom. There were two beds for our parents, one on one side and one on another side. I slept in a bed sort of at right angles to my parents' beds. There was a sheet drawn in front of my bed right across the room. That was the privacy.

There was another room that my mother rented. We rented it to a whole family: a mother, a father, a daughter about my age, and there was also a son, but he was a mental patient. He was very seldom home; he was in an institution. I remember once when they came for him because he was violent. They tied him up with a rope. The family used the kitchen. They would eat separately in their own room with a table and dishes. Their whole room was about as large as our kitchen. They kept food in their room and ate in their room.

I think my mother went shopping every single day. The kosher butcher shop was right around there. There were stores with no door, just an open space: a butcher shop with a butcher block, a round one, was standing in the doorway. I remember seeing someone standing there and chopping with a cleaver. She always bought live fish and kept it in a huge kettle, a huge round tub, and it swam in there until she was ready to chop its head off and cook it.

In contrast to Sadie Rehstock, Jennie Grossman and Morris Hochstadt, brother and sister, were shtetl Jews. They came from a small rural village, Lulieniec, which was Polish in their day (Polish was the language spoken by the non-Jewish population of the surrounding countryside) but is now part of the Soviet Union. Morris was born just past the turn of the century; Jennie, a few years later. Their father was a carpenter; like many carpenters, he traveled during the week (most likely there was not enough work to occupy him in his home village) and returned for the Sabbath.

MORRIS HOCHSTADT: *As a child, to me that house was—well, I lived there, there was nothing special. The floor was plain wooden boards,*

7

slats. I remember they were roughly made, and there was earth in between too, plain earth so that if you walked in you walked on the boards but there was also plain earth. The whole house didn't have more than three bedrooms if I remember: my father and my mother, and the young children, and the grandparents.

They had their own bedroom, the grandparents, and my parents had a bedroom, and the children had a bedroom, and there were beds in what you would call the living room, but it was a workshop because my grandfather Wolf Meyer was a harness maker, and he dealt with the peasants—made harnesses for their horses. So they used to come in to Wolf, I remember, once a month, to check on their harnesses.

We also had a little room in that house, the kitchen, an oven, and we'd bake. On top, the oven was flat. My grandfather used to climb on top of the oven and sleep there because it was warm from the cooking, especially on weekends, where you had the fire going all Friday and Saturday. I remember sleeping with him up there. He used to go up there and sleep. With me it was a big deal to go up there and sleep. It was something different just to sleep with grandfather. I think he went up there because he was advanced in age and the house probably wasn't very warm. He used to get up early in the morning and say his prayers. As kids it seemed he went, "mm ummm mmmmmm," like this. And I remember he used to put us to sleep like that, too: the buzzings. He used to get up before the sun came up and start saying his morning prayers. Later on, when the sun came out, he first went to the synagogue; these were just the preliminary prayers.

JENNIE GROSSMAN: I remember the windows, thick windows, the windows with the glass that when you looked down you saw ridges. That used to be a form of play for me, for I would stand near these windows and move my head up and down, and I'd see the yard change, and it was very fascinating. I wove all sorts of stories; later on I discovered it was fairy tales. I remember, too, we had some cows. Every evening they would come back. I hated milk ever since. I hated the warm milk. I was never able to drink milk until skim milk came on the market. I could not stand that rich foamy stuff. Never had it. And even now I put an ice cube in my milk.

Then I remember a room, a huge room, and I remember partitions hanging, fabric sort of partitioning off sleeping areas. I slept with my sister Edith. *Poppa would build a* sukkah *[temporary booth in which to celebrate* Sukkot, *the autumn holiday of thanksgiving] on the outside, and that was it; the* matsos *[unleavened bread] we baked in the community bakery; they all did. The toilet outside, outside. I had a cold* tush. *If that's all that is available, you survive. You don't think about it, you don't know any better.*

And also I remember the kitchen. It had a big fireplace, a pripitshik. *On the back end of it, there was a ledge, and when it was cold the children could get up there and cuddle up and lie there. It could have been five feet wide. For little kids to get up there and snuggle up. I remember my mother boiling things and cooking things in the fireplace with a swing iron bar. She had big heavy pots and she would make the* cholent *[stew made with carrots] that way. The Saturday dish, you know, you have it cooking all day. All I remember is the fire always going and the huge wooden table with wooden benches, that was our everyday eating. But for the Sabbath there was a table set in the other room, in the big room.*

Don't you know the song about the pripitshik? *I can sing it for you.*

"Oyfn Pripitshik" ("In the Fireplace") is not, strictly speaking, a folk melody but rather a song written by a Polish Jew who emigrated to America—Mark M. Warshawsky (1840–1907). It evokes memories of the characteristically Eastern European brick fireplace/stove that was the heart of a shtetl household but was not duplicated either in the cities of Eastern Europe or in America. "Oyfn Pripitshik" is the song most likely to bring tears of nostalgia to the eyes of anyone steeped in Yiddish-American culture and born before 1920; discovered by Sholom Aleichem, the music was used as a theme in a movie based on the life of George Gershwin.*

> A flame burns in the fireplace,
> The room warms up.
> As the teacher drills the children in
> The aleph-bet.

---

* During the Holocaust, "Oyfn Pripitshik" became a ghetto song, with the words slightly altered: "At the ghetto wall a fire burns, the surveillance is keen." Recently the song has recurred, also slightly altered, among refusniks in the Soviet Union: "Even should they beat you or throw you on the pyre, repeat 'komets-alef-o.' "

Remember, dear children, what you are learning here.
Repeat it again and again.
Kometz-aleph is pronounced "o."
Learn dear children with great eagerness
So I am bidding you
Whoever will be first in learning [to read the Jewish letters]
he will receive a little banner.
When you grow older you will understand
That this alphabet contains
The tears and weeping of our people.
When you grow weary and burdened with exile,
You will find comfort and strength
Within this Jewish alphabet!
Look into these letters.

Oyfn pripitshik brent a fayerl,
Un in shtub iz heys.
Un der rebe lernt kleyne kinderlekh
Dem alef beyz.
Zet zhe, kinderlekh, gedenkt zhe, tayere, Vos ir lernt do,
Zogt zhe nokh a mol un take nokh a mol: Komets-alef-o!
Lernt, kinder, mit groys kheyshek,
Azoy zog ikh aykh on,
Ver s'vet gikher fun aykh kenen ivre, Der bakumt a fon.
Az ir vet, kinder, elter vern,
Vet ir aleyn farshteyn,
Vifl in di oysyes lign trern,
Un vi fil geveyn.
Az ir vet, kinder, dem goles shlepn,
Oysgemutshet zayn,
Zolt ir fun di oysyes koyekh shepn,
Kukt in zey arayn![1]

Tess Egrovsky, on the other hand, lived in a "mixed town," a place inhabited by both Christians and Jews:

I was born in 1902. I lived in a small town in the Ukraine, in Podolia Gubornia [a province]—Kalus, the town was called. It was a wonderful town, a very wealthy little town, we were about five hundred families, but we had what you would call in America a resort place that people used to come to us from all over Russia, like you go here in the country. Like it was a healing resort—pine trees. Very sick people used to come and stay there over the summer. We also had a vineyard. They came from the biggest towns in Russia, and that, of course, was very profitable for the town.

My father died when I was very young, probably four years old. The only thing I remember about him is what my mother told me; I don't even remember the funeral. After he died, my mother was left with seven, eight children, but we had plantations, tobacco plantations. We used to rent the fields from a Christian, a Polish high *mache* [someone with status], who had a lot of land. He actually owned part of towns there where the gentiles lived. We were very friendly. My mother dealt with him for many years, and he had only one little girl, and we were the same age, and whenever we came up, whenever work had to be done, he didn't know what to do for us; he used to make spreads for us, the most wonderful dinners. From him my mother would rent fields, and we planted tobacco, and that's how my mother made a living. There were a lot of wealthy Christians who used to deal with my mother. We had all kinds of fields, at different times, different kinds: tobacco, corn, peanuts, and I don't know what you call it in English, you make oil from it [probably rapeseed]. Sometimes she had partners and sometimes alone she rented the fields.

I don't remember what my father did, but I know one thing, that he built a beautiful home, a brand-new home. My father went to a different shtetl and ordered someone to come and build a house, and it was a new house. The other houses were plain old houses, but we had two porches, one in the back of the house and one in the front. Our house was brick. The other houses were painted, I think. It was a long street. The other houses had porches on the second floor, and you had to walk up to the porches on the outside and walk into the house.

He bought furniture from the biggest cities. We had a very large room that here is called a living room, a front room, a *zoll*, the main room; a master bedroom was right next to it, and from the main room you can go into the kitchen, the dining room, the *stalava*, an eating room, whatever you want to call it. And from that room another room, a child's room, another big bedroom with two beds in each bedroom.

In the kitchen was a stove, a built-in stove, a European-type stove, with coal, with wood. We had working cabinets with doors. The top of the cabinets were used as a working area. Baking bread, preparing food, for Passover you had to bake, we baked from the stove. It was made out of bricks, and then painted over with paint; they had a different name for it, but I would call it lime. We didn't eat in the kitchen, we ate only in the dining room. Wood was on the floors. All the house, parquet wood, and you covered them with carpeting.

The windows were big, double like here, one big glass but double, you could open it up and down just like here, you could open from the bottom to the top and the top down to the bottom. No small panes, large panes. In wintertime we put on storm windows, on the inside were storm windows, inside not outside, one pane on top and one pane below. It covered the whole window. Our front room had two large windows; actually going down the steps we could look into the house in those two windows. The other wall to the side street had three large windows, and you could not look in from the outside because they were away from the sidewalk. We had a fence all around.

The house that we lived in was a big house. We were three girls— four girls but one was married—and three boys. The girls had their own room. My oldest brother I really don't remember. When he got married, my mother was pregnant with me and when I was born, he left for Argentina. I never saw him; we used to correspond, sure, but I don't know him. He went because he didn't want to go into the army, to serve for the czar, so he left.

The children who did not sleep in the children's room slept in the living room. We had two couches that opened up to sleep, they were made from leather, a sofa, when it opened up you were able to put away your linens, some clothes in the top, like here you use your dresser, there we used the sofa that you slept on. We had movable closets. We had mirrors, family pictures, not paintings—no paintings—and two beautiful mirrors.

We also had wonderful places to go bathing, swimming. We had a mill in the city, and in the back of the mill—it was worked with water—there was a pond where people used to go swimming. Of course, men were separate and ladies were separate; in Europe they separate. We were wearing something, but some people were bathing nude. We used to go bathing summertime; in wintertime we had to use whatever we had in the house.

You are making me homesick. If I had this house here, how happy I would be instead of living in an old jalopy apartment, that is what I think comparing it with my home. It is only too bad I had to leave it in such a peculiar way with a pogrom [murderous anti-Semitic riot] and a war and all. If I could have the house that I left in Europe here, I would be the happiest person in the world, because that house is comparable to any private home you see here in America. It was a beautiful house, a comfortable house, and a happy house until the revolution and the war started.

"Friends or Enemies": Their Christian Neighbors

Even in the most insular shtetls, Eastern European Jews could not avoid contact with the Christians who were their neighbors. Christians often worked as servants in Jewish households, even though the practice was proscribed by law. Christian peasants came, regularly, to the shtetls to trade; Christian landlords, to collect their rents and otherwise manage their estates. In the cities and mixed towns, Jewish and Christian children played together in the streets, while their parents did business in the shops and the marketplaces. Christian apprentices sometimes worked for Jewish craftsmen (although rarely the other way round); and Jewish bankers, large and small, underwrote Christian enterprises, large and small. However much they all might have wished to keep their distance from each other, economic and physical reality made the gaps rather small, often breached.

Like all neighbors, the Christians and Jews of Eastern Europe were sometimes good friends and sometimes not, more often not. Both parties were caught in a historical imbalance that bred enmity between them. Since the Middle Ages, Christians had been "in charge," and Jews had been "different." The Jews did not go to church or celebrate Christmas; they spoke a strange language, worshiped their God in a "peculiar" way, ate unusual foods. Some Christians believed that Jews needed fresh Christian blood in order to bake one of those unusual foods—*matsos*; this was the famous "blood libel" that was the excuse for many Eastertime pogroms. Having been hated by their neighbors for centuries, the Jews of Eastern Europe responded by hating their oppressors, regarding the *goyim* (literally, "strangers"; figuratively, "anyone who is not Jewish") of Eastern Europe as little more than idol-worshiping barbarians, and stupid ones at that.

These ancient and divisive myths were reinforced by the real economic changes wrought by industrialization in the late nineteenth century. Long a weak rung in the economic ladder, the "trading and managing middle" that the Jews had occupied for centuries suddenly became, at least for some Jews, a relatively secure place to be. Industrialization tends to favor those who have had long experience in a cash economy (who know how to save, borrow, and spend money—instead of trading in kind), those who know how to be geographically mobile (who can travel to where the factories are opening, who can locate rentable housing for themselves, instead of remaining on ancestral farms, tied to the land). In Eastern Europe—until the governments of successive czars began actively interfering with the process—those people were almost always Jewish.

In the last decades of the nineteenth century and the first of the twentieth, religious and cultural resentments were exacerbated by social and economic dislocation. As just one example, take the matter of domestic servants. Many American descendants of Eastern European Jews have the impression that "in the old country" most of their ancestors were poor. Thus it comes as something of a surprise to learn that as poor as the Jews may have been, many of them employed servants—Christian servants—who were, by definition, even poorer. Domestic service was a source of abiding friction between Christian and Jewish communities of Eastern Europe at the turn of the century, and the irritation it created has still not been pacified. Claude Lanzmann's film *Shoah* (1985) depicts a group of elderly Polish women in the town of Grabnow who, when asked in the 1980s to recall the Jewish women who had been their neighbors fifty years earlier, remarked that the "Jewesses were more beautiful than the Poles." When asked why this should have been so, they replied, "Because the Jewesses did no work, not the way the Polish women worked. They hired us to do their work for them." Both Esther Ginsburg, who comes from a small Lithuanian city, and Max Hirsch, from a rural village in the Ukraine, have strong memories of their parents' servants.

ESTHER GINSBURG: *In Lithuania we lived with my grandmother who was running a bakery. Mother was running a dressmaking establish-*

"The work was the difference between the Jew and the non-Jew."
Jewish merchant in a marketplace in Poland,
early twentieth century.

ment in that house. It was quite a big house; she employed five girls to sew. And she had, of course, a woman to take care of the house and someone to take care of us [Esther and her sister].

We had a beautiful home and a beautiful garden. The house adjoined the armory. I recall Friday nights, beautiful memories. All the tables, the machines were covered, the tables were laden with homemade cookies and cakes and tortes and fruits and liquors and wine. The samovars were going, and Mama would invite the officers from the armory next door to be companions for the five women that worked for her.

My mother felt she owed them that, you know, they were working very hard and the days were long, they didn't have eight-hour work days, they put in all kinds of hours, living with mother. And, you know, I suppose they were exploited to an extent, they did a whole day's work, that was from dawn to dusk, and so Friday night was party night for them. Well, that was the way of life there. They came from out of town, from small villages, and they lived with Mama. She fed and lodged them and gave them their clothes and maybe a few rubles at the end of the year.

I remember the funniest things. I remember a tar salve my father used to have, and you stood in front of the open fireplace and let the heat go through you and the tar. And I remember roses, we had the most beautiful roses—gardens smelling with roses. And mother would make preserves; those were the roses that you made into preserves. And the ice cream, where the man would come around with a little wagon, with a bell. I have never in my life, and I have eaten ice cream all over Europe and in Israel, I have never tasted ice cream like that, that was sold to me as a child, the most unusual flavor, nothing ersatz in it.

And another thing, when mother would look for me, well, this nanny that I had, who was Polish, was very Orthodox, devout, I should say, devout Catholic. And she went to church every morning. Well, what is she going to do with her two charges? She had to take them to church. So, I would love the scent of the incense, and when I was lost, and I would walk off, my mother was sure that I was somewhere in church; I would go off on my own. I loved the quiet, the coolness, the darkness, the smell of it, it did something to me. I don't know, maybe I should have been born a Catholic—it lured me.

Mother never did the cooking. Mother never did a stitch of work in the home. She was a lady. She ran an establishment. She designed and

16

she cut and she doled out the work to the girls. When we came to America, our first apartment was a walkup: three flights of stairs, and Mother never walked upstairs in her life. And she had to make a coal stove, which she never did in her life. And I know it was a very short-lived romance there: she quit. She developed migraines; she always had a *shmatte* [old rag] on her head, soaked in vinegar. It was a terrible, terrible letdown, because at home, there, she had help.[2]

MAX HIRSCH:* *My father was a rich man. We had a general store and besides we had 600 acres of land. He had also forests. In this town there were about 250 Jews and about 2,000 non-Jews. The non-Jews were farmers, about 95-percent Ukrainian, maybe 5-percent Pole. The non-Jews were farmers; some had 8 acres, 9; the richest, 20. He was a rich man already if he had besides the 20 acres land, a few pairs of horses, two cows and sheep, a few of them. And they [the non-Jews] worked in summer in our place because they were needed for harvest. We needed daily, for instance, 60 or 70—most of them women; they came to cut the grain.*

Most of the Jews in our town were poor, but they were better off than the Ukrainians. Every Jew went on with his own profession. For instance, what profession he had? He went to the village, he bought wool, from the sheep. If they had to sell a small calf, the non-Jew, he sent it to the Jew. And the Jew brought this to the slaughterer or to the shochet [ritual slaughterer]. The Ukrainians they worked much harder than the Jews in our village. Much harder. He [the Ukrainian] worked day and night. At winter they had, in the forest, was enough wood to carry out, to sell. So the Ukrainians cut wood, and he had to go with his pair of horses about nineteen kilometers to the city to sell it. And it was slow because it was very heavy. But not the Jew! The Jews had no horses, no wagons, and didn't work such work. The work was the difference between the Jew and the non-Jew.

The girls took care of the store, Ukrainian girls. And we had Ukrai-

---

* Max Hirsch was the only person we interviewed who did not spend at least part of his or her youth in the United States. We decided to use excerpts from his interview because he provided us with unique and valuable insights into schooling (see chapter 3) and medical conditions (chapter 4) in Eastern Europe. Hirsch, a physician, immigrated in 1928 (he was then twenty-nine) after he had completed a residency in Germany.

nians to milk the cows. This was no problem like you have today to have a girl in your house.[3]

In 1918, two sociologists, W. I. Thomas and Florian Znaniecki, published what was then a pioneering and is now a justly famous investigation of Polish peasant culture, a culture from which one of them (Znaniecki) had recently emigrated. Their remarks on the status of various occupations that young Polish men might pursue indicate one part of the reason domestic service in Jewish homes was a sensitive issue for Christians. Apparently, only abject poverty or the total lack of other opportunities could drive a Pole to such employment:

As the peasant is particularly susceptible to ridicule, this is often sufficient to hinder a marriage. A girl will hardly ever marry a man if she suspects that for any reason her choice may be ridiculed. The reasons are various. The most frequent is the inferiority of social position. . . . The occupation is also very important. There are occupations which make a good marriage impossible for the man. Among these are catching stray dogs in the streets, sterilizing horses and cattle, serving in Jewish houses, and in general occupations having a connection with Jewish business. (This last prejudice tends to disappear except in connection with personal service.) There are other occupations to which only a slight ridicule is attached, such as shoemaking, tailoring, peddling. Another source of ridicule is physical defect, however slight. Similar prepossessions are found against girls, but the lack of variety in woman's occupations makes them less pronounced except as against servants in Jewish houses.[4]

Later in the book, Thomas and Znaniecki reproduce, at great length, a letter from a local Polish newspaper (they attribute the letter to an anonymous parish priest) that provides yet another part of the reason at least some members of the Polish community were displeased when their young people chose to serve in Jewish homes. The year is 1898, and the subject is sex:

18

The priests even today maintain, with a few exceptions, the mediaeval exemptions against the Jews, trying on the other hand to inculcate the Christian spirit of charity with regard to them also. But in this they have much less success. The peasant cannot be persuaded by any means that the Jew is a man like himself. And even if sometimes theoretically he acknowledges his equality "before God," he never introduces this theory into practice in his relations with the Jews. But poverty or the need of earning make him often a real Jewish slave. From this precisely, from this material slavery, moral depravation and social degradation, the Church wants to save and to preserve its members.

A young boy (about 20 years old) confesses that he behaved indecently. During the examination it proves that he is serving with Jews and that they scandalize him, try to modify his ethical views. Thus, for example, he sleeps in a room adjacent to a Jewish bedroom where two conjugal couples are sleeping. In the same room with him sleep three young Jews who every evening undress completely in his presence, make fun of the uncircumcised, tell him to listen to what is going on in the conjugal bedroom and persuade him to bring a girl of his acquaintance. They creep upon his bed and touch him, even give him liquor and push him out to bring a girl, etc. Moreover they abuse him at work, tell him to do the dirtiest and heaviest things, call him stupid, treat him with scorn and make him work on Sundays, but also on Saturdays. . . . The priest orders him to search for another place and if he does not find any to come to him, and promises to get work for him. This boy came to the church, but many who have served for a time with Jews never show themselves in a church, become quite irreligious, and what is worse, grow completely worthless. Sometimes at the end of his life such a moral and material wreck finds himself again in the church and the confession of such man justifies completely the fears of the Church about the lot of Jewish servants. Therefore priests frequently admonish poor parents who want to give their children to serve not to give them to Jews. They charge the Jews with material exploitation (bad pay, poor lodging and food), contemptful treatment, demoralization, and destruction of health.

. . . The fathers and mothers of our peasant children are sometimes rather indifferent, if not blind to the danger menacing their children if given to Jews. Getting rid of a burden from home and sometimes the hope of some income make them ignore the possibility of evil and they complain only when the consequences appear and when, moreover, they do not get any money, for the demoralized daughter or son who "spit" on everything that used to be holy for them, do not care for their parents who gave them away, and prefer to dress for the few pennies earned with the Jews. Then only begins weeping and complaining, "Why did we not listen to the priest when he told the truth?"[5]

Recounting another incident, the priest continued in the same vein, reflecting—yet again—the depth of the prejudice that existed against Jews in the Christian community:

A girl allowed herself to be tempted by a rich Jew who rented a room from the Jewish family with whom she served. The girl had a weak point; she like to dress herself. He promised her a dress and also to give her medicine to avoid a child. She received the dress all right, but when he got tired of her he moved away and sent her to his friend. The latter promised to marry her (though he also was a Jew), lived with her for about two months and left her. The girl was very good by nature, she was pained that she had fallen but already it was difficult for her to withstand or to refuse anybody. The Jews have this peculiarity that they teach the appreciation of the body and of sexual relations. They bring into the mental horizon of the Polish peasant girl the erotic element (in spite of the brutality and coarseness with which they treat her) which is unknown to the soul of the Polish peasant and so different from the severe Christian view upon the body and sexual functions. She did not see in her actions the "moral ugliness" which the Christians usually feel, but only the transgression of a law, of a cruel law that forbids her such a good thing and moreover brands her, particularly for the relation with a Jew. (The sexual relation with a Jew is in the eyes of the Church a particularly aggravating circumstance in view of the familial connection established by the coitus, the danger of the child being educated in the Jewish religion, and the "mixing" of Christian and Jewish blood.)[6]

Another source of the abiding friction between Christians and Jews was the fact that the Jews of Eastern Europe were engaged in two activities doomed to engender resentment: moneylending and the sale of liquor. Those to whom we owe money are always despised, especially when they ask that their money be returned, with interest. Those who sell liquor will frequently be despised, most especially by those who perceive alcoholism to be undermining their communities. Irving Farber, who was born in a "mixed" village just before the turn of the century, remembers the liquor and the inn where it was dispensed:

I came from a small [Polish] village, close to the Russian border, in eastern Galicia. The village, in itself, was probably more poverty than anything you've ever seen or you can imagine. The peasants were so poor, although they had no problem for food—you can always find something to eat, cabbages and potatoes—the problem was matches, soap, oil for the lamp, clothing. Out of the four hundred people, must have been about four or five families which we would call middle-class.

We were the only Jewish family in that village. We did everything. We had our inn. We had our milk business, which used to deliver to the city. We had a farm. We had the harvest every year. We had horses. We were, by comparison, very prosperous. We had enough food to eat. It was a large house. In that house lived my mother and father, my grandmother, two brothers of my mother, and an aunt of mine, an old lady. All lived, all derived their livelihood, mostly from selling alcohol, drinks, alcoholic drinks.

From what I understand, my grandfather was favored by the authorities, and they gave him a concession to sell drinks and tobacco products. It required definite concessions, and you only got it with very great difficulty. And with that he was prosperous enough to buy this house, in that village. We had in the front, the kretshme, the inn—and outside of that we had four rooms. And nobody [in our family] slept in the kretshme because the peasants might come in as early as five in the morning for a shot of whiskey. I've seen it done.[7]

21

Simon Dubnow, who wrote a history of the Jews of Russia, early in this century commented on the profound social implicatons of the liquor trade, in which many of his contemporaries were involved:

Speaking generally, the economic structure of the Russian Jews experienced violent upheavals during the first years of Nicholas II's reign. The range of Jewish economic endeavor, circumscribed though it was, was narrowed more and more. In 1894, the law placing the liquor trade under Government control was put into effect by [Count Sergei] Witte, the Minister of Finance. Catering to the prejudices of the ruling spheres of Russia, Witte had already endeavored to convince Alexander III that the liquor state monopoly would have the effect of completely undermining "Jewish exploitation," the latter being primarily bound up with the sale of liquor in the towns and villages. . . . In consequence of this reform, tens of thousands of Jewish families who had derived their livelihood either directly from the liquor trade, or indirectly from occupations connected with it, such as the keeping of inns and hostelries, were deprived of their means of subsistence.

It goes without saying that, as far as the moral aspect of the problem was concerned, the best elements of Russian Jewry welcomed this reform, which bade fair to wipe out an ugly stain on the escutcheon of the Jewish people—the liquor trade bequeathed to the Jews by ancient Poland. Known as the most sober people on earth, the Jews had been placed in the tragic position that in their search for a piece of bread, thousands were forced to serve as a medium for promoting the pernicious Russian drunkenness. The memory of the days when the Jewish saloon was the breeding-place of pogroms, in which the Russian peasants and burghers filled themselves with Jewish alcohol to fortify themselves in their infamous work of demolishing the homes of the Jews, was still fresh in their minds. Cheerfully would the Jewish people have yielded its monopoly of the liquor trade to the Russian barroom keepers and to the Russian government who seemed genuinely attracted toward it, had it only been allowed to pursue other methods of earning a livelihood. But in closing the avenue of the liquor traffic to two hundred thousand Jews, the Government did not even think of removing the special restrictions which barred their way to other lines of endeavor.[8]

Thomas and Znaniecki viewed the same phenomenon from a different perspective, that of men who hoped to forestall the disintegration of Eastern European peasant communities, and who regarded liquor, as well as other goods that Jews sold, as agents of that disintegration:

> The Jewish shopkeeper in a peasant village is usually also a liquor-dealer without license, a banker lending money at usury, often also a receiver of stolen goods and (near the border) a contrabandist. The peasant needs and fears him, but at the same time despises him always and hates him often. The activity of these country shopkeepers is the source of whatever anti-Semitism there is in the peasant masses. . . . The shopkeeper teaches the peasant boy smoking, drinking, and finally stealing; the connection established in youth lasts sometimes into maturity, and almost every gang of peasant thieves or robbers centers around some Jewish receiver's place, where the spoils are brought and new campaigns planned. . . . Usually Jews manage only the commercial side of the questions, leaving robbing or transporting of contraband to peasants.[9]

Since moneylending is an activity carried on privately, away from the observation of children, none of the people we interviewed could remember much about it. Thomas and Znaniecki did, however, preserve something of the nuances of the relationship when they transcribed this letter, written by a Jewish shopkeeper in Poland to a young Pole then living in Chicago:

Wojakowa, July 15, 1914.

Dear Wojciech [Hedmej]:

First I thank you for your letter which I received on July 2, and I thank you for remembering us. As to our health, about which you ask, it is as usual, and our success, as in Galicia; it cannot be praised, because in Galicia there has been always misery and there will be further misery. Money is always lacking. There is nothing new. As to weddings . . . we covered (with a veil = married) today the daughter of Kacola from Moskowska. We have a new priest. And there is nothing more of interest to write. We have very nice crops, and harvest is beginning. And I inform you that I received 120 crowns by money order from you on July 15, for which I thank you heartily. And there is great heat in our country. And you ask why I did not want to accept 20 gulden from your wife. You ought to know yourself that she did not offer me any. If she had offered me, I would surely have accepted, even a single gulden, for who is the Jew who does not want money? And you write me not to give anything on credit (to your wife). I don't want to give on credit much, and your wife owes me already for a shawl and for different smaller things. And if you send any money for me, send it to my address, it will be the best. . . . My wife greets you and thanks you for the letter that you wrote to us, and we beg you to write us more, whether your condition is getting better. And when you have money, send it to us, because we need it much and we have waited a long time. And when God grants you to come back to our country, then I will relate to you everything. And I write you that you have a nice daughter, because when there was a May-festival, she came to us for candies.

I finish this letter. Be healthy and please answer to your Jew who is very well-wishing for you.

Kalman Metzendorf[10]

Most of the Jewish moneylenders of Eastern Europe were not, strictly speaking, bankers; most did not earn a living lending money. Rather, they were shopkeepers who, given the nature of their business, might be expected (at least in good times) to have a little extra cash on hand. Usually they worked in their homes; usually they knew each of their customers intimately; frequently they were women. Hannah Toperoff, who was born in the Volhynia region in the northwest Ukraine, can recall the physical context in which such moneylending might have proceeded:

We had a very spacious home, a tremendous dining room and a kitchen, and then we had something like a parlor, we used to call it a

24

zoll. Three bedrooms. . . . Sometimes merchants would come to our shtetl, and they probably also had a great contact with the peasants, and through them we had peasants in our home also. They were usually hiring woods, forest, for wood, so they would come to the shtetl and see when the time of chopping of wood would come, and then they had to tie the logs, and these logs they used to export through the river.

We had no kretshme at all but because we had a spacious home and because we had spare rooms so those people who had to come for business—big merchants, not everybody—they used to stop in our place. And we would accommodate them and give them a bedroom to sleep in, and I think mother would also give them meals but that was just as an accommodation. It was not a livelihood.

My father was a rabbi, and he was also a shochet: he was a slaughterer. My mother had a store. We had a store also attached to the house. It was just like one unit, and we had yardgoods there, of the best possible kind, and it was rather a general store because you could find anything there. We girls [there were five daughters and two sons in the family] used to help out in the store, especially after father was gone; that was the main livelihood.

Now you must understand it was not the kind of store you were busy in day and night. The store was attached to the place, you see, and you hardly stayed in the store at all. The outside door was open. If somebody came in, you would hear the ring on the bell, so somebody would come into the store and help the person with whatever they wanted to get. One room that I mentioned to you was right next to the store, so all you had to do is just get up, even when you were at the meal sometimes in the dining room, you heard the ring, you just got up and you went through that room and there you were, in the store, no problem. However, there were some holidays—they were called the peasants' holidays—when they all used to come. It was bazaar day, so to speak, but all the peasants from the vicinity used to come to the shtetl. Then it was busy, and everybody, the whole house, even the servants, would be in the store. Some watching and others selling and so on. That's the kind of store we had.[11]

Even when moneylending is not involved, ordinary commercial transactions can lead to friction when one party is convinced of the stupidity of the other, a conviction many Jews shared about their neighbors, as Morris Hochstadt's recollections of his maternal grandfather reveal:

My other grandfather's name was Ovraisky. He was a teacher. He used to teach children. Besides, he was also a cantor. Of course, he was in business making caps for the peasants. For anyone, but generally he worked for the peasant trade. He worked out of the home; he had machines there, boys—men who worked for him. He used to go to Pinsk to buy material, for that was a big city—bring it back and make caps. They were all one size. One size, and many times when the goy would put the cap on his head and complained that the cap was too big, my grandfather would say, "Don't worry. Your head will swell." And if the cap was too small, he would say, "Don't worry. Your head will shrink." They bought it! They bought it!

They also had an extra room downstairs where they had machines. The goyim at a particular flea market used to come in with a lot of wool which they had shorn off their sheep. And it was rough. This grandfather Ovraisky had machinery where they took the wool on canvas, and as they turned the machines, the canvas rolled, the wool kept going in from different rollers, and by the time it came out a whole bale was pure wool. He use to weigh it and charge by the pound. So he had several different businesses. The combs would comb out the roughage [debris in the wool]. And only the pure wool remained. And of course he made the goyim turn the wheel, it wasn't electrified. He was the only one who had that machine. They turned the wheel for their own wool. My grandfather didn't do anything; he just let them use his machine, and got paid for it. I remember there were extra rollers standing in the corner so if one broke down there were others.

Pogroms, War, Revolution, Emigration

Many Christians in Eastern Europe resented Jewish prosperity. When Alexander III acceded to the Russian throne in 1881, he was determined to right the balance, to find an answer to "the Jewish question," to solve "the Jewish problem." Whatever religious and political grudges he may have borne against the Jews, the fundamental, and oft-repeated, intention of his anti-Semitic policies (including the pogroms) was to put an end to the prosperity enjoyed by at least some segments of the Jewish community.

On 22 August 1880, Count Nikolai P. Ignatiev, minister of the interior, sent a memorandum to Alexander III, outlining a rationale for what were to become the infamous May Laws of 1881:

> The principal source of this movement [the recent pogroms], which is so incompatible with the temper of the Russian people, lies in circumstances which are of an exclusively economic nature. For the last twenty years the Jews have gradually managed to capture not only commerce and industry but they have also succeeded in acquiring, by means of purchase and lease, a large amount of landed property. Owing to their clannishness and solidarity, they have, with few exceptions, directed their efforts not towards the increase of the productive forces [of the country] but towards the exploitation of the original inhabitants, primarily of the poorest classes of the population, with the result that they have called forth a protest from this population, manifesting itself in deplorable forms—in violence. . . . Having taken energetic means to suppress the previous disorders and mob rule and to shield the Jews against violence, the Government recognizes that it is justified in adopting, without delay, no less energetic measures to remove the present abnormal relations that exist between the original inhabitants and the Jews, and to shield the Russian population against this harmful Jewish activity which, according to local information, was responsible for the disturbances.[12]

Apparently neither the May Laws (which prevented Jews from engaging in business on Sundays and Christian holidays and—worse—made it illegal for them to move from one house, or one town, to another) nor several subsequent amendments (which, for example, established restrictive Jewish quotas in secondary schools, professional schools, and universities) succeeded in adequately curbing the "prosperity" of the Jews. Alexander's successor, Nicholas II, who became czar in 1894, was also greatly troubled by the Jewish question and continued to search for new and more stringent answers. In 1903, Count Arthur Pavlovitch Cassini, who was then Nicholas's ambassador to the United States, again dwelt on economic imbalances in trying to explain, to the Associated Press, why the Kishinev pogrom of 1903 (one of the most murderous and destructive pogroms ever recorded) was a justifiable form of homicide:

> There is in Russia, as in Germany and Austria, a feeling against certain of the Jews. The reason for this unfriendly attitude is found in the fact that the Jews will not work in the field or engage in agriculture. They prefer to be money lenders. Give a Jew a couple of dollars and he becomes a banker and money broker. In this capacity he takes advantage of the Russian peasant, whom he soon has in his power and ultimately destroys. It is when the patience of the peasant is exhausted that a conflict between peasants and Jews occurs. Ordinarily the Russian is a patient person, but it is only natural that he should entertain a feeling of resentment for the one who has wrought his ruin.
>
> The situation in Russia so far as the Jews are concerned is just this: It is the peasant against the money lender and not the Russians against the Jews. There is no feeling against the Jew in Russia because of religion. It is as I have said—the Jews ruin the peasants, with the result that conflicts occur when the latter have lost all their worldly possessions and have nothing to live upon. . . . The Russian readily assimilates with the people of all other races, and if he cannot assimilate with the Jew, it is apparent that the fault must be with the Jew and not with the Russian.[13]

In the face of such official provocation, any cordial relations Christians and Jews had managed to establish with each other proved fragile. Many elderly Jewish immigrants can now recall, with pleasure, Polish and Russian playmates of their youth. They also recall generous and kindly gestures—especially protection offered during riots and pogroms—but they also recall the riots and the pogroms, as well as the "gentler" forms of harassment that, in those days, became part and parcel of everyday life. On the first day of her interview, Sadie Rehstock depicted the pleasanter aspects of Jewish-Christian relations:

"We looked across the village and we saw them kill our grandparents."
Aftermath of the Kishinev pogrom, 1903.

There was a little old gentile woman who was a washerwoman, and she sometimes came when my grandmother was alive. She would get our things to be washed and bring them back clean. This woman was very fond of my grandmother, and I used to be amused by her husband. I used to see him hold a chair onto his backside and walk around the room with the chair. This was in his own apartment. His wife was very fond of my grandmother and came and cried when she died.

The janitor was Polish. The Poles that we knew as neighbors we were friendly with. I never saw a pogrom; when it came to Easter we had to stay inside, that's all. I had a little Polish friend in another apartment and we played on the same landing. I must have been five years old. They had a Christmas tree, and I used to play on that tree in the landing, after they threw it out, after Christmas. They used to invite me into the house for Easter, and they had delicious candy, and I wouldn't eat anything because it was not kosher.

Yet when asked, on another day, for some of her earliest memories, Sadie Rehstock recalled the other side of the picture:

Polish I didn't talk at all. I refused to say a word in Polish, 'cause I hated it. I hated the Poles. And I hated the language. Everybody did, everybody hated the Poles. Anti-semiten. Nobody told me, I saw what was happening. Well, the attitude. When they had a parade, an Easter parade, and they took their images out of the church and marched through the streets, they [her parents and grandparents] wouldn't allow us to open a window and look out at it. They would make us go away from the windows, and we didn't dare look at them. They [the Poles] would threaten to throw stones. There wasn't a law against it. When we came to this country, I told my mother that if anybody talks Polish to me I wouldn't answer. And in one year I forgot every single word except the catchphrases like "thank you" and things like that.

Few American descendants of Eastern European Jews understand—in part because our own childhoods have been so different, in part because our parents refused to talk about it—the extent to which the immigrants' sense of themselves and their religion was wrapped up, from the time that they were first conscious of the world around them, with the sense of being victimized by Christian indifference and brutality, with the sense that the people who are your friends on Friday can turn out to be your enemies—perhaps mortal enemies—by Sunday.

SAM REISS: *Litna was a large Jewish community as communities went in Poland. On the map it is a half-inch below Warsaw, near the Vistula River. In Poland there was a constant climate of fear. There wasn't the relaxed feeling that I have now where I live in Jerusalem. I recall when the Cossacks invaded Poland during World War I [probably late 1916; Reiss was about twelve]. They came on horseback. Their arrival started in the afternoon. They kept coming on their horses all the day and all the night. The stench of the horse's droppings on the streets—there were cobblestone streets—was tremendous, it was paralyzing.*

My father—his name was Yitzhak, he was twenty-nine years old then—was walking along the street, and a Cossack came along and kicked him in the face and knocked out every one of his teeth, and my father lies in the gutter with all of his teeth lost—at twenty-nine. Whereupon, this Cossack got off his horse, pulled off my father's boots and his coat, and then rode away.

There was no appeal from that. This is what I mean when I say the climate—no standing, no recourse.

I remember in my own personal experience. It was around Sukkos time when Jews build a booth to commemorate their sojourn in the desert and their exodus from Egypt. I was sent out to get some nails. I was a youngster, I must have been six, seven. On the way home I was jumped on by a bunch of these shkotzim [Christian bullies] who would run in gangs. I was beat up but I saved the nails. I got home with the nails, a little late, a little bloodied; they jumped on you and each took their turn. At a certain age the shkotzim would attack only certain levels. When they grew bigger, we called them pogromchiks, they would not hestitate to attack. Some of the adult Polacks would throw rocks at the synagogue. There were many Poles who had a high respect for religious places; religion they would never permit themselves or anyone else to attack or be abusive of. So sometimes—my father was the shochet for the town, the ritual slaughterer—sometimes when he had to go to the slaughterhouse, he was accompanied by soldiers because he feared for his life. It seemed that every week some Jew is attacked or killed or found dead in the forest. It had reached a point where the community had a fear; they were not relaxed. The political and economic situation always predicted the reaction of the non-Jewish population to the Jewish population.

The only time I remember getting in some licks was when the Balfour Declaration* came—I think it was 1918—on the day when the declaration became public, we—I and my gang of boys that we used to play with—we went out into the street and we jumped on the *shkotzim* and we jumped on these guys, and we took a beating but we enjoyed the fact that we took the aggressive steps of jumping on them, and they chased us and we ran into the *shul* [synogogue], which was our place of refuge.

When we left Poland, we were searched at the border. I had been given a silver dollar by a man who had lived in our town, had gone to America, and had become a successful clothing manufacturer. I treasured that silver dollar. I used to look at it every night before I went to bed. When we got to the border, they searched me and took that dollar away from me. Then they proceeded to cut the buttons open on my jacket; since I had one dollar, maybe those Jews are smart enough to hide it in their buttons. They found nothing except a cut button. I remember that very distinctly. I was so pained, I was so hurt. I couldn't do anything, I was a little kid. An American silver dollar! I never forgot that, I remember to this day. I must have wept bitterly, bitterly. I remember to this day the frightening look of those people, the stern look of those people.

MORRIS HOCHSTADT: *My earliest memory? Let's see. Well, we were sitting in our house—Shabbos [Sabbath]. We were having a bite around three or four o'clock in the afternoon, my father and my brother and my mother and me [he was nine or ten]. And we look out of the window and we see a Polack soldier running after a Jew who was going to shul with a beard. A new sideline of ripping Jews' beards out! Off the face! So my father saw him attacking this yidl [a small Jewish man] going to shul. So my father jumped out of the window, through the window, to stop this soldier from doing that. So this soldier left the*

---

* The Balfour Declaration, issued by the British cabinet in November 1917, expressed the intention of creating a national homeland for the Jews in Palestine, which the British had just recently wrested from Turkey as one of the spoils of war.

other Jew alone, and with the back of his rifle he hit my father over
the back. But my father grabbed the rifle in midair, and my father took
out his paper to show that he was a civil worker [the elder Hochstadt,
at that time—about 1910—was making coffins] working for the civil
government, and he left him alone after that.

We used to walk to cheder [religious elementary school] with a lan-
tern. My brother and I, we went to cheder together, and on the way we
picked up some more boys going to cheder. Coming back at night, the
peasants in their wagons with hay or whatever used to see a Jewish kid
and take their whip and fling it at him, wherever they struck. I don't
remember being struck, maybe we were too fast for them, but they
would swing their whips. We were cold and frozen and running with
a lantern, in the snow, when the goy passed on the wagon. He was
sitting on top, he saw kids and tried to hit them with a whip.

Some observers of the Jewish communities in turn-of-the-century
Russia (officials of the Jewish Colonization Society,* for example) believed that this kind of harassment and the pogroms were more devastating to the Jews than was long-term poverty. The psychic damage,
they suggested, was more terrible—because irreparable—than the
physical:

> The most terrible feature of the lives of the Russian Jews is the
> "pogrom." Protection of life and property are two things which
> even the rulers of barbarous countries feel called upon to guarantee
> their subjects. But this protection is not accorded the Jews in Rus-
> sia at the present time. . . .
> In order to show in figures the extent of the pogroms let us
> mention that from the 17th day of October, 1905, till the end of
> 1906, 661 towns and cities were devastated, and the 38,000 famil-
> ies, or 162,000 persons, suffered. General loss during the last po-
> groms amounted to 54,153,853 rubles, 985 persons were killed,
> 1,492 wounded heavily, while the number of those wounded in
> a lesser degree amounted to many thousands, 387 women were

* The goals of the Jewish Colonization Society, founded in 1891 by Baron Maurice de Hirsch
(a British Jew) with an enormous endowment, were to promote the emigration of Jews from
Russia (or anywhere else in Europe or Asia where they were oppressed) to form colonies in various
parts of North and South America.

widowed, 177 children completely orphaned, while 1,474 were deprived of one of their parents.

But one cannot estimate the damage done by the pogroms in mere figures. Completely destroying the safety of property the pogrom ruins credit, brings about an economic crisis, and throws tens of thousands of unemployed workmen into the streets. Still more terrible is the effect of the pogroms upon the moral atmosphere prevailing among the Jews. The knowledge that in the full light of day in the sight of everybody, a crowd of the lowest rabble may burst into your house, plundering and murdering, destroying all that you have toiled for, may violate the honor of those who are dearer than life itself, may maim or kill you . . . the knowledge that it is useless to struggle because behind the pogromists armed force is ranged against you—such knowledge paralyzes the energy of the people.[14]

Obviously, the energy of the people was not completely paralyzed. Some (although, grievously, not all) chose to emigrate—hardly a form of paralysis. But even those who fled were touched traumatically, their memories indelibly imprinted.

JENNIE GROSSMAN: *I do remember as a child that the soldiers would come into the house and just commandeer the entire house. They took it over. It was a frightening experience. They slept in our house, and my mother had to cook for them. Maybe I'm some soldier's child, God forbid!*

I remember stories my mother and father told me about when I was an infant. There were times when they had to run and hide. They had a hiding place in the barn, underneath. They took refuge there. As an infant I would be crying, and they would hold their hands over my mouth to keep it in, and I nearly suffocated several times.

And I remember my father telling stories. In fact, all his life, he would wake up with nightmares—screaming—they were 'killing him!' Wake up just screaming. Many nights I would go running in. He had those nightmares all his life.

As a child, after coming to America, I used to dream about Poland, but what I dreamed about was the terror of the gypsies.

34

HANNAH TOPEROFF: *I was born in 1914, and we lived in that town, Proskurov [in the Ukraine], until the Russians began to persecute the Jews and we escaped to America. My father left separately. It was my mother and five young girls. We looked across the village and we saw them kill our grandparents—they fell over dead. Then they came after us. They asked for money but my mother had money. I saw them shoot [my grandparents] and then they fell down. I was a block away by today's measurements. They would stop people and ask for money and if they didn't get money they would rape the young women that were rapable—not children. But we escaped because we had money. My mother paid them off. They let us go. We were lucky. They could have done that. We walked through. Where we walked there were woods, and there were sharp bushes and the bushes made our legs bleed. We went to Rumania first. I don't remember how we got to Rumania, I only remember walking.*

For many years I couldn't remember all of this. My mother throughout her lifetime in America always had nightmares. And we as children were so accustomed to it: when she had a nightmare it was like standard procedure to walk in and wake her up because she would scream. And one night in the process of waking her up, it is the tendency that when you dream about something and you are awakened you will talk about it. I said, "Mama! Mama! What is the matter?" And she woke up and she described this scene to me that I thought that I had dreamed—that I didn't actually think I had lived through. And she described the scene of this entire incident to me. And then I remembered.

Historians have estimated that roughly one third of the Jewish population of Eastern Europe emigrated in the fifty years between 1880 and 1930. Such a massive migration must have many causes, but the statistics of immigration clearly demonstrate that the overriding cause was fear for their lives. After each wave of pogroms, the number of Jews coming into this country (and others) would rise sharply. Thus, whatever terrors emigrating Jews may have faced paled in comparison to the terrors they had left behind. Etta Soschin, for example, was eighteen years old, just on the edge of maturity, when Ukrainian nationalist soldiers burst into her home in Felshtin:

The first intimation that I had that anything was amiss was that three soldiers burst into our home at about 9:30 A.M. on a Monday

35

morning. At the time, our family, with the exception of my father, who had not come home the previous night, were all at home. I distinctly remember this because the samovar was prepared for tea at the time. On the entry of soldiers, the family dispersed in fright, running in different directions. I ran into the room of our tenant and hid in a wardrobe in his room. I heard a voice calling to me to come out, and stepping out I was seized by a soldier who dragged me into the dining room and began questioning me roughly. This soldier I remember as being tall and red haired, with a forage-cap with a red center piece extending down one side of the head.

The soldier then asked me whether I was Christian or Jewish. I replied that I was a Christian and was the tenant's daughter. This the tenant denied. Thereupon the soldier demanded that I make the sign of the cross, saying that he would release me if I were a Christian child but would kill me if I were Jewish. In terror, I kissed his hand and called him "brother" and begged him to release me, but the soldier replied using the Russian slang term "that a goose and a pig have no relationship!" (*gus svinye nye tovarisch*). He then shouted *"lozhish"* (lie down).[15]

Many Jews, like Etta Soschin, Hannah Toperoff, and Jennie Grossman, must have departed from their homelands in Eastern Europe with a mixture of fear and hatred in their hearts: fear of what lay ahead, hatred of what lay behind; hatred not so much for the place in which they had been born, as for the people who had lived there; a hatred born of harassment, oppression, and terror. But all the children of the emigrants, those born in the United States as well as those born in Europe, those who experienced pogroms and those who did not, the five- and ten-year-olds who subsequently became Americans, lived their earliest, formative years in the shadow of the pogroms, in the shadow of fear, oppression, and terror. That shadow clearly did not paralyze their will—as some had feared—but it did distort their existential understanding of themselves, a distortion that those of us who have been born and raised in relative security can barely begin to comprehend.

LIFE IN THE OLD COUNTRY

TESS EGROVSKY: *So then there came the trouble and we had pogroms, and my mother felt, you know, they used to rape girls, and my mother decided they should send me here [this was 1904 or 1905]. I didn't have a chance to get the passport and I went to the borderline, stealing. Oh, my cousin found a man who took me to the borderline. You paid for that. In those days, they were afraid for girls. Something might happen to them. It was dangerous just to be.*

And so they left, large numbers of them. The best estimates suggest that one third of the Jews living in those parts of Eastern Europe that belonged either to the Russian or the Austro-Hungarian empires in 1914 emigrated between 1880 and 1925. The children, carried along by their parents' decisions, left—insofar as they can now remember their feelings about it—with fear and loathing. The adults were more ambivalent. The Old Country, after all, was home: the place in which they had been raised, the place where beloved relatives still lived. Happy memories—before the pogroms, before the trouble started— were just as plentiful as unhappy ones. Jennie Grossman recalls the emotional difficulties emigration created for her mother:

It was traumatic for her. She was saying goodbye to her father. She really adored him. I remember all the relatives around the train and saying "goodbye," and the waving and the crying. My mother's father accompanied us to Danzig. We get on the train, and the first thing that happens is that I don't feel well, and by the time we get to Warsaw I had the measles, and we were stuck in a bedbug-ridden hotel in Warsaw for three weeks. My grandfather stayed with us, he wouldn't leave, they adored each other.

So finally we got going to Danzig. On the train going to Danzig— the sons-of-bitch Polacks!—we get on the train, and my grandfather was supposed to get on the train with us, and soldiers get on board the train and start throwing off people because they needed the room. He was thrown off the train. My mother and we three were allowed to get on. And they never had a proper goodbye because they were torn from each other's arms. He was dropped in Poland, and we continued to Danzig. It was heartbreaking. My mother cried all her life, for the rest of her life, at the farewell she did not have with her father.

And I remember my mother dropped—she was carrying a bundle, there was a mirror in there, and you know other personal things—the things fell to the floor and the mirror cracked, and she picked up the pieces and took them with her to America. For years she had them with her. It was dreadful. She kept those pieces—she couldn't bear to part with anything that had anything to do with her father.

Despite her mother's travail, however, the emotional difficulty that Jennie Grossman faced, along with other immigrant youth (whether born abroad, or born to parents just recently immigrated) was not longing for the Old Country but the need to adjust to the New: "becoming American" was just as fraught with danger as "being European."

"TEMPEST TOSSED": LEARNING TO LIVE IN AMERICA

IRVING FARBER: *At sixteen I went to America. My older brother was there. He sent tickets for me to come to America. Just me. My father was here before; he didn't like it there and came back. He didn't say nothing. He just didn't like it and went home. On Saturday, before I left, I said, "Let's have a treat on me." On Saturday, in the shtetl, you didn't pay money—Shabbos—and the next day I said to my father, "I need a ruble. Give me a ruble—a dollar—to pay." "So! You're a spender! You will never go to America!" I said, "If you won't give me a dollar to pay I won't go to America." He gave me the dollar in a hurry; they were waiting to take me to the train. I went to the train and I went to Europe [Russia, from Farber's perspective, is not in Europe]. I got on the boat at Antwerp.*

Irving Farber's story is emblematic of dozens of immigration stories we heard, of thousands we might have heard: family lost and family found; *here* confused with *there*; the pleasures of being young and brave;

the terrors of being lost and frightened. But Farber's story is not unique. By the time he arrived at Ellis Island, millions of immigrants had preceded him; immigration procedures had long ago been routinized. For more than fifteen years, New York had been functioning as the only port authorized to receive immigrants from Europe. Shipping companies had gotten into the practice of giving each immigrant a health examination at the port of embarkation, since the U.S. government required that each person rejected in New York on grounds of poor health be returned to Europe at the expense of the company. A second—this time the official—health exam was performed on Ellis Island, to search for any communicable or chronic disease, most particularly the eye infection trachoma. Immigration officials at Ellis Island were responsible for ensuring that each immigrant had financial resources sufficient for at least a month's food and lodging and also provided temporary identification papers. Ferries plied the waters between Ellis Island and Manhattan throughout the day and night; hustlers, pimps, and thieves plied the ferry slips, searching for hapless immigrants. Representatives of charitable organizations—the Hebrew Immigrant Aid Society, or HIAS, was one—regularly patrolled the same territory in order to protect those, like Irving Farber, who did not yet have the skills necessary to protect themselves.

When I came here, I take the ferry boat to go to New York—in 1913. They asked me, "Do you have any money?" and I said, "Five dollars," and they said, "Go ahead." I stayed on the boat with my suitcase, and a young man came over to me and said, "Mister, I see nobody came to pick you up." "I came to my brother and he sent me a ticket but he didn't come." He said, "You come with me." I said, "What was the point?" "Come with me. Come with me. I am from the HIAS."

He took me to the HIAS, they had a place on East Broadway and I stopped, and the minute I put down my suitcase, I went out looking for my brother.

I sent him a postcard that I was coming, but he didn't get my postcard yet. So when I came there [the address on the postcard], it's a bank. I say, "Mister, do you have a letter for Morris Farber?" "Morris Farber? Oh, he gets his mail over here. He comes once a week and he gets his mail." So he shows me the letter I sent him. The name of the bank was Barish Savings, a Jewish bank, at 77 Ridge Street. I took chances: they come here once a week; they make their deposits here; they get their mail here. I said, "When he comes, tell him his brother is here."

And about an hour later, a man comes in the HIAS and asks to see Itzhak Farber. They have a microphone: "Itzhak Farber! Itzhak Farber!" I come out, and they say, "Do you know this man?" I say, "I don't know." How do I know? And he says, "I am your uncle, I am your father's brother. Don't you remember me? I was on the picture with your father." I says, "No, I don't." Then he says, "Come with me. I'll take you home."

His name was Israel Farber. So I went with him to his house. And I say, "Take me over to my brother's house." And he says, "No, you wait here. I want your brother to come here." 'Cause they were on the odds. "The only way I will get him here is if he know you here so he will come." So he calls up Morris: "Itzhak came." There was a telephone outside; they lived in a building with a walking up. So he [Morris] came and he [Israel] wouldn't let him [Morris] go away and he [Israel] made supper for me and him [Morris].

My uncle brought Morris back to me. Listen, my brother is dead now, but he was happy to see me then.

When Irving Farber landed on Ellis Island, William Howard Taft was president of the United States. Theodore Roosevelt had preceded him, and Woodrow Wilson would follow. In those years—the first two decades of the twentieth century, sometimes called the Progressive period—the United States underwent tremendous changes. From the time of the Revolution until the start of the twentieth century, American politics had been dominated by the politics of land, American culture had taken the yeoman farmer as its ideal, and American economic power had depended upon what its farms and forests could produce. But as the nineteenth century turned into the twentieth, the farm was yielding pride of place to the city, the small businessman was yielding to the trusts, and the United States was becoming an industrial, not an agrarian, colossus. The steam engine had replaced the water wheel; Schenectady, Trenton, Evansville, Birmingham, and Grand Rapids were spewing forth manufactured goods with which to supply not just the nation but also the world. The frontier having closed, youngsters of many ethnic stocks were becoming laborers and union members in Pittsburgh, Cleveland, Detroit, and Baltimore, instead of homesteaders and grange organizers in Sioux City, Portland, and Boise. At the moment Irving Farber stepped off the boat, young ladies in pleated shirtwaists and young gentlemen in knickers were somewhere sipping lemonade in each other's company—and 1 percent of American companies were turning out 45 percent of the nation's manufactured goods, 5 percent of the population owned nearly half of the nation's property, nearly one third of the nation's seventy-six million people—many of them recent immigrants—subsisted below the poverty line, and one and one half million children—Irving Farber's age or younger—were toiling in the nation's factories.

Reform was everywhere in the air; Republican Progressives (like Roosevelt) wanted reform just as much as did Democratic Progressives (like Wilson). The reformers themselves were, in some ways, a diverse lot, ranging from crusading journalists to dedicated social workers, from novelists to politicians, from school superintendents to public health nurses. All had looked about them and decided that the country was changing in terrible ways; all had decided that they were the people specially chosen to repair the damage.

Much of domestic politics in the Progressive period resulted from the sudden discovery that the cities were not at all like the countryside, big businesses not at all like the general store, urban political bosses not at all like the authors of the Constitution, and immigrants not at all like the native born. As diverse a group as they may have been, the Progressive reformers had a few things in common aside from their passion for reform. Virtually all were Protestant and highly educated and had their social roots in the prosperous rural middle classes: they were the children of teachers and ministers, shopkeepers and small businessmen, farmers, doctors, and country lawyers.

Progressive reformers came from—and hoped to preserve—the social world that had once been the heart of American culture. Children of small businessmen and farmers, the reformers had watched the great trusts grow—steel, oil, railroads, sugar, meat, banking—and wished to return to the status quo ante Vanderbilt, Rockefeller, and Morgan. Children of the countryside, the reformers had also watched as the lumber companies felled the forests and the coal companies pockmarked the valleys; they wished to conserve for future generations as much as possible of the natural beauty of the land they had known.

Similarly, the reformers had watched in horror as the nation's great cities became dirty, overcrowded, garbage strewn, unhealthy. They blamed urban havoc on the political bosses who traded votes for favors (a boy in trouble here, a father without a job there, a grocery bill unpaid around the corner) and contracts (a sewer to be laid in the next ward, coal to heat the schoolhouse, sidewalks to be created up the block), simultaneously making a travesty of the democratic process and turning the once-elegant cities into slums. The reformers were determined to take it all on, the bosses and the slums: they wanted direct election of senators and pasteurized, certified milk; they wanted laws that would allow voters a choice about major bond issues and laws that would require tenement landlords to install flush toilets; they wanted recall elections (to oust corrupt politicans) and public health clinics (so that poor babies could be saved).

Immigrant children met the reformers, and reforming attitudes, at every turn: in the classroom, in the library, in the civics book, in the newspapers, even at the movies. If they spoke and read English, if they went to school, immigrant children could not have escaped the dominant political and social messages of their time. But the world the reformers wanted to construct was not a world with which immigrant parents had either much familiarity or much sympathy, a discordance that put immigrant children of all ethnic stocks in a terrible double bind. Were they to listen to their mothers or to the teachers? To their fathers or to the doctors? Whose language should they speak? Whose country, whose world, should they try to be living in?

For Jewish immigrant children, the choices were doubly difficult, doubly wrenching, because the world the reformers were trying to build was a world relentlessly and resolutely Christian. "Observing closely the life of the children of the Jewish poor," a sympathetic commentator remarked, "we cannot help noticing the extreme contradictions existing in their very surroundings. The Jewish home, synagogue and cheder, the Jewish traditions and ceremonies on one hand, and the Christian, nay Gentile world on the other, are two incompatible influences tossing the Jewish child hither and thither."[1]

"Hither and thither." "Here and there." "Tossed"—perhaps "tempest tossed"—may be just the right verb; "contradictions," just the right noun. As much as Jewish parents may have tried to protect their children from it, in America the Gentile world was everywhere omnipresent and insistent. In the old country, you could send your boy to a

Jewish school, the *cheder*; in the new, he had to learn from the *goyim*. In the old country, you could send your daughter to the rabbi when she needed advice; in the new, she read magazines, or asked a friendly librarian. Reformers wanted, sincerely and urgently, to help immigrant children; but the help they offered, the advice they gave, the future they desired for these needy children, was not quite what immigrant parents had in mind.

Thy Brother's House

Take the matter of housing. In Eastern Europe, what Progressive re-formers might have called "overcrowding" was simply a way of life.

MAX HIRSCH: *In Russia, let's see, we had [counting] one, two, three, four rooms. We slept—for the period, it was very big—six; two uncles was eight; my grandmother was nine; and my aunt was ten. And we had four rooms. And I don't ever remember going to sleep with only the four children and parents. There was always somebody else, some-body else. Was it a cousin? Was it an uncle? One of them. We had them, very many. Some lived away, so if they came, if they came to the town, they stayed over by us, and that's the way it was.*

I mean, there wasn't no room to dance. We had a bunkbetl, which opened into a bed, made with a cover, so when you pulled it out you slept in it. And then we had two beds and we had a sofa. The kitchen was the part that you cook in, and the rest [of the house] was to be used.

In Eastern Europe, poverty was not the fundamental reason for shar-ing beds and bedrooms. Those shtetl Jews who were not poor—the Hirsches for example—might have added rooms to a house for purposes of entertaining or establishing a business or housing servants or bathing, but they did not add rooms so as to provide privacy at night. Tess Egrovsky, whose family was unusually wealthy, recalls that her house in the Ukraine had not only a separate bathing room but also a separate and permanent *sukkah*, which (when it was not being used at *Sukkos*) served as bedroom and classroom for the private tutor her mother regularly employed. Her mother, wealthy mistress of an extensive household though she was, nonetheless slept in what would otherwise have been called the living room of the house; and Tess, daughter of wealth, shared a bed and a bedroom with two of her sisters. Personal privacy was simply not high on the Eastern European list of priorities.

In the New World, of course, poverty was more pervasive, at least at first; and the immigrants had to make do with whatever housing they could find. Few could afford spacious housing. Some—those who came earliest and were poorest—lived in multiple dwellings, tenements: one or two stories in Chicago and Philadelphia; four or five stories in New York; and two or three, sometimes five or six, apartments to a floor. Others, those who left the large cities and landed in smaller towns—Lowell or Trenton, Atlanta or Durham—might occupy a house, but it would have been small, unkempt, on the wrong side of the tracks.

In all of those places, crowding was the rule. Immigrant parents and children slept wherever they could find, or create, a flat surface: a folding cot in a hallway, a mattress stretched over three chair seats, a fire escape platform in the summertime. Thus, Esther Ginsburg remembered an apartment she and her family of seven lived in after leaving Lithuania.

It was in a brand-new tenement. Very clean. We had a toilet inside the apartment. It was on the fourth floor, but we had a dumbwaiter* in the house. It was so cold in the wintertime; we had no heat at all except from the stove in the kitchen. It was just a few years after we came. I must have been fifteen, maybe sixteen years old [about 1916].

There were two bedrooms. Three of my brothers were in one room; they all slept together in one bed, a double bed. I slept in the other room with my mother, because I was the only daughter with four sons, and I couldn't share it with my brothers. My father slept on what you call an oyfshtelbetl [folding cot] in the dining room with my youngest brother.

One day I had to go to the bathroom, and I saw them having sexual

---

* A dumbwaiter was an internal delivery system, used in apartment buildings that did not have elevators. Each apartment had a door in a wall; when you opened the door, you had access to a shaft which contained a wooden box on pulleys; items placed in the box on the entry floor or the basement could be hoisted up to the apartment—and vice versa.

intercourse on the kitchen floor. Where else could they go? They didn't have a bed to go to unless they kicked me out. I just passed by and saw them lying on the floor and that was it. I didn't say a word, just ran into the toilet, flushed the toilet, and ran back into bed, and I don't know what happened after that. They never said anything to me, and I never said anything to them.

This kind of crowding was distressing to Progressive housing reformers. Privacy and serenity were the two things that native-born Americans valued most about their homes. In America, the reformers believed, no one needed to be crowded: there was lots of land for houses, lawns, and gardens. Building materials were cheap, and so was labor. Sun-filled, spacious, well-ventilated houses, houses in which every person could lay claim to a room of his or her own, were essential, the reformers thought, not just to the good health of the population but also to the sustenance of family life. Prosperous Americans built their suburbs, planned and decorated their homes, as if they all agreed with the English architectural critic John Ruskin, whose many books appeared in hundreds of American editions between 1850 and 1900:

> Home is the place of peace; the shelter, not only from all injury, but from all terror, doubt and division. In so far as it is not this, it is not home; so far as the anxieties of the outer life penetrate into it, and the inconsistently-minded, unloved or hostile society of the outer world is allowed by either husband or wife to cross the threshold it ceases to be a home; it is then only a part of the outer world which you have roofed over and lighted a fire in. But so far as it is a sacred place, a vestal temple, a temple of the hearth . . . it is a home.[2]

Housing reformers understood spacious homes to be vestal temples not only for families but also for Uncle Sam. The sustenance of democracy, they believed, also required good housing. American children needed to learn what it means to separate private behavior from public behavior, one person's belongings from another's—the essential meaning of the term *private property*. "Homes are quite as much needed to make good citizens as to make good men," two housing reformers asserted, "for according as the working people are provided with better

"Then we moved to a house of our own. . . .
to my friends it was a mansion. . . .
The place was magnificent."
Child's birthday party, single-family home, Brooklyn, 1920s.

or poorer homes will the government and the morals of the country be better or worse."³

To the Jewish immigrants, however, there were some values more important than the privacy of property, and one of them was hospitality to relatives and friends, especially relatives and friends who were—temporarily or permanently—without homes of their own. Hospitality was more important to the immigrants than single-bed occupancy.

TESS EGROVSKY: *When I came to this country I went to live with my aunt who lived in a very small, little house in Philadelphia. I stayed there for six months. There were five girls in one room—three in one bed and two in the other bed. I was sixteen, the older one was under twenty, there was one about twenty, another fourteen, eighteen. The room, I can say, was about twelve by twelve.*

It was very nice, sleeping in a bed with two other people, but in the morning, when we used to get up, then it was very cold; we didn't have no heat. Only in the bottom; upstairs there was no heat. On the ground floor was the dining room, the kitchen, the summer kitchen [which was outside], and a front room. In the front room was my cousin, with her three children; she had three little boys. She slept with three boys in one room. And then there was another cousin and her husband and three children in another room, but they stayed there only about three months.

Sometimes we were fourteen, fifteen people in that little house.

Progressive reformers referred to all those aunts, uncles, and cousins as "boarders" or "lodgers." One famous study of living conditions in New York in 1910 reported, with considerable despair, that almost 80 percent of Jewish households included boarders—while only 25 percent of the "Colored," 24 percent of the Italian, and 6 percent of the Irish did.⁴ The reformers did not think it was wise for strangers to be sharing tables and beds with members of the family—or for distraught housewives to be spreading their already thinned-out energies on such a large number of souls. "Room overcrowding," one reformer asserted,

is bound up with another social problem, namely, the lodger evil. This prevails chiefly among the foreign elements of the population . . . especially among the Jews in the larger cities. It is fraught with great danger to the social fabric of the country. It means the undermining of family life; often the breaking down of domestic standards. It frequently leads to the breaking up of homes and families, to the downfall and subsequent degraded career of young women, to grave immoralities—in a word, to the profanation of the home.[5]

The Jews, of course, did not see things quite that way; making space for the *mishpoche*—uncles, aunts, first cousins, sixth cousins, even next-door neighbors from the shtetl—was not profanation of the home, but rather glorification of it, virtually a religious obligation: had not Abraham spread out a table for the angels? Unbounded hospitality had been part of the Eastern European Jewish housewife's routine for centuries upon centuries, ever since Jewish peddlers had gotten in the habit of traveling around the Polish countryside, and Jewish merchants had learned to search for bargains in far-off places. In the New World, hospitality was even more valued; you may have hated Yussel in Vilna, but in Chicago he became your friend. He was in need, and—who knows?—he might be the key to a good job for your son or a good match for your daughter—not to speak of a few extra dollars with which to supplement your husband's meager earnings.

Thus, it happened that, in the New World, even when Jews had struggled somewhat up the housing scale, even when they had indoor toilets and gas ranges, dumbwaiters and sun-filled rooms, steam heat and bathtubs, they still chose to double up in bed—and, not incidentally, enlarged the family purse in the process. Virtually none of the first generation of children to grow up on these shores knew what it meant to have his or her own bed, let alone his or her own room. And no one, except the reformers of course, thought that this was particularly strange.

JANET SOMMERS: *There were seven children. We lived on the Lower East Side of Manhattan, on Rivington Street. I have a feeling it was the top-floor apartment. There were not many rooms, and it was crowded sleeping there, but we did have a bathroom in the apartment.*

Then my father bought a house in Brooklyn. My father had saved his money and bought the building: twenty-eight apartments, seven to a floor. We lived on the first floor. Not only did we have an apartment there, but we broke through into another apartment to add another room for all of us. My first memory of that apartment was the telephone that was put onto the wall. It was not a crank thing, but it was a gooseneck thing. We had help in the house.

Then we moved to a house of our own. The things that come to my mind about that house. . . . It was a house, but to my friends it was a mansion. Murals on the wall. There was, in the living room, a candelabra, a chandelier, with twenty-four lights. When the previous owner left, he left with the chandelier and they sued him for it and got it back. They put down on the floor, not a Persian rug but a Chinese rug. The place was magnificent. We even had a white toilet seat.

In our new house, there were three bedrooms and a bathroom on the second floor. Only one bathroom. Oh! How I used to suffer! They [her brothers] all got in together and stayed there for hours.

. . . In the bedroom facing the street my mother and father slept. Next door to my parents is a small bedroom and for the most part I slept in that one bed. There were two beds—how we got them there, who knows? They bought me kiddy furniture because it was the only thing that could go into it. Two of my brothers slept in the other bed.

And all the people who came from Europe, there was always room for them—my father's nephew, my mother's sisters. One sister stayed until she was married. Another stayed quite a while. When I was thirteen, my cousin came from Europe, and they made me sleep with her. She was a nice enough person, maybe she was seventeen or eighteen years old, but I hated sleeping with her. Her feet smelled. I liked her, but I didn't want to sleep with her. I used to cry to my mother, but where else could she sleep? Not with my brothers. So she slept with me until she got married—three years, maybe four.

The back room was slightly larger, and the other four boys slept there. And at that time four boys, four big boys, occupied the back bedroom. Two in a bed each. There was no thought about minding; that was the way it was. And one drawer each for all of them. When I think of the four boys sleeping in two beds, and all of their possessions going into one drawer each and sharing that one closet, my hair stands on end! They argued constantly.

In spite of the reformers' fears that crowding would stunt their development, these children do not recall, now that they are elderly, much discomfort arising from it. Occasionally there were complaints, like Janet Sommers's, but none that we heard—either about stolen covers or about smelly feet—seemed of much consequence to the complainers, and many people we interviewed did not complain at all. Occasionally, we heard pleasure ("Snuggling with my sister was nice. We kept warm that way") but most frequently, resigned acceptance ("Well, that just was the way it was").

JENNIE GROSSMAN: *We [she and her younger sister] were accustomed to sleeping together. We slept in the same bed until we were teenagers. None of us stole the covers, but we did fight about making up the room. If I was angry at her, I would make up only half the bed. I was just making up my half. And she would make her half. And then maybe when she was twelve or thirteen, she wanted to know how babies are made. I did know but what I told her was that if you sleep in a bed with somebody, and you sleep tushy to tushy you have a baby. Well, that poor kid! She never turned her back on me again!*

Eventually, of course, the desire to assimilate proved more powerful than the force of tradition. By the time the immigrant youth had become adults (roughly between 1930 and 1950), starting their own families, choosing their own apartments, buying their own small houses in the suburbs, the American ideal had become their own: houses were better than apartments; houses with lawns and gardens were better than those that were attached; houses with separate bedrooms and separate beds for each child were best of all. Or perhaps the discomforts of overcrowding had made more of an impression than anyone is now willing to admit. Whatever the reason, privacy and serenity—Ruskin's vestal, familial temples—carried the day, as Sol Meyrowitz and Jennie Grossman attest:

SOL MEYROWITZ: *Our first apartment, after we got married, was a one-bedroom, but when the baby [his son, Joel] got sick, we moved in with my mother for a while because the bills were too high. My*

51

mother had a two-bedroom apartment then, but she also had a boarder, so we had to live in the living room, only about a month, I guess—and then Sally [his wife] took the baby and went to the country for the summer.

When she came back we found a nice apartment across the street from my mother, and we lived there all during the war. It was three rooms. Barbara [his daughter] was born there. She had a crib in the bedroom, and Joel slept on a kind of folding chair-bed in the living room. The springs hurt his back, and he used to cry about it a lot.

We wanted a larger apartment. We wanted the kids to have bedrooms, separate, but the landlord wouldn't give us a better apartment unless we paid for the stove and the refrigerator. So we decided to look for a house.

We used all our war bonds. We bought one of those attached houses, you know the kind, it had a rental below and we lived above. We wanted to stay near my mother. So we got this house and it was wonderful. It had three bedrooms, a den, a kitchen, and a living room—all on one floor. And it was near the school, so the kids didn't have to cross any streets. And they had their own bedrooms.

We lived there until I retired. I loved it there. Nobody ever worked on it but me—no plumber, no carpenter, no roofer, no painter, nobody. I did all the work myself. Who could afford a plumber?

JENNIE GROSSMAN: One of my sisters married a man, he was a nice man really, but not very successful. His father owned real estate—you know, apartment buildings. So they had an apartment in one of his father's buildings, but his father was a stingy old bastard, he charged them rent anyway.

Well, their first child was a boy, my nephew Stanley. And when Stanley was about three or four, my sister got pregnant again, and she got really upset. They couldn't afford another baby. And they only had one bedroom, and they were worried that if the baby was a girl they would need even a larger apartment. So she had an abortion. I remember the whole thing. It was awful. But she decided to have an abortion, and her husband agreed with her and she went and did it. She just couldn't stand the idea of those kids having to share a bedroom.

Later on, when her husband started to do a little better, then they had another kid. And it was a boy anyway.

A Uniquely Hebrew Habit: Working at Home

Yet another facet of immigrant Jewish life that native-born Americans found disturbing was the sweatshop. In Eastern Europe, Jews had been accustomed, for centuries, to working in their homes. Men and women, boys and girls, grandmothers and grandfathers, none of them understood what it meant to distinguish between "workplaces" and "homeplaces."

TESS EGROVSKY: *In our house, the beautiful house [in the Ukraine], my mother had a mill that we made kasha [groats; coarse-ground wheat]. We had a man working for us. By foot he ran it, not by mechanical; he was working the machine by foot. He made kasha in a building next to the living quarters; it was a big extension, and that's where the kasha was being produced.*

He was working for her for many, many years. He was a very dependent man. He was almost like one of the family. He had one little girl, and every time he came to work he would bring her because she was my age and he felt that we could be very friendly. As a matter of fact, in later years, when the pogroms started [about 1919], this particular Christian fellow, he would take as many as he could—my sister, myself, especially myself—to his home that he lived in out of town. And he would keep us there until they went away.

SADIE REHSTOCK: *The kitchen [in Warsaw] had a stove and beside the stove was a little table, a working table, with a sewing machine standing in the kitchen. A stand really, with a machine on top. It was used to make buttonholes on men's shoes. It was a whole shoe without buttonholes; my father had to put the buttonholes in. That machine was owned by my father who employed someone to help work it. He came several times a week; he was Jewish. My father did the buttonholes, but he also had a man who helped him.*

My mother was also a capitalist. My mother hired some young girls, sometimes four at a time, which made her a capitalist. My mother sewed white collars and cuffs. She was a contractor. A contractor gets material from a manufacturer and takes it home. These girls finished up the work; they sewed the collars and cuffs. They were friends or relatives—all Jewish. Once in a while there were men, too—my mother's cousins. They would sing songs while they worked—Yiddish songs, sometimes Russian folk songs. We were very friendly; when we came to America, we kept up the friendship. They were friends who worked for my mother.

ESTHER GINSBURG: *My mother was a dressmaker [in Lithuania]; we had five sewing machines in the house. It was a two-level building with an upper and lower level, and the entrance was through a staircase into the main room—and then we had a bedroom, a living room, and a kitchen upstairs. The living room was also the working room where the people used to work. In the bedroom my father and mother slept. The children slept in the living room; there were six of us. Five machines and six children.*

When the people who operated the machines left for the night, the children moved in. We slept in a bed, the room was rather large, and all you had to do is push the machines to the side and put up a bunk; it wasn't a real bed; it was a convertible thing. You were sitting on it during the day, and at night you had straw, spread straw on the thing, and that is where you slept. It looked like a bench, an ordinary bench, and you put straw out and just lie down and slept. To make the bed you picked the straw up and put it someplace.[6]

When they moved to the New World, the immigrants tried to reproduce the way of life they had been accustomed to in the Old. Not infrequently they succeeded. One reason the needle trades attracted many Eastern Europeans (not all of whom had previously made a living as tailors) was that much of the work could be done at home: sewing machines could be operated at home, buttonholes stitched at home, stockings and petticoats sold from home. However horrendous the sweatshop may have been, it at least replicated the work habits to which some of the immigrants, like Esther Ginsburg's mother, Sam Smilowitz's father, and Etta Levine's parents, had become accustomed.

ESTHER GINSBURG: *The first apartment we had was in Boston; we had a four-room apartment, and my mother sold from the house. Underwear. She sold stuff right out of the house; she couldn't wait [to start a business].*

LEARNING TO LIVE IN AMERICA

The apartment was two bedrooms, a front room and a kitchen; she used the front room. All day long there were people coming in and out—women mostly. One bedroom my brothers, and one bedroom my father and my mother. In the living room—the front room—me. They had all beds in the bedroom. I slept on a cot in the living room. My three brothers slept in two beds.

In the kitchen was a coal stove. We had a table. We had a black sink, and we used to make hot water in the boiler, in the stove. My father was a presser; my mother sold, mostly underwear. She washed, she ironed, she cooked, and she sold underwear.

Without me my mother couldn't get along because I spoke English after a while. She couldn't understand the yentas [gossipers] when they spoke English, but I started to speak English right away. After a while she got a store by herself, but for the first few years she sold right from the house.

SAM SMILOWITZ: *My father had been a capmaker in Galicia, and he got a job in a factory here making caps, too: soft caps, with a little peak—the kind the taxi drivers wore. And he worked at home, too: piecework he would bring home; and some of his friends would work at our house, too. There was a machine in the house, and at night I heard it going when I went to sleep. Foot operated. We had no electricity then; we had gas lights. My father's sewing machine was in the kitchen. I remember lying awake at night and wishing they would stop, already, with the machine and go to bed. I slept in the same room with my mother and father and when he finally came to bed, I always woke up, and then I couldn't go back to sleep again. I hated that sewing machine.*

ETTA LEVINE: *I remember the first butcher shop my father had. We lived behind the store. The store had three rooms in the back, and you got entrance into this apartment only through the store. And there was a refrigerator in the little hallway that separated the apartment from the store. Oh! I used to hate that apartment. I hated it because my parents worked so hard. And I hated to bring my friends home through that store, all the garbage—the bones and the fat—in the back, right in front of our apartment.*

I hated to see my parents work so hard. Long hours and very little profits. My mother would be always in the store. She was never one who cut meat or chopped or did anything like that. After my father weighed the meat, she would wrap it—and in those days they wrapped it in newspaper. She would prepare the newspapers, tear the papers, and then would wrap it. She took the money, too. My father never liked that part of it. You see my father was really a scholar. My father, he would prefer anything that was connected with books. We were very, very poor. We never thought about it.

Fifteen dollars a month—I think that fifteen dollars a month was for the store and for the rooms behind the store.

Like Etta Levine's parents, many immigrants (and their children, too) worked long hours at home—taking in other people's laundry, for example, or making artificial flowers; but those long hours did not unduly distress the Progressive reformers: "admirably industrious," they might say, "demonstrating a thoroughly American desire to get ahead." No, the good-hearted social workers (and many were unendingly patient and good-hearted) were not opposed to having women and children work at home for wages; what they could not tolerate were men who worked at home. Men who work at home, the reformers thought, turn what should be a woman's world into a man's world (privacy, again!) and bring strangers into places where strangers should never tread. The sweatshop was evil because, as Ruskin might have put it, the sacred was contaminated by the profane.

The Progressives had a vision—children of industrialization that they were—that "workspaces" ought to be separate from "living spaces" (hence their passion for zoning laws), that husbands and fathers ought to go off every day to factories and offices, that children ought to go off to schools, that mothers ought to be the only ones left at home, protecting and polishing the hearth. Immigrant children ought, Progressive reformers thought, to be raised precisely the way they themselves had been raised, but this could not happen when fathers stayed home to work and—worse yet—brought strange people into the kitchen as well:

One drawback to improving conditions in tenement house life for the Hebrews has been their peculiar devotion to the occupation of tailoring and to the "sweat shop system." This is also growing among the Italians—more among deserted or widowed women, as a stopgap occupation, however, than among the men as a regular trade, as it is seen among the Hebrews. . . . In time it may be supposed that this particular form of occupation, with the evil conditions depending on it, will be outgrown—a process which may be materially hastened by proper sanitary laws and the proper enforcement of them.[7]

Eventually the Jewish sweatshop went the way of prosperity and Americanization. In various cities across the land, Progressive reformers (with the help of some labor leaders) managed to pass ordinances that restricted the practice: ordinances that prevented businesses from functioning in residential districts, or that required provision of ventilation for workrooms and toilets for workers. But the positive incentive of prosperity was more effective than the negative incentives of fines, for as Jewish families became more prosperous they chose to keep their children in school for longer periods of time, and as those children began to enter the labor force, they chose the American "way of work," not the European.

"Water, Water, All You Want": Keeping Clean

Cleanliness—especially personal cleanliness—was one of the few prosaic yet crucial matters on which the native-born Americans and the immigrant Jews saw eye to eye. Wealthy Americans had started to enjoy the comforts of private plumbing in the middle of the nineteenth century; most substantial dwellings built in American cities after the 1870s made provision for a hot water boiler in the basement or the kitchen (the water was provided, often free of charge, by the city), a footed bathtub located somewhere on an upper floor, and a flushing toilet connected to a sewer line. By the 1890s, even rural and suburban houses of some consequence came outfitted with an electric water pump and a toilet that drained to a dry well.

By the 1890s, many Americans had also come to understand that toilets that flushed and bathtubs that spouted hot water were more than merely comfortable. The germ theory of disease (first propounded by

Louis Pasteur and Robert Koch in the 1880s) had convinced many people that good sanitary practices were the key to good health—and that such practices extended well beyond matters of personal cleanliness (see also chapter 4). If germs were indeed invisible and omnipresent, as the scientists stated, then an overrunning cesspool in one neighborhood could cause cholera or dysentery or typhoid in another, and a laundress's sneeze could well lead to her mistress's pneumonia. The Progressive campaign to clean up the slums—to provide sunlight and ventilation in every apartment, to ensure that flush toilets would be installed in all tenements, to build public bathhouses on every corner and public laundries on every side street—was thus as selfish as it was altruistic. If the germ theory of disease were true—and no one doubted this for a moment—then making America clean for the poor would make America healthy for the rich as well.

Immigrant Jews at first knew little or cared nothing about the germ theory of disease, but the set of religious rules and regulations they had carried with them across the Atlantic had been requiring personal cleanliness for more than two millennia:

> Philanthropists and reformers, particularly those of the fair sex, are apt to regard the immigrant Jewish population as a "slum" population; as degraded residents of narrow and filthy streets, whose foul general habits are beyond their power to describe. . . . In fact, of the homes of the poor population of the city, the Jewish home is the cleanest. . . .
>
> The personal cleanliness of the Russian Jew is far above that of the average slum population. The pious use the bath as often as possible, and as required in the form of the Mickva. . . . It also must be borne in mind that the religious Jew cuts the nails of his fingers and toes at least once a week, because, according to the rabbinical teaching, dirt under the nails contains "devils," or "evil spirits." Before each meal he must carefully wash his hands, and repeat this operation immediately after meals, and must then also rinse his mouth; and he must not walk four steps from his bed in the morning without careful ablution of his face and hands. A Jewish woman must visit a bath at least once a month; the nails of her fingers and toes must be cut off completely. All these religious rites and customs are carefully observed by the older generation

58

"I went to the bathhouse with my father, but the little kids used to take baths in the copper sink."
East Side, New York City, 1905.

who are generally pious; the younger people, though they do not observe all these rites religiously, still follow them more or less.[8]

In the villages and towns of Eastern Europe, private plumbing systems were nonexistent. Jews were in the habit of bathing regularly, but not in their own homes. Every town of any size had a bathhouse (with a steam room) as well as a *mikve* (for the ritual immersions required of women). Some of the people we interviewed recall the trip to the bathhouse as a special occasion: once a week perhaps, or once a month. But only the wealthiest families, who had many servants, bathed at home: and even for them, there was no easy access to water, as Tess Egrovsky recalls:

There used to be a man delivered water to all the neighborhood. In Europe we called him a vaserfirer—he delivered to everybody. This water was in a big tank, and he would fill up our barrel. And from that we used it in the house. These containers were in the kitchen and my parents' bedroom.

And we also had to take a bath, it's not like here where you had bathtubs. We were very well off. We had a separate room just for taking baths. It had a tub in it and a stove. The tub you filled up with water and placed near the hearth, and it heated up, or they poured water from the pot.

And we had sinks, yes. The sink was a little cabinet, a wooden cabinet with a door that had a pail standing there, and it was made on the outside just like the sinks are made here. It was a cabinet sink, you could move it anywhere you want. It was not attached to the wall, it was a piece of furniture. And it had on the outside, it had a little shelf with a glass, or whatever you want. The sink was used for washing and cooking. You had to wash your hands in the morning. The European people wash their hands the very first thing in the morning, and then they say their morning prayers.

The toilet was outside the house, partially. If you had to go, you had to go outside the house. You could go inside the house, but in the morning you had to clean it up.

In European cities, sanitary facilities were only a bit more advanced. In Warsaw, Minsk, and Odessa, the city government provided steam-engine–driven pumps that sent cold water to rooftop holding tanks, whence it flowed into taps in each apartment (in the United States, this was called a "cold-water flat"). Most of the sinks in those apartments did not have drains (that is, there was no sewage system) and toilets were still both outdoors and unflushable. Sadie Rehstock, in recalling the slum her family lived in in Warsaw, spoke of how the windows of the main apartment faced into the courtyard:

A very large, wide courtyard, with four different buildings around it. When I looked out the window into the courtyard, I saw the toilet that everyone used, so when I looked out the window I saw people doing their business in public.

I was a child, so I never used the outside toilet. I used a potty in the house and it was carried out to the toilet. I don't remember who carried the potty out—probably some adult. I guess we must have had cold running water because I remember a faucet; in the summertime we let the faucet run and left food in the sink so there was always cold water running into the sink, keeping the food cold.

And there was slop water outside in the courtyard in a huge tank, a huge tank for the slop water. That tank had an interesting name: in Yiddish, it was pomeshov. And there is a saying about it in Yiddish. In the building, on the top floor, was an attic that was used to dry the clothes that were washed, a boydem, and when something is washed not very clean it was pomeshov gevashn, oif dem boydem getrukn [washed in slop water and dried in the attic].

In America, in the first decades of the twentieth century, the plumbing systems available, even to the poor, were a considerable improvement over what even the rich had been able to acquire in Eastern Europe. Gold may not have been lying in the streets, but flush toilets could be found in most tenements. Irving Farber, for example, had heard about the plumbing that he could expect even before he emigrated:

My father [who had been to America] told us that we led a very primitive life. We didn't understand what it means, how to get steam or hot water. We didn't know what that meant, what he saw in America, where somebody opens up a certain screw, opens up a valve, and water,

water, water. The laughing of the people there rings still in my ears to this very day. "How is that possible, you open a valve, and water, water, all you want?" That's how primitive we were.[9]

By 1905, virtually all American cities had banned outdoor privies and required landlords to install indoor toilets, connected to sewer lines. Compliance was not perfect, but nearly so—since fear of cholera and typhus had galvanized even the most recalcitrant landlords and bureaucrats. Progressive housing reformers hated the sight and smell of tenement hall toilets; some were made of wood and tin (and thus leaked and sweated), many—apparently—were rarely cleaned, and all served more residents than the reformers thought either appropriate or sanitary. But to people who were accustomed to cold weather and outdoor privies, a hall toilet, no matter how filthy, had the distinct advantage of being indoors.

And other benefits quickly became possible as well. Our grandparents, with their children tagging along, moved about—from one apartment to another, even from one community to another—with extraordinary frequency. One of the things they moved in search of was better plumbing. If the first apartment was a cold-water flat, the next might have running hot water; the one after that might have a toilet exclusively for the use of the family; and the third (or fourth or fifth) might have a bathtub as well as a toilet.

Charlie Moses was born in New York City in 1903, the third child (but the first to be born in the United States) of parents who had emigrated from the Polish city of Lodz:

Our first home was on Pitt Street, on the Lower East Side [in New York City], but I was too young, I don't remember that apartment. Then we moved to Cherry Street, opposite the printing-press people. That apartment had a toilet in the hall. When we went outside to the bathroom in the winter, the water would freeze, so we had to run into the house to fill up a bucket. It happened more than once.

That apartment had no bathtub, not even in the hall. We had a toilet in the apartment [house] there, but no bathtub. All the baths were taken in the bathhouses. Sometimes I went to the city baths.

From Cherry Street we moved to Harlem, 98th Street, and from 98th Street we moved to 94th Street. We had four rooms, an old-

fashioned sink and stove—a copper sink, with faucets. The bathroom was still in the hall, but at least we had hot water. I went to the bath-house with my father, but the little kids used to take baths in the copper sink. The washtub had a center that came out and that was the bathtub. The laundry was done at home, and some went to the [commercial] laundry [for] the larger things that could not be done at home.* But we had no bathtubs in the house.

After we were on 94th Street for a while, we moved across the street. We had, in the first apartment, a copper-colored sink—a dark sink— and they also gave us hot water, but my father and mother decided to pay an increase of fifty cents a month for a white sink and hot water. We wanted more conveniences, more modern, so we moved across the street.

The public baths that Charlie Moses remembers patronizing were an important facet of the reformers program for the slums. "The need exists," one reformer asserted in 1903, "and it is clearly the duty of the municipality because the health of the whole community is concerned. The frightful congestion of humanity, resulting in physical conditions that lead to degeneracy, poverty and crime, should at least be alleviated by opportunity for cleanliness."[10] Since the 1880s, all large American cities had attempted to meet the need: in 1902, there were already four public bathhouses in Chicago, five in New York, two in Philadelphia, and one each in Buffalo, Rochester, and Yonkers, New York; in Pittsburgh, Pennsylvania; and in Brookline, Massachusetts. Each dispensed soap and towels, and one was allowed a fixed number of minutes in a shower stall. Private bathhouses also existed in tenement districts, and these offered the additional luxury of a steam room. Jews were frequent visitors to both kinds of establishment:

> The Russian baths are very numerous in the Jewish quarters, and very much frequented. "I cannot get along without a sweat (Russian bath) at least once a week," many a Jew will tell you. On the days when these Russian baths admit only women, they are

---

* Commercial laundries (also called "steam laundries") could be found, in those days, in every urban neighborhood, rich or poor. Using steam engines to drive huge washing machines, and gas-fired boilers to heat the water, they provided many levels of service: "finished" (which meant ironed); "dry" (dried and folded); and "rough dry" (unfolded).

also crowded with women and children. During the Summer, the public baths on the East River are crowded with Jewish humanity from daybreak till late in the evening.[11]

SADIE REHSTOCK: *In the first apartment we had a bathroom in the hall. We used to go to the baths outside in the bathhouses; we had just a toilet. All the baths were taken in the bathhouses. I used to go there for a bath by myself. Sometimes I go to the city baths. Sometimes if they weren't busy they let you stay a little longer; if not, they would say, "Time up!" They gave you enough time to take a shower and get dressed. If they weren't busy, they give you two minutes more.*

When we lived on Third Street, there was a private bathhouse on the middle of the block; we would go in for a bath once in a while. Saturdays, Sundays, we would go into the private bathhouse. They gave you twenty minutes to get washed, and we had to clean out the tub; you did it yourself, and then they would do it. You have to bring your own towels, or you pay five cents a towel. Sometimes when I was working already, I used to take the bus home and stop on Avenue D and pay for a towel and take a shower there.

"The Children Seem To Have Been Forgotten": Street Life

If the reformers approved of the ways in which young immigrant Jews bathed, they did not similarly approve of the ways in which they played. In the world of Ruskin, childhood was supposed to be a time of rustic pleasures, with children enjoying fresh air, lots of exercise, and convivial companions—gamboling in pastures, tramping through woods, skating on frozen ponds, cavorting with dogs and horses. Scenes and pastimes remote indeed from tenement children such as Charlie Moses, Aaron Katz, Hannah Toperoff, and Sam Smilowitz.

CHARLIE MOSES: *Before I was able to talk practically, I was in a street fight, with kids from the next block who came on with stones and with garbage-can covers to use as shields. I had a shield in my hand. I was a pishe [small boy; literally, one who still pees in his pants] but I remember it. But I never found out where they got the stones. On the East Side there were no lots. Everything was covered with a building—whether it was a private house or a tenement.*

I played in the streets with other kids. You know how we played basketball? We couldn't get into the school grounds; they must have locked the gates. So we made up our own. Across the street from our house there was a fire station, and outside there was a ledge, maybe about five or six inches. Well, that was the basket. And the basketball was—we took a stocking filled with rags—thrown against the ledge.

AARON KATZ: *After school I was an errand boy, because they had no telephones. I did that even when I moved to Brooklyn, when my father bought his own home; I continued spending some hours of the afternoon answering the telephones. I earned money by walking over to the corner drugstore and waiting for a telephone call: pick up the receiver, and ask who they wanted to speak to—which was generally confined to the block. I would run over and get the person they wanted to speak to, and usually was rewarded with a penny or two. There were four or five telephone booths. At times I would handle all five. I had competition but I was fast; I turned out to be a sprinter. I remember once earning fifty cents.*

That money I spent on myself. I ate a lot of charlotte russes. I went into the candy store and bought pencils. Oh yes, I distributed amongst a great many strangers, too. In the candy store I used to get ten pieces of bonbons or hard candy for one penny, and this is something you couldn't resist—the greedy eyes. You couldn't resist being compassionate, even at that age. I distributed a good deal of candies and loved doing it.

I wasn't beat up as frequently as some of the others. After I started buying candies I wasn't hit any more; I'll put it that way. I was beat up by a great many people, older people. In those years it was commonplace for the older boys to kick one in the asshole, to strike out at the younger people. It was commonplace; it was a form of release for them. And it was commonly done. We never stopped looking over our shoulder.

And, oh yes, we gambled a little bit. We played pennies: odds or

65

evens. I didn't always win until I learned the tricks of the game. So that is the way our pennies were dissipated.

HANNAH TOPEROFF: *Once we went home [from school], we didn't see the other children; we had chores to do. If they lived next door, then O.K., but I didn't see the other kids in the class. I didn't see too many of the kids outside of class.*

On one of those big holidays, when the straw-hat season would be over—I guess Labor Day—and these old men would come through our street, poor people, still wearing straw hats, and the kids on our block wanted to make a bonfire and they would go around stealing these straw hats from these poor people. They would clip the straw hats off their heads. And the poor man would be running after. No way would he could get that straw hat back. The kids would fly and save it for the big bonfire. Anybody with a straw hat. Oh! The bonfire was in the alley way, they would have it right in the beginning of the alley way. We only had this one alley. All the kids would use whatever wood they could get. They would collect it for weeks in preparation for this big fire. Just for the fun of it. Seeing flames.

SAM SMILOWITZ: *On my block I was the power. I was the boss. Street gang. We had gang fights. Rocks, bottles. Against the Irish. It was rough stuff. The apartment houses were put together; the janitor used to live in the cellar, in the back. And then there was a little passageway, from the front of the house to the backyard, so we loaded up the back of the yard with all kinds of junk, mainly broken bottles, that we could throw, or use for stabbing. The plan was when they come we all act scared and let them get close. And run down the passageway. Those kids came through the building, and we were waiting. We did a job on them. And that was the last we saw of them. I prefer not to recall exactly what happened to them. A lot of mussed-up faces. They got the message to pick on some other gang on some other block.*

We had great names: Jew Boy, Skinny, Fatso, Ginso.

Although Sam Smilowitz remembers all this name calling fondly, other people we interviewed do not recall taking kindly to being called "Jew boy"—or anything else that smacked of anti-Semitism. Many people we interviewed recalled that one prominent aspect of all the tomfoolery in the streets was ethnic hostility—much of it expressed in a fashion all too reminiscent of Eastern Europe. Janet Sommers says that when she was quite young, she did not really know that there was much difference between Jews and gentiles; the subject was never discussed at home. But then one day:

A bunch of kids ganged around me—I was six years old—and called me a Christ killer. And I didn't know what the hell they were talking about. I started to cry because they said I killed somebody, so when my father came home, my eyes were all red, swollen from crying. He said, "What's the matter, bubbula?" I said, "Poppa, they said I killed somebody." That is when I found out we were Jewish, and then I found out there were Jews and non-Jews. So then he explained to me that we were born Jews and they were Gentiles and they said that the Jews killed Christ. But actually we did not; it had happened centuries ago and I was not responsible for it. He said it to me in a quiet way, but he was angry. He used to let me play with some of the kids in the evening but that day he didn't let me play with anybody.

If Jewish parents were distressed about the activity in the streets, so too were the reformers. They wanted to create a gentler environment for immigrant children, to build parks and playgrounds all over the tenement districts: a tiny bit of the countryside within the city, places in which poor immigrant children might learn to play in a more "civilized" fashion, without beating each other up, without gambling, without harassing their elders. At the turn of the century, as dwellings encroached upon the few open spaces left in cities—and as the dwellings themselves began to be built without backyards or courtyards—children were increasingly confined to alleys, hallways, and streets, a form of confinement that—according to the reformers—was undermining their health as well as their "proper social development":

In the original plan of the city of New York the children seem to have been forgotten. . . . The unoccupied space has been covered by improvements which have left to the children no other opportunity for play but such as can be found in the streets. The streets themselves have been largely occupied by car tracks and new servitudes [that is, electric poles, telephone lines, and so on], so that it is dangerous as well as obstructive to traffic for the children to use them for games of any kind, without incurring the interference of the police.

A sense of hostility between the children and the guardians of public order is thus engendered, leading to the growth of a criminal class and to the education of citizens who become enemies of law and order. Nothing can be worse or more to be deplored than this state of affairs, whether regarded from a moral or economic point of view. The outlay for police, courts, reformatories, hospitals, almshouses, and prisons is thus largely increased, while outside of these safeguards against poverty and crime is bred a general feeling of discontent, which is the cause of much misery, poverty, and danger to society.

. . . Our failure to provide for the reasonable recreation of the people, and especially for playgrounds for the rising generation, has been the most efficient cause of the growth of crime and pauperism in our midst.[12]

Such rhetoric apparently did the trick, for many parks and playgrounds were constructed during the Progressive years. Those new facilities did not, of course, bring an end to crime and pauperism—or live on in the memories of the people we interviewed. None could remember anything much about swings, seesaws, or fountains—although one or two could recall adolescent flirtations that were mediated by white skirts and public tennis courts. Apparently, even after the playgrounds and the parks were built, immigrant children continued to play in the streets and continued—if their memories now serve—to play in a fashion that neither their parents nor the reformers were likely to approve.

Becoming Americans

As they came to maturity, immigrant children and the children of immigrants began to understand themselves as caught between two worlds: the world their parents had come from and the world toward which their teachers were pointing. Which would they choose to emulate?

Some reacted as if neither was particularly attractive. The world their parents had come from was one in which men were still rigidly separated from women, in which girls wore demure clothing and marriages were arranged, in which holidays were celebrated only in the company of relatives and picnics were arranged by the burial society. To many Jewish youths, this world appeared tainted, if for no other reason (and there were many other reasons) than that it was their parents'. But the world of the high-minded social reformers was not the right choice either, for it seemed to consist entirely of libraries and lectures, concert halls and tea dances, playgrounds and good intentions, a world that was, on the one hand, entirely too tame for an adolescent, and, on the other—like the blond and blue-eyed romances of many Jewish dreams—both entirely seductive and entirely out of reach.

Between these two poles, however, lay a third possibility. Children who had been born just before and after the turn of the century came to maturity in a world that contained the new media: silent films, cheap monthly magazines, inexpensive illustrated newspapers. The newspaper publisher William Randolph Hearst had discovered the value of a titillating headline sometime in the 1890s; *Boy's Stories* began publication in 1899; *True Romances* in 1902. Mae West made her debut in 1910; Rudolf Valentino started making women swoon three years later. On the screen, in the pages of magazines, some Jewish adolescents discovered a world they cared to emulate, at one and the same time thoroughly exciting, thoroughly American, and completely accessible to the children of the poor.

It was the world of the "flapper." Janet Sommers recalls precisely what image the word *flapper* was meant to convey: the image of an adolescent—male or female—who, contrary to the instructions of both parents and teachers, allowed the high tops of galoshes to go unfastened, flapping open. Hannah Toperoff recalls something of the hijinks that were involved when the adolescent children of recently immigrated parents learned to flout the values of both the cultures in which they had been raised:

When I was fifteen or sixteen [1925], it was popular to be a member of a [high school] sorority. That was the way; that was the social pat-

tern. And I remember vividly, once, my sister and I smoking away at one of the meetings and then hanging out of the window to vomit. Yes, sir! We were very sick and we had our heads out of the window. We both tried it together.

We got into a sorority, the two of us. All sororities were "alpha" something or other. But the interesting part about this sorority was that the girls in it were referred to as "fast." And I remember vividly going to my first dance, a sorority dance, and I would like to describe what we wore.

We were clothes' horses, and we had our own private dressmaker, whose name was Mrs. Dragon, and she was a Polish woman and an excellent dressmaker. We were *fancy fancy*. And to this first sorority dance I wore a green, what was referred to as *metalisé*—this was material that had gold and silver threads in it and was a rather showy kind of material. It was green with all kinds of highlights.

And I wore that dress without a stitch of clothing underneath! No bra, no nothing; without a stitch. I don't think I was even wearing underpants.

The youthful memories of Esther Ginsburg, Sol Meyrowitz, and Morris Hochstadt convey, each in a different way, the extent to which popular media were teaching Jewish youths to behave in untraditional ways. Necking, going to night clubs, experimenting with makeup, these were more than untraditional; they were positively contrary to tradition, a deliberate defiance of parental values, a deliberate—as with the galoshes—effort to define oneself as an American, not perhaps the model American the teachers, librarians, and social workers were trying to create, but an American nonetheless.

ESTHER GINSBURG: *I started going out with Willie when I was still in high school. I went to places I never went before. Oh! He used to take me to the movies. We always sat halfway down—no necking. I was just so happy to be in places that I never went to and never thought existed. He took me to the Pageant, which is a Chinese restaurant. He took me to other movie houses. I used to love it. I went to places that I never saw in my life. I loved him, I really loved him. And every Friday night he used to take me to basketball games in his high school.*

We never necked in the movies. But I had a friend in high school.

My parents were American but not as American as her parents. She was pretty wild; she dated, she necked, she did things I would never dream of doing. My mother made sure I wasn't going to do anything wrong. I guess her mother didn't talk to her that way.

SOL MEYROWITZ: *My father and mother didn't do things the way Americans did things. My sister was very aggressive: she used lipstick at thirteen, fourteen. Well, it was considered indecent. Sometimes I was scolded and sometimes whipped for what I did. She left home and joined the stage for a period of several months when she was fifteen, sixteen—a dancing troupe, a chorus line. Oh! I had a miserable time of it. She was very modern; she used lipstick and went to burlesque shows. In those years, in our house, it was verboten. In those years, she went to dances and all the things that were frowned upon she went to. I don't know where she learned it—maybe from the movies.*

MORRIS HOCHSTADT: *I had a good friend named Jack, and on one vacation he and some other fellows took a drive down south. Anyhow, we stopped at a cabaret, which was something new in my life. And in the cabaret—I never drank, except soda, ginger ale—but then there were others who drank stronger drinks. And then came the cabaret girls. And they came around the tables nude. Nude! I didn't know where we were, but my friends did—they knew where to go.*

I remember these girls, how they came to the table. A guy put a quarter, and she went over and with her vagina she was able to pick it up. That's some vagina! And I saw them do that! It was the kind of place they went to, not the kind of place for a yeshiva bokher [student in a traditional religious academy] to go to!

Yet whether they chose the "way of the flapper" or the "way of the reformers," Jewish youths were eager to assimilate. Many observers noticed this. "No other race responds so quickly," one American noted, "to the influence of environment. The young Jew adjusts himself with incredible facility to the conditions of modern life and while adopting our customs he appreciates our thoughts and feelings to a greater extent than we imagine."[13] Some Jewish adolescents experimented with holding hands in public (strictly forbidden in the Orthodox code), and others ate pork chops in college dining halls. Some tried

71

horseback riding, ice skating, and tennis; others, agnosticism, socialism, and birth control. As they grew older, they stopped visiting public
bathhouses and started insisting on separate beds; some took apartments of their own as soon as they could afford to.

Each of these steps along the road to Americanization was fraught
with emotion, no matter how trivial its content might appear. The
way of the flapper and the way of the reformers were both incompatible with the traditional world of Jewish parents. Each step on the road
toward becoming an American thus widened the gap between parent
and child. Sensitive observers of the immigrant scene were well aware
of the special difficulties that this created for Jewish children trying
to assimilate in a Christian world, for Jewish children whose religion
governed even the most mundane aspects of behavior:

> At home the child is taught certain moral precepts, he becomes
> used to a certain mode of life, he knows and believes in the distinc-
> tions of the milk and meat diet, he understands the significance of
> kosher food, he observes the sanctity of the Sabbath. . . . All these
> seem to him his own and are dear to him. No sooner does he
> come in contact with the world at large, than his entire being is
> shattered. . . .
>
> There is now a contradiction between his own self and the sur-
> rounding world. With him it is not a question of theological ab-
> stract discussion; it is a problem of practical significance. . . .
>
> Quite frequently the Jewish child finds himself a stranger both
> to his own fold and to the Gentiles that surround him. The home
> that was so attractive and sweet to him becomes a burden; he is
> ashamed of his own parents and their mode of life.[14]

Of all the forces working for assimilation, the most powerful, for
the Jews, were the schools. As powerful as the influences of the streets
and the media may have been, nowhere were the contradictions between the New World and the Old more apparent—and more con-
founding—to Jewish children than at school. To Jews a "school" and
a "synagogue" are equally sacred places; indeed, in Eastern Europe they
were frequently one and the same place, which is why—even to this
day—older Jews still say that they are going to "*shul*," when younger
ones insist that the buildings be called "synagogues" or "temples."

Jewish parents may have been appalled by the American streets, indifferent to the English-language newspapers, ignorant of the movies, but they were determined that their children do well in school, a determination that had been ingrained in their culture for centuries. But in American schools, the reformers reigned supreme. American schools did not teach Torah and they did not preach Orthodoxy. This meant, inescapably, the worst contradiction of all: in order to please their parents by doing well in school, Jewish children were forced to reject the other traditions that their parents prized.

3

BREAKING AWAY FROM TORAH: THE IMPACT OF AMERICAN SCHOOLING

WE ALL KNOW the stereotype; we have all heard the jokes. The Jews love learning. They are the people of the book. Jewish children excel in school. The Jews revere scholars and scholarship. "What's a Jewish dropout?" "Someone who quit after a master's degree!" "You got a ninety-eight! That's nice, but what happened to the other two points?"

Like all stereotypes, this one has a base in reality, but—like them, too—it also lies, disguising part of the truth. Some Jews love learning—but others scoff at it. Some Jewish children excelled in school, but others failed, a failure honored more in silence than in celebration. Some of the Jewish children who excelled in school paid a terrible, haunting, alienating price for that excellence. The pedagogic practices common in our parents' youth were (as often we have been reminded) more stringent than those with which we as children were familar, but that stringency was enforced by physical abuse—the whip, the ruler—and emotional humiliation (often delivered as sarcasm), a fact often left out of nostalgic memoirs. Was it love of scholarship that really motivated many Jewish immigrants toward scholastic excellence? Or fear of the whip? Or love of the dollar? Or a desire to escape the world of their parents? Or a desire to succeed in the world of the gentiles?

From *Cheder* to *Gymnasium*: Education in Eastern Europe

In the shtetls of Eastern Europe, Jewish boys began going to religious school, *cheder*, at the age of three. The *cheder* was not a nursery school: the children did not play and run and sing ("Running, playing, athletics: it just wasn't done," Max Hirsch recalls), or attend for two hours in the morning or an hour and a half in the afternoon. In the shtetl, little boys (rarely little girls) attended school ten to twelve hours a day, six days a week. The schools were not bright and airy places; in fact, most were not really schools at all but classes that met in the kitchen or the parlor of the man who did the teaching, the *melamed*. Such instruction as there was consisted entirely of repetitive drill. Max Hirsch recalls starting *cheder* at the age of three:

I remember that the first memory that I have was standing in front of a little room and crying all day, crying the whole day. This was the house of the rebbe [rabbi]. You had to go there for the day and sleep there too, because there was no cheder in our little village. For Shabbos we went home. It was a great shock to me. It was the whole week we lived with the rebbe and his wife.

But that doesn't count, you know. What counted is that at the age of three, me darf shoyn onheybn tsu lernen [one should already begin to learn]. I remember once, I was about six or seven, and after the cheder was over, we still had to stay there. And it was a summer day and it was still light so they let us play. "Geyt aroys [go out]," the rebbe said.

75

We had a game, we played it with a hoop, a circle, and you chased it with a stick. Well, the cheder was not far from the mikve. I never expected to meet my father because my father used to come to town, but around four or five o'clock he used to go home. But this time he stayed, he went to the mikve. It was about six-thirty and there, as I was chasing this hoop, my father comes. "A Gemore bokher! [Young student of the Talmud!] Zol arumloyfn vi a shaygets! A shaygets! Shkotzim loyfn arum! A Gemore bokher, mit di payess! [You run around like a Christian peasant! Only Christian hoodlums run around! A Talmud student with side-locks doesn't do that!]."

It may sound funny now; it wasn't funny then.[1]

The *melamed* was not a respected member of the community; he was not a scholar but, rather, a teacher, a drill sergeant, who subsisted on the meager fees paid by the parents of his pupils: "To share a wealth of knowledge is among the most 'beautiful' of deeds; to sell a meager stock of it is unworthy."[2] The *melamed* kept his young students at their stultifying tasks by beating them—frequently.

MORRIS HOCHSTADT: *I remember going to cheder, my brother and myself. We went to cheder on the other side of town. We were only probably six or seven years old. There was a teacher on the other side of the shtetl where my grandfather was, and we must have paid him, and everyone had to bring their own kerosene for the week. We brought it in a bottle, and that was the kerosene we used. And every boy had to bring kerosene for when his time came. It lit the lamps. We used to walk there early in the morning at eight o'clock and come back about ten at night. We used to walk back and forth with a lantern.*

That was our formal schooling. The cheder school was taught by a melamed. He was my uncle and he was a mean son of a bitch—to the kids. If you didn't know it, you got a shot on the side. Belted you, sure—a mean son of a gun! He hit his own nephew; as a matter of fact, my father had him as a teacher too. Actually he was my father's uncle; he wasn't my uncle, he was my great uncle. If you didn't know your lesson, came Friday, if you didn't know your lesson, woe to you! Shame on you! But not enough to kill you. You can be the biggest dummy, but something is going to remain with you after twelve hours a day like that.

76

"The cheder *school was taught by a* melamed. *He was my uncle and he was a mean son of a bitch."*
Cheder, *Lublin, Poland, 1924.*

Most shtetl boys stayed in *cheder* until they had learned to chant (without comprehension) the Hebrew of the prayerbooks and to read and write a little Yiddish. Most girls escaped the rigors of the *cheder* altogether; some may have acquired basic literacy in Yiddish at home (many could repeat the Hebrew prayers from memory but could not read them with comprehension); and beyond that, little was expected. In some parts of Eastern Europe, at some times, children—both boys and girls—may also have been required to attend state schools in which they were taught to read and write in a language the state approved— Russian, Polish, German, or Hungarian; but this practice was never universal.

Most children, and this was even more true of the Christians than of the Jews, were either totally illiterate or only barely literate when they began their working lives; only the most exceptionally brilliant and amenable students were encouraged to continue their studies. Some Jewish boys—actually very few, although we hear a lot about them—survived the basic *cheder* and went on to advanced religious education, first in an advanced *cheder* (in which the Torah might be read) and then in a *yeshiva*, where, in an atmosphere of comparative freedom, they could apply the tools and the discipline they had acquired in *cheder* to the task of analyzing and commenting on the Talmud, which is itself a set of commentaries on the Torah. Other Jewish boys attempted to find places for themselves in the secular (or, to be more accurate, Christian) school system, either the *gymnasia* which prepared students for the universities, or the trade schools which prepared them for one of the more specialized crafts or demiprofessions. Unfortunately, in Eastern Europe the demand for places in the secondary schools almost always exceeded the supply, and competition was very keen. As a result, most children—Jewish or Christian—had no opportunity for secondary schooling, but the opportunities for Jews were restricted even further in Russia and Poland after 1887 when the first of several successive school quotas were introduced. Most of those Jews who immigrated as adults were thus not themselves highly educated. The men could read and write, at least in Yiddish—accomplishments that set them apart from the illiterate Christian peasants who had been their neighbors—and perform rudimentary calculations. Many of the women, perhaps a majority, were completely illiterate.

On the other hand, poorly educated or not, most Jewish immigrants respected education. In the culture of the shtetl, no young person was more admired than the studious boy, as Max Hirsch recalls:

In the shtetl any occupation that called only upon physical strength and exertion was considered low. Anything that rises from that level up to the Talmud, a Talmud khokhem [wise one], his social prestige was in proportion to the distance from physical effort.

You see, if you wanted to say, for instance, something derogatory about a man, you said grober yung, a fat fellow. In the United States it is the opposite; you venerate physical strength, athletics, and so on. But we didn't. The Jewish term for being noble is eydl, pale. A German term, an edele mensch, a noble man—when we saw somebody emaciated and on the verge of tuberculosis or what have you, it's an eydl. Pale. Emaciated. Because that was associated with studying all the time.[3]

One of the unique features of shtetl life was the glorious future it promised for the studious boy who succeeded in becoming a *yeshiva bokher*, a student in one of the advanced religious academies: no matter how poor he had been as a child, his adult years would be made comfortable—not through his own exertions but through those of either his wife or his wife's father. He could teach without asking for fees—"sharing" a wealth of knowledge; he could lead his neighbors in prayer without demanding recompense; he could spend his entire day reading and writing; he did not have to sell his mind to the highest bidder because the bid had already been settled at the time of his marriage.

MAX HIRSCH: *My brother did not go, ever, to a secular school. He went to cheder. From cheder to a higher cheder and then to a yeshiva where he studied Gemara [part of the Talmud]. And when he reached the age of eighteen, the shadkhn [matchmaker] and the mekhutn [potential father-in-law] came and farhert in der Torah [gave him a test in the Torah]. Yes, that was part of the qualification as a potential son-in-law. He had to pass the test in Hebrew learning if the mekhutn wanted somebody who was a scholar. And most rich Jews wanted at least one son-in-law to be a scholar. And the yeshivas became, to a very large extent, matrimonial, pathways to being a groom.*

They tell even a story, that a Litvak [a Jew from Lithuania] came to a yeshiva and says, "I want a look. Have you a nice yeshiva bokher for a son-in-law? Well, he must be——" And they showed him one and he tested him and talked to him. He was very choosy. So they asked him, "Listen, what kind of a daughter do you have that you're so choosy?" "A daughter?" he says. "So, who has a daughter? Zol zikh arumdreyen a gelernter eydem in shtub, ver darf a tokhler? [Let there be a learned son-in-law in the house, who needs a daughter?]."[4]

In the culture of the shtetl, a learned man, devoted to study, had considerable status. So worthy of emulation was he that even a baby's lullaby reflected the desire to have such a person in the family:

> Under Gitteleh's cradle
> Stands a snow-white kid
> The kid went off to trade
> With raisins and almonds
> But what is the best trade?
> Gitteleh's bridegroom will study
> Torah he will study
> Holy books will he write
> And good and pious
> Shall Gitteleh remain.

Or:

> My Yankele shall study the law
> The Law shall baby learn
> Great books shall my Yankele write
> Much money shall he earn.[5]

Even in the cities, among Jews who were somewhat assimilated, education—secular education now—was still prized, because the further a young man progressed in it, the closer he came to achieving a professional position, as a physician perhaps, or a lawyer or a banker—and thus to potential wealth. The school quotas imposed under Alexander III (and reduced further under Nicholas II) were thus particularly devastating to the Jews of Russia because they blocked one important avenue to economic security.

Thus, whether they lived traditional lives in the shtetls or modern lives in the cities, most Eastern European Jews were convinced, realistically, that the path to riches ran through the obstacle course of schools—an attitude reflected in Isaac Babel's story "You Must Know Everything."

Written in 1915, when Babel was twenty-one and had just finished studying at the Institute of Financial and Business Studies (roughly what an American business school would be if it accepted undergraduates) in Odessa, the story is a vignette: a young boy, likely the author himself, is spending a Saturday at home alone with his grandmother, who will silently supervise his studies.

Grandmother, in a good humor, sat in the corner in her silk Sabbath dress and I was supposed to do my lessons. It was a difficult day for me, I had already had six lessons at school, and now my music teacher, Mr. Sorokin, was supposed to come, and so was Mr. L., my Hebrew teacher, to give a lesson we had missed. Peysson, the French teacher, might also come, and I had to prepare a lesson for him. . . .

Grandmother did not interrupt me—God forbid! Her face was drawn and blank because of reverence for my work. She fastened her round, bright yellow eyes on me. Whenever I turned over a page, they followed the movement of my hand. Anybody else would have been made very ill at ease by this fixed and ever-watchful gaze, but I had grown used to it.[6]

Later in the afternoon, as the light dims and the boy grows weary, his grandmother begins to tell stories. One of the stories is about the boy's grandfather who apparently had an insatiable thirst for knowledge, but died a failure. To the boy's surprise the old woman begins to cry—and then:

"Study!" she suddenly said with great vehemence. "Study and you will have everything—wealth and fame! You must know *everything*. The whole world will fall at your feet and grovel before you. Everybody must envy you. Do not trust people. Do not have friends. Do not lend them money. Do not give them your heart!"

She said no more. There was silence in the room. She was thinking about years gone by and all her troubles. She was thinking about my future, and her stern commandments pressed down heavily—and forever—on my weak, untried shoulders.[7]

As Babel's story indicates, by the turn of the twentieth century the winds of change were already beginning to blow across the educational systems—both Jewish and Christian—of Eastern Europe. Urban Jewish families, like Babel's, were encouraging their children to learn French, as well as Russian, and discouraging the use of Yiddish. *Cheders* for girls were established in some of the more progressive villages and towns; and some Jewish girls, either the most radical or those with the most assimilated parents, were demanding—and getting—a secondary education. As state-funded primary education improved, increasingly large numbers of Jewish boys desired places in the *gymnasia* and—eventually—in the universities. Rebellion was everywhere in the air, and secular education was everywhere one of the touchstones of the rebellion.

Ironically, and often to their horror, Jewish parents discovered that the cultural conditions that made good *yeshiva bokhers*—compulsive discipline, argumentative discourse, respect for literacy—also made good *gymnasium* students; and good *gymnasium* students tended to want to continue on to university. This meant a sharp break with tradition. To attend the *gymnasium* (where uniforms were required), a Jewish boy had to cut his *payess*, the twin locks of hair he traditionally wore over his ears, and remove his *yarmulke*. He also had to violate the Sabbath, since classes were held on Saturdays; if he boarded at the school, there would be no time for morning and evening prayers. The fabric of traditional relations between parents and children would be rent, all because the child had done precisely what the parents had expected him to do—studied hard.

In the United States—where secular education was not only required but also free—this pattern of parent-child relationships subsequently became the norm, but it was already manifest in the shtetl; long before most European Jews had heard of American public high schools and colleges, they had discovered that the invocation to study could also be an invitation to rebellion.

MAX HIRSCH: *I had ambitions to go to the gymnasium. But at the end of the fourth year, when I began talking about it—I was about ten years old—my grandfather, my mother's father, said, "No." But then in January my grandfather died, and then I said, "Well now, this is my time. My time has come." And I brought up the whole question again, and*

I said, "I'm not going to continue. I'm quitting school in a week or so." I wanted to dramatize, to make my point.

So I spoke to my father, and he finally agreed that I should start preparing, and he even was very helpful. He had friends among the civil servants, and he bribed them; he liked to kvell [to boast or swell up with pride] about my accomplishments in school. So every day I went to a tutor for an hour or two. His name was Ostrowski. He was pleased that I wanted to go to gymnasium; he was pleased that I wanted to study Russian and study it well. And he noticed, of course—he knew that I had resistance at home—so he, in a way, he admired my determination and courage. So by the end of August I had prepared myself for the examination, and I had to present myself for the examination. And sure enough, I passed: one day of written exams and another day of oral exams.

But I had to overcome certain difficulties. I had the payess. Now, if I presented myself for the examination with the payess, they would probably have failed me right away. I was told this; there was no law against it, but I would surely fail. I couldn't cut off my payess, because then how could I come back to town and face the families, in shul? So my sisters came to my aid. First of all, they thinned out the payess; they didn't cut, but they thinned out. And then with prune juice, sticky, they combed it back. Since I had long hair (this was a constant source of irritation, of argument, between me and my mother and grandfather: "Farvos darf men hobn azoy fil lange hor? Shkotzim hobn lange hor! [Why does his hair have to be so long? Gentile boys have long hair!]." Jewish boys were supposed to have short hair because if you put the tefillin* close to the brain and the heart, you serve God with the brain and the heart, then there should be no interference, nothing between you and communing with God), I could comb the payess back and it would mingle with my hair.

I cut off my payess as soon as I passed the examination. School started in September, and Rosh Hashonah was about two weeks after school opened. I had to go home but I already didn't have the payess. And I

---

* *Tefillin* are two sets of phylacteries used by Orthodox Jews during morning prayer. The phylacteries consist of two boxes, with straps attached and made out of cowhide parchment inscribed with sections from Scripture. One box is placed on the forehead, and the straps hang down the side of the face and over the shoulders in front; the second box is placed on the left arm, and the straps are wrapped around it.

*had my uniform. Well, I wouldn't dare go to shul, Rosh Hashonah, in
uniform. That was out of the question. But I wore trousers and a shirt
and a jacket and a tallis [prayer shawl worn by men in synagogue]. But
as we were walking to shul, in the market square a Jew came along, an
old man, a devoted friend of my grandfather, a self-appointed trustee
of my father's correctness. So he looked at my father and he looked at
me, without the payess, and he spat. I didn't know what to do with
myself. These things stick to your mind; this happened sixty-eight
years ago, but I still remember it.[8]*

On the question of secular education for Jewish youths, the czar's
government sided, ironically, with shtetl tradition; the elders of the
shtetl did not want Jewish boys to go to the *gymnasia*, and neither did
the czar. Since only a minuscule portion of the imperial budget was
spent on education, there was not enough room in any of the secondary
schools or universities to meet the demand burgeoning in all quarters
of the population. Wherever competition was based on merit, there
lay the possibility that the Jews, who started preparing their children
for educational competition in the cradle, would succeed. And wherever the Jews might succeed, there the czar had to intervene.

And intervene he did. In 1887, Alexander III imposed the first of
the infamous school quotas: no more than 10 percent of the places in
secondary schools and universities in the Pale* were to go to Jews; no
more than 5 percent outside the Pale; no more than 3 percent in St.
Petersburg and Moscow. A few years later, under Nicholas II, the quotas were reduced even further: 7 percent, 3 percent, and 2 percent, respectively. Jewish mothers, it was said, would stand weeping for hours
in the offices of the minister of public instruction, hoping to get an
exception certificate for their sons. In some of the commercial schools,
schools of the sort that Isaac Babel had attended, it was said that
wealthy Jews had provided endowments so as to enlarge enrollments,
thereby increasing the number of Jews who could attend.

Simon Dubnow, the Russian Jewish historian, must have known
whereof he spoke when he remarked that "it was scarcely to be expected that the Jewish youths who had been locked out of the Russian
schools should entertain particularly friendly sentiments toward a re-

---

* Legally defined early in the nineteenth century, the Pale of Jewish Settlement was a geographic area containing most of the seventeen far westerly Russian provinces and all of Poland.
Jews had to obtain special permission to reside outside the Pale.

gime that wasted their lives, humiliated their dignity, and sullied their souls."[9] The school quota was the single czarist regulation the Jews hated most. The quota meant that the doors to learning—as well as those to respectability and wealth—were slammed in Jewish faces. While pogroms, war, and the threat of starvation spurred many Russian and Polish Jews to leave their homelands, many decided to emigrate to the United States in part because of the rumor that school quotas did not exist there.

"God, Country, and Home": Jewish Children in American Schools

Indeed, it was true. In America, school quotas did not exist (at least not yet)* and certainly not in the public lower schools. In New York and Illinois and Pennsylvania and Massachusetts (as well as in most other states of the Union), elementary schooling was required for everyone—girls as well as boys; and no tuition was charged. Secondary public schooling was also free, and no one could be excluded, except—perhaps—for misconduct. Higher education—business schools, colleges, law schools, medical schools—was expensive, but even here there was hope: perhaps a scholarship could be had; perhaps (in New York) the child could go to City College (if a boy) or Hunter College (if a girl) for they, too, were free.

The schools our parents confronted when they arrived here from Europe were physically very different from the ones they had left behind: large, imposing buildings, several stories high. There were *cheders* in the New World, to be sure, and *yeshivas* also; the first Jews to come from Eastern Europe had begun to establish these traditional institutions as soon as they arrived. But the "jargon schools," as unsympathetic German Jews liked to call the schools where Yiddish was the language of instruction, were no match for the public schools. When we asked people to tell us about the schools they had attended as children, it was always the public schools that came first to their lips.

Reformers disliked intensely the public schools in urban immigrant districts: the buildings were decrepit, they said; the sanitation, primi-

---

* In the 1920s, some colleges created anti-Semitic quotas, some of which were not removed until the 1960s.

tive; the heating system, worse. Children were crowded into poorly ventilated rooms; there were not enough desks; there was no place to play. "Not conducive to the best development of the child," was their charge. Perhaps so, but Jewish parents were satisfied; in America there were no quotas, and the schools were free. Immigrant children were sent to school, often right off the boat.

SADIE REHSTOCK: *My first day of school I remember as if it were yesterday. We arrived at the end of the summer so we were only here a few days when they told me that I had to go to school. Well, I went to school with a girl who lived in the apartment we were staying in. They were some sort of relatives—not relatives, but relatives of relatives. I was told that she would pick me up when it came time to go home for lunch.*

I came out of the school door and I didn't see her, and I didn't know where I lived. I could hardly speak English; the only word I knew when I came off the boat was yes. But I remembered the little girl in whose seat I was sitting; it was so overcrowded that there were about fifty children in that room, all girls. I had to sit in the same seat with her and put my arm around her waist so that I shouldn't fall off the other side.

I followed her home. I didn't know why, but I assumed that I am a Jewish girl, she is a Jewish girl, we were all Jewish children, I followed her home. And when I got to her home, sure enough they were eating lunch, they were a Yiddish-speaking home. I told them where I lived. I didn't know the street, but I said there is a bathhouse right next to where I live. And they knew where that was. It was number 15 Rutgers Place. After lunch, they gave me some applesauce (I think I had applesauce), and they took me home.

As physically different as American public schools may have been from the *cheders* of Eastern Europe, they were in many ways pedagogically similar. *Cheder* boys were not allowed to run and play, and neither were second graders on the Lower East Side—at least not during school hours. Education meant "book learning" in Poland and Russia, and that was precisely what it also meant in the immigrant districts of Philadelphia and Chicago. In both Eastern Europe and America, children had to sit still and keep quiet for long periods; they had to commit to memory huge amounts of material; they had to demonstrate respect for and subservience to their teachers, even when the teachers caused them severe, and unwarranted, embarrassment. John Dewey's message had not yet penetrated American pedagogy; "progressive education" was avant-garde in the Progressive period. Discipline was the goal, not nurturance. The "developmental needs of the child" were poorly understood and barely considered. Once one got past its massive doors, the American public school was just a *cheder* with girls.

CHARLIE MOSES: *In first grade, we had to sit down and keep very quiet, no talking, and follow suit and imitate the letters that the teacher put on the board.*

We had a book, story books, a progressive reader. We didn't have a formalized reading method. You had a primer. In the primer were stories: "The sky was falling down." We children actually repeated that story with the teacher, so we learned it by repeating it. We would match the words we had learned with the words in the book, and this way we acquired a vocabulary. It is like when you learn a song and match the words you learned by heart with the words on the page. You learned it by faith, it is the gestalt method. A lot of kids learned these stories so well they very often would be reading to you, and if you looked you would see that they were reading from memory.

SOL LEVINE: *I had a fourth-grade teacher, Miss Peterson. She wasn't a good teacher. She hit us with a pointer if we talked at the wrong time. Talking was illegal, and hitting was common. Oh sure, most of the time I got hit for reading under the desk.*

Later on, I had a teacher named Miss Bower and she was worse: she broke a ruler on me. She struck out left and right. She induced us to be bad; she hollered; she bullied us.

SOL MEYROWITZ: *My first-grade teacher, she was part of the old school; she was the kind of teacher who walked up and down the aisle. She looked like a witch, and she would walk around with a ruler in her hand. We were supposed to be looking at our book and I had another book besides that book and she came behind me, I didn't see her, and she hit me in the hand, actually cut my hand with the ruler, my hand was bleeding. "That's a lesson to you"—something like that.*

I was afraid of her. I use to pee in my pants. Actually peed in my pants, actually wet my pants, and she give me hell for it. I would say, "I got my hand up. I want to go!" And she would say, "You sit there and read that." I couldn't hold it any longer, but she scared me anyway, so I would sit down and as soon as I sat down after she screamed at me, I urinated, soaking my pants.

SADIE REHSTOCK: *I do recall some behavior on the part of teachers that I subsequently understood to be very, very egregious, very insensitive. On one occasion in the lower grades, the real lower grades—oh! the lessons I learned in grammar stayed with me forever. I raised my hand and the teacher said, "What is it Sadie?" "Can I leave the room?" She said, "Yes, you can leave the room." So I picked myself up and I go and she said, "Where are you going?" And I said, "I asked you and you said I could leave the room." And she said, "Yes, I said you can leave the room, but you didn't ask me whether you may leave the room!" I was so embarrassed with the whole thing, I never forgot the difference between can and may. She made the point—but at what a price! I remember it, and every time I recall it I get that feeling again, that feeling of being embarrassed. But I have never forgotten that grammar lesson.*

SAM REISS: *They were very strict, they were very strict in discipline. And we feared our teachers because they would send you up to the principal, and the principal would beat the hell out of you. I almost got beat once, for standing out of line and looking out the window or something like that, or talking to some of the other boys. Our room was below the principal's office and I could hear him beating kids.*

But the teachers were tough. You didn't sass a teacher in those days like you do now. You had good respect for your teachers.

In the early decades of this century, all American schoolchildren were subjected to this form of pedagogy, but not all American schoolchildren had parents willing to reinforce it because it was so closely akin to the pedagogy of the *cheder*. "Whether it is because of the repression that existed in the foreign lands from which they are gathered," one school superintendent observed, "or because of the racial sadness that seems to have been their heritage since they wept by the waters of

Babylon, there is no class of people who do so much to honor the teacher . . . as do the Jews."[10] "I remember the attitude of the parents toward the teachers," reports Max Weiner, who was born in Chicago, to immigrant parents, in 1908:

Most of the parents had no education or very, very little. The teachers were looked up to as if they were God, and the fact that they were not Jewish had nothing to do with it. The teacher knew best.

And the teacher was going to educate your child; therefore your child better obey the teacher. And whatever the teacher did was wonderful in the eyes of the parents. So the fact that your child was singing non-Jewish songs and celebrating the birth of Jesus and making Christmas decorations would never offend most of the people because this was like part of your education.

They didn't think, "This was something against the Jews." They thought, "This was the way a child was taught in schools."

Rebecca Green, who was born in Odessa but emigrated as a small child, spent all her school years in American public schools and subsequently became an educator herself. Her career caused her to reflect, in a particular way, on the implications of all that reinforcement:

Adults don't seem to be too aware that it is registering on the child— the impact of all these little things on the child—that it is bringing into being, in terms of her own needs, to be liked and so on. This is where the impressions are laid down and you carry them through life.

You don't question what the teacher said. If your teacher told you that you needed something, then you told your parents—and boom! you have it. Later on you learned that that was a way to get goods, material goods, things that you needed.

When you come from the kind of background I came from, you know that you have to do your best. My father was, and I perceived it as a child, he was in the top echelon of the Jewish people. People came to him and sought his opinion. The household was on a high level. A child gets that opinion from the way her parents live; you had to do your best.

One result of the mutually reinforcing attitudes of schoolteachers and Jewish parents was passivity. Contemporary observers noticed that immigrant Jewish schoolchildren were remarkably passive, an observation absent in many nostalgic recollections of the "good old school days":

> These children, their teachers report, are singularly docile—not the girls only, but the boys as well. In some cases, indeed, this docility amounts to a defect (of which, however, teachers are not wont to complain)—the children seeming to lack those healthy instincts for mischievous play that are the accompaniment of a happier childhood. . . . They are more receptive than self active.[11]

Charlie Moses, who was born in Manhattan in 1905, recalls one good example of that passivity:

I remember, when I was in kindergarten, being told to go upstairs to the office of the assistant principals, their names were Fanny Decker and Eugene Callahan.

I was told to go up and make a left turn, and I remember going up one flight of stairs and then I couldn't make a left turn because there was a wall. I was so literal-minded and infantile that I didn't realize that I had to climb another flight of stairs to reach the second floor. So I just stood there—until a teacher realized that there was something wrong, and she opened the door and motioned to me to come down.

And Sam Smilowitz, born in Brooklyn in 1911, vividly remembers how some parents managed to ensure passivity:

Our parents respected the teachers, and teachers were authority figures for them. In junior high, I just remember one teacher, Miss Freed. There were empty lots near the school and I had to urinate, and went to an empty lot and went against the wall, and Miss Freed came along and she saw me, and called me over and said, "Sam, what are you doing?" I said, "Miss Freed, I am not on school property." She said, "Bring your father! Bring your father!"

And when I had to bring my father to school, it was rough: he lost half a day's pay. He went down there. When they said, "Bring your father!" you couldn't substitute by bringing your mother. And when he came back that night, he said to me, "What you did was not so terrible. I used to do it myself. I do it myself." But he explained that she is trying to make a human being out of you, and while he is talking, he is punctuating with bang! bang! slaps on my face!

When the occasion demanded it, he did it; he wasn't bashful. I didn't cry and I wasn't humiliated. Not at all. That's the way life was in those years. I did wrong, that's all, and that's the end of it. I took my punishment.

I had a cousin that lived with us at the time; he was about fifteen years old. One time one of the teachers, Miss Robinson, told him to bring my father to school. Miss Robinson said that my cousin is running around with bad company. Meanwhile my father is walking and looking around the room. And then he says, "You mean running around with that bum over there?" And she said, "Yes." And then he calls my cousin up. "How many times have I told you to stay away from those two bums? And you won't listen!" Wham! Bang! Wham! Bang! Right in front of the class! Slapped him right in front of the class. And he was the oldest boy in the class. In later years he would say that was the most humiliating moment he ever had in his life. But he said he learned a lesson.

Miss Robinson knew every member of our family. She lived near us, and you would tip your hat at Miss Robinson. Everybody was very respectful of Miss Robinson.

Sam Smilowitz also recalls the end result of all that reinforcement, however brutal it may have been:

In high school we used to think that if you got less that ninety on a math test, you had disgraced God, Country, and Home. I remember I got a one hundred on geometry, algebra, intermediate; ninety-eight in solid; ninety-four in trigonometry; and ninety-two in advanced algebra.

And we used to think that the school could be divided into two groups: the Jewish boys and the non-Jewish boys. The non-Jewish boys used to hang out together in an ice cream parlor across the street. And they used to wear what we called "pork pie" hats, flat hats. We had nothing to do with them; they were not particularly interested in studying. And all we did was study.

During the first two decades of this century, many observers noted that Jewish immigrant children were better students, on the whole, than their Italian, Irish, Polish, and black slum contemporaries. Teachers, principals, policy makers—even the children themselves—knew it at the time. And no one has denied it subsequently. All the historians and sociologists who have examined the question have concluded that the Jews were simply better at schoolwork than any other ethnic group.

Many Jews, of course, like to brag about this conclusion, especially when trying to persuade their own children to strive for the same educational excellence. But early in this century, there were Jewish children who hated school or who did not get remarkably good grades or whose parents were not willing to sacrifice everything so that a son or daughter could stay in school. Janet Sommers, who was born in 1910, had just such a father. "I took a commercial course in high school," she recalls, "but he was annoyed with me. He was angry because he thought I should go out on my own and make a living. I was fourteen, maybe closer to fifteen already. He was a dictator, a tyrant really." After two years, Janet Sommers quit high school and went to work—although years later, she took a high school equivalency exam, went to college, and became a teacher. Her father, however, did not discriminate on the basis of sex; one of her older brothers was not even allowed to enter high school:

And my brother Joe, he resented it all of his life. Because my father decided that he needed someone to help him in his real estate work, and he elected Joe to do it for him. He said: "You're the one." None of my brothers could contradict my father. I don't think Joe ever went to high school; he was taken out from elementary school to help his father. He resented it all his life.

If there were Jewish parents, such as Janet Sommers's, who did not fit the cultural stereotype, so too were there Jewish children who rebelled against it. Their voices rarely get heard, in part because they have not been willing to make them heard—ashamed perhaps, or fearful that their own children might be tempted to follow the same path—and in part because the pattern of their lives pokes discomforting holes in the stereotype. Sam Smilowitz, for example, went to college, but his brothers did not:

They didn't want to. My middle brother won a scholarship to Cornell, but he never went. The reason he attempted to win the scholarship and succeeded was because my father had a brother who had a son— my cousin—who won a scholarship to Cornell. My father reproached my older brothers for the fact that they never won a scholarship, but their cousin won a scholarship. Out of pride my brother determined to win a scholarship, which he did, and then never availed himself of it. My father was furious.

And you look at the two men now, my brother and my cousin, and my brother is a lot better off—money-wise.

And Charlie Moses, who later became a physician, in his youth simply, and atypically, hated school—all of it, from elementary school through college:

When I was in elementary school it was a hostile environment. I thought it was highly circumscribed. I was a free kid out on the street, in the lots, call it the woods, a lot of open spaces. I guess I like to play. The kindergarten wasn't so bad because they gave you a little more latitude, but when first grade came and they wanted you to read, and they wanted you to write, sit at a desk . . . and gradually, as you get harnessed to it, the second grade, third grade, fourth grade, you are chained to the book—and they won't let you take your nose out of the book. You go from one book to another book, from period to period. "Keep your eyes on that book, for whatever it's worth!" As the disaffection grows, by the time the kid is in the fifth grade, he has had enough school to last him a lifetime. He still goes because he has no other alternative.

It was boring, there was nothing really interesting. I would read independently. I was an average reader, but school intefered with my reading. I got hit all the time, for reading a book under the desk. I got hit in school, a couple of times, smacked hard, because I was caught in school reading a book behind the geography book. And I found ways of beating the system by writing out the notes myself, notes that I signed myself—my parents could not write in English—notes that said

93

that I had to leave the room a number of times a day, whenever the pressure got too tight, I would get up and go for a walk, leave the room, walk around upstairs, downstairs—get out of that atmosphere. Sitting up, for half an hour, looking straight ahead. A very cruel life we impose on children. School is not meant for children, not for me or for any other child. School is meant for adults, for the convenience of adults. What I learned in school was useless, a lot of useless information. What you learn by yourself you own; what you learn in school is not yours, just something you give back. And you lost it; it is gone; it is inconsequential—trivial.

And do you know what education really is? It's a way to get a respectable job at low pay. My friends who did not go to high school, the ones who went out to work, they have an economic life as good as mine. My contemporaries, whether they went to high school, college or not, their economic status has very little bearing on where they went to school.

Education is a big myth. Schooling is overrated, which we set store by!

"My Teachers Really Gave Me Everything": School for Jewish Girls

Perhaps Charlie Moses was right. But there was one group of immigrant children who adored school when they were young, who did not chafe at the manifold restrictions on their behavior. These were Jewish girls, whom Judaic law had barred, for many centuries, from occupying the one social role their culture favored above all others—the good student. Sadie Rehstock, born in Warsaw but educated largely in the United States, recalled, when first being asked about her school experiences, "My grandfather, when I was young, used to say to me in Yiddish, 'If you had been a boy you would be a genius, but a girl . . .'" American schools opened new vistas for Sadie Rehstock:

In Warsaw I didn't go to school. My aunts taught me. They taught me Polish, my grandmother taught me Yiddish, then a friend of hers came

*"She was beautiful, very beautiful, a young girl, and I kind of
adored her. . . . I had her as a teacher in the sixth grade.
She played the piano in the assembly."*
New York City classroom, 1906.

from Palestine and she taught me a little Hebrew, and my aunt also taught me a little Russian. I was able to read in these languages, so when I came here I thought I was an educated person—but I wasn't quite up to the mark. . . .

My first teacher was a Jewish teacher, her name was Miss Rothschild, and she was darling. She used to put me on her lap after school and teach me English words. She was a nice, kind person. Maybe she knew I was a smart kid, I don't know, but she taught me. I loved Miss Rothschild.

Etta Levine, born in New York, recalls the effort made by her much older cousin, who had been born and reared in Rumania (the cousin who shared Etta's bed for many years) to dissuade her from pursuing a college education:

Cousin Sophie used to give it to me because I had the nerve to go to college. She didn't believe in education for girls. On Thursdays, when my mother was working late and I would come home from college and prepare supper, I would hear, "A girl doesn't let her mother work so hard and she go off to college. Some educated lady you are!"

Etta Levine's reaction was typical of many young women in her generation: "I used to take a book and bury my head in it." Education was extremely important to these young women. Their American teachers—the Miss Rothschilds of their new world—had become significant role models, mother substitutes, representatives of a different, ineluctably more attractive way of life. They touched a nerve, these beautiful young women, satisfied some deep need that the daughters of Jewish immigrants—many of whom later became teachers themselves—can still remember nearly three quarters of a century later. Rebecca Green and Hannah Toperoff were born abroad; Rose Janofsky, in Boston; they all spent their formative elementary school years in American public schools.

REBECCA GREEN: *School was always, always exciting. It was exciting carrying the books, many more books then I needed. I must have carried all the books in the house; it was wonderful carrying lots of books.*

I loved it. I loved to write and was one of those perennial students—that is not a compliment—I had a need to go on and on.

I must have walked to school and must have walked with my two older sisters. School was an important place to go to; my parents kept telling me this. My big sisters were going and I was going too; you can't escape recognizing that it is important to go to school. You are going with your big sisters. If school is perceived in the home as a very important place, then you have a value system. You are going there, you are worthy enough to go to that place. You have achieved, at the age of four or five, these things, all these have registered; the more books you carry the more along the ladder you have gone. This was your work, going to school; it was your job. That's what my parents kept telling me.

ROSE JANOFSKY: *I had a teacher called—this goes back, I remember her so clearly—Elizabeth A. Bliss. Nobody I knew was named Elizabeth; this you only read in books. We had kids named Jennie and Sarah and Beckie, Tillie—but Elizabeth A. Bliss! She lived in the suburbs, and she had a garden, and she came into the city in the springtime with an armful of peonies that to me was just beauty incarnate. She would walk in, and they would just perfume the room. And she would just assign me to take a little bunch of these peonies and give them to each of the teachers.*

Now remember I have never in my life seen a flower, you must know this, never seen a flower. I am not saying that I never passed a florist shop, I may have passed a florist shop, but that was not the sort of thing immigrant parents went into business doing. They went into business to eat not to sell flowers.

And I used to pray that she would let me bring these flowers to Miss Lowenstein, who was sort of the youngest member of these teachers; she must have been twenty. She was beautiful, very beautiful, a young girl, and I kind of adored her; she was beautiful and young. I had her as a teacher in the sixth grade. She played the piano in the assembly, and it's funny but I can remember some of the songs she use to play. "Elegy"—la da da da da, dum da dum la la da dum—Massenet, I think. And I remember her hands, and I thought that was the greatest.

I was very musical at that time too, and we had music appreciation, and I remember tutoring all the kids at that time too. I had a fabulous memory for all these little songs, and Bizet and Massenet and *Carmen*, and all the popular things, they would play them for you, and you had to recognize them, and I won all the prizes.

HANNAH TOPEROFF: *I had a teacher, Fanny Silverman, who lived in our neighborhood, and I think I once went there with her to help her take something, deliver something, and she lived two blocks from where we did, and she was very wonderful to me, and she was very nice to me. She would help me: she would hug me and take me in her arms; she would nurture me. My mother was not a nurturer. I always managed to find somebody who would take me under the wing.*

For example, I remember we had a spelling bee and I won first prize, and the prize was they would give you stationery. Fanny Silverman took me into the small supply locker and said, "Take what you want. Anything!" It had pencils, paper. You know, paper to us was not the sort of thing you came by easily, or pencils, for that matter. You had to go out and get a pencil. Crayons? Unheard of. And she gave them to me.

As Rose Janofsky is aware, many of the young Jewish women who were so deeply touched by their teachers had mothers who were remote, from whom they felt estranged:

I loved my teachers. I loved them. I always sought a surrogate mother. My whole life, my mother was not demonstratively an affectionate person. I always attribute that to the fact that she started out with so many problems. It wasn't that she was critical of me; she was nothing, she didn't pay attention. My mother never paid attention to what was going on in school. My teachers would give me books to read and take home. They were very, very good, very nice to me, and I remember them fondly for the rest of my life.

I think they did influence me to some extent, in many areas: well, love of reading, music, which I otherwise would not have had. Everybody talks about Jewish homes which are always filled or crammed with things cultural. It is just not so. In my home there was nothing cultural. I forgave my mother for it eventually—what could she do?— but my teachers really gave me everything.

Making Good American Citizens

As caring as the Miss Rothschilds of American public schools may have been, they clearly had something in mind besides the formal curriculum. Along with reading, writing, and arithmetic, they were teaching "Americanization," making a deliberate effort to wean immigrant children away from the cultures of their parents. "You cannot catch your new citizen too early in order to make him a good citizen. The kindergarten age marks our earliest opportunity to catch the little Russian, the little Italian, the little German, Pole, Syrian and the rest and begin to make good American citizens of them," one educational expert asserted[12]; and others—quite clearly—agreed:

A story can illustrate the influence the tactful teacher may have in the tenement home. One day a girl, ragged, dirty, disheveled, was brought into a class taught by a bright young teacher who had already become noted for her success with foreign children. Leah, for that was the girl's name, could speak no English. She at once manifested, however, a strong liking for her teacher and, drawn by this affection, mastered the intricacies of English speeech in an incredibly short time. As soon as she could make herself understood, she would lie in wait for her teacher and walk with her part of the way home. Slowly, at first, more rapidly afterward, Teacher began to drop hints as to how Leah's personal appearance might be improved. Every hint was acted on, and soon Leah began to wash her face and comb her hair, to tie and polish her shoes, and to have her clothes clean and neatly mended and held in place by hooks and eyes instead of pins.

One day when they came to the door of the tenement where Leah lived, Teacher expressed a desire to pay a call on Leah's mother. The sight that met her eyes was not a pleasant one. The family contained many children of whom Leah was the eldest, and there were two boarders besides, all domiciled in two rooms. Out of a confused mass of bedding, children, rickety furniture, and broken cooking utensils stood the inevitable sewing-machines out of which the family earned a living.

In subsequent afternoon walks, Teacher began to throw out

99

suggestions as to how Leah might reform her home. The child immediately set to work. The mother regarded Leah's doings askance, but nothing could withstand her enthusiasm and she soon won her father's support. The boarders were turned out. Another room was hired. The rooms were cleansed and put in order. Even the small brothers and sisters were subjected, at first greatly to their disgust, to the scrubbing brush, and were obliged to learn how to comb their hair.

About this time Teacher showed Leah an illustrated magazine. It contained a picture of a dinner table set with silver and cut glass and garnished with flowers. By this time Leah had learned to cook in the cooking class. With the picture as her guide, a larger and bolder scheme than any yet entertained entered her little brain. There must be a dinner table with a white cloth and garnished as nearly as possible like the picture. When this triumph was complete, Leah wrote a letter, which her father signed, inviting Teacher to dinner. Teacher accepted the invitation. What a change met her eyes! Instead of the squalor of her earlier visit she beheld the neatness of a poor but well-ordered home.

The father and mother were a bit stiff in their reception, because they had but a few words of English, but they treated Teacher with all the reverence due to a queen. And she was a queen, for was she not to those poor Russian Jews the distillation of American civilization?[13]

By 1900, "Americanizing" teachers and principals were trying every means at their command to acculturate immigrant children, pushing the children out of the past and into the modern era. As they set about molding their young charges, the teachers kept in mind a specific ideal: their new young American would be modestly dressed and, above all, clean.

SOL MEYROWITZ: *Oh, I remember the routine so clearly! There used to be morning inspections. The teacher would start the day with a reading from the Old Testament, then she would inspect our hair, turn our hands around, look at our ears, examine my neck to see if it was dirty. One day she sent me home because I had a dirty neck. And she actually rubbed my skin to see if it was dirty.*

100

We were just a bunch of sad kids, you know, snotty little sad kids: always poorly dressed. We were dirty, dirty. You had a bath maybe once a week, and you wore your underwear all week. The teachers used to come at us; they had a school nurse who would come and look at your hair, with two little wooden sticks, because lice was common among these kids, and she would pick apart your hair to see if she found a louse. She would send you home immediately, and your mother would have to go through some ritual to get you deloused.

And they would look at your hands. I remember turning them over in front of the teacher. I remember kids used to shine their shoes; you had to make sure you came to school with clean shoes. We were checked for lice until the fourth or fifth grade. Clean, we always had to be clean.

At least one of the people we interviewed believed that all this emphasis on cleanliness was implicitly anti-Semitic. When they first arrived in America, Esther Ginsburg's family lived in a town in Massachusetts in which there were no other Jews:

The principal must have told the teacher to "send the Jews home because they are dirty and bugsy." Two of my brothers were sent home from school because they were supposed to have nits in their hair. And when they got home, my father went right back to school and said to the teacher, "Madam, I would like to talk to you. Why do you send my children home?" And she said, "I am so sorry, but the principal told us we had to." And he said, "I want you to go through their heads and show me where you found nits." And she said, "I didn't even look through their heads."

Aside from the need to keep clean, teachers encouraged children to speak unaccented English, so as to mask their immigrant origins.

AARON KATZ: *The teachers were mostly WASP, but nevertheless they knew their immigrant children. Some were very kind to us and helped, and others were rough. In the fifth grade, I had a teacher, a Miss Prescott, who was forever telling us that her great-great-grandfather was the General Prescott of the battle of Bunker Hill. She would always talk to us in a very precise way; she always made us talk precisely, too. And she would tell us about the battle of Bunker Hill, and we were*

*absolutely certain that she had been there herself. She was an old
biddy, but she made us talk precisely.*

In the pursuit of cultural uniformity no stone was left unturned, not
even the child's name.

REBECCA GREEN: *On my birth certificate I am Beckie. My Jewish
name is Bayla. I should have been called Bayla, but the doctor transferred it to Beckie, and I was Beckie all my life until I had to graduate
from elementary school. Then Miss Hagerty who was a wonderful old
lady, the 8-B teacher, asked to see me and I got scared to death. She
was a very severe disciplinarian. I was a goody goody, and I thought,
"What can Miss Hagerty want with me?" And she very angrily said,
"What is your real name?" And I said, "My name is Beckie." And she
said, "It can't be Beckie! That is a nickname. What is your real name?
Is it Rebecca?" I said, "No, no, it is Beckie on my birth certificate."
"You can't put Beckie on a diploma so I will call you Rebecca. How
do you want me to spell it?" And I guess I became Rebecca. When I
went to high school, all the teachers called me Rebecca; it must have
been on my transcript or something—but my parents never stopped
calling me Beckie.*

And perhaps without thinking too much about it, Americanizing
teachers also assumed that immigrant children were, or would become,
Christians.

ETTA LEVINE: *I have a very clear memory of one time that I got into
trouble. I don't know if I was in fourth grade or fifth grade and we
were singing the "Battle Hymn of the Republic," and I wasn't singing
and the teacher asked why. "Well, I am Jewish, and 'he has seen the
glory of the coming of the Lord' is about Jesus Christ, and I don't
believe in Jesus Christ. I am Jewish, and I don't believe that he was a
god."*

*In those days, a great many of the teachers were Catholic, and so I
was sent to the principal, and I must have been very little because she
took me on her knee and said, "Don't mind her. Don't worry about
her. Just go home and come to school tomorrow. I'll talk to the
teacher. She'll understand that I'll have told you to come back to*

school." But when I came back to school, the teacher was very angry at me because she had expected me to apologize to her, and I said that I didn't do anything that I had to apologize for. That was the only time I can remember being in trouble.

In New York, and perhaps also in other major cities, a small but not insignificant number of teachers in the public school system were themselves Jewish, the sons and daughters (or grandsons and grand-daughters) of German Jews who had immigrated much earlier in the nineteenth century. By the beginning of the twentieth century, these Jews were already assimilated: some had converted to Christianity; some had dropped religious affiliation altogether; some had become Reform Jews and appeared, in all outward matters, to be indistinguishable from their Christian contemporaries. As a community, the German Jews were discomforted by their newly arrived brethren; indeed "discomforted" may be too mild a term. German Jews (in New York they were called "uptown Jews") had hidden their Jewishness in order to avoid anti-Semitism; they were terrified that the new immigrants, so obviously and openly Judaic, would foil the ruse. "Those advertising signs in Hebrew letters," one German Jew remarked in 1889,

> that jargon [Yiddish] . . . those remnants of Russian dress and manner, those loud ways and awkward gesticulations, are naturally repulsive and repugnant to the refined American sensibilities. . . . The jargon homes and schools will tend to stifle every growth of Americanism and encourage the generation of Orientalism. We need strong forces to counteract these influences.[14]

The schoolroom was one battlefield on which some German Jews waged their war against "Orientalism," although, as both Rose Janofsky and Charlie Moses tell us, the end result may have been a stalemate.

ROSE JANOFSKY: *I don't know why I remember this so clearly, but I do. There was one teacher who taught economics. Her name was Rothstein, but later she changed it to Ralston. We subsequently found out that she converted to Christianity, too. She was a nasty piece of work. I remember when we had an extended holiday because of Yom Kippur, she said, "Well, how did you enjoy your extended weekend?"*

103

"Well," I said to myself, "here is an enemy. It is bad enough she became a Christian, but why is she also an enemy? What is this with her?"

CHARLIE MOSES: *I remember one teacher I had. She was always making the nastiest remarks about Jews and revolutionaries. She called them the "bêtes noirs." And I remember my father telling me that she was one of those Jews who had changed her name so that no one would know she was Jewish. She was a Jewish anti-Semite. I remember continuously the disparaging remarks that she made against Jews.*

Some Progressive reformers, aware of the destructive effects of the Americanization campaign, cautioned against accelerating it. Such social workers, many of whom knew immigrant families more intimately than the teachers did, understood that, in the effort to make immigrant children into good Americans, teachers were encouraging them to be disrespectful of their parents, were driving unnecessary and potentially harmful wedges between the children and their parents. "The public school is the great savior of the immigrant district," Jane Addams (founder of Hull House, the most famous of the Chicago settlements) believed:

> . . . but there is a certain indictment which may justly be brought, in that the public school too often separates the child from his parents and widens that old gulf between fathers and sons which is never so cruel and so wide as it is between the immigrants who come to this country and their children who have gone to the public school and feel that they have there learned it all.
>
> The parents are thereafter subjected to certain judgment, the judgment of the young which is always harsh and in this instance founded upon the most superficial standard of Americanism. And yet there is a notion of culture which we would define as a knowledge of those things which have been long cherished by men, the things which men have loved because thru generations they have softened and interpreted life, and have endowed it with value and meaning. Could this standard have been given rather than the things which they see about them as the test of so-called success,

then we might feel that the public school has given at least the beginnings of culture which the child ought to have.

I do not believe that the children who have been cut off from their own parents are going to be those who, when they become parents themselves, will know how to hold the family together and to connect it with the state.[15]

Yet even without the Americanization campaign, the end result, at least for Jewish children, was probably inevitable. Given Jewish devotion to schooling and the fact that American schools were secular, Jewish students were going to be drawn away from the traditions of their parents, no matter what their teachers did and did not do, simply by the process of education itself. The more time the immigrant child spent reading the central texts of Western civilization, the less time he or she spent reading Talmud; the more the child came to respect the secular leadership of the country, the less need he or she had for a rabbi's judgment. As the child progressed farther up the educational ladder, each rung brought with it some new break with tradition—and each led in the same general direction. Both Sam Smilowitz and Charlie Moses recall some of those apparently insignificant steps, although the fact that they have been stored in memory for so many years suggests the deep meaning lurking behind their apparent insignificance.

SAM SMILOWITZ: *I remember—isn't it funny how the littlest things stay with you—I was in high school, and the high school had a cafeteria, and sometimes I would buy a lunch for myself. And once I just reached in for a sandwich and didn't look at it, and paid for it, but when I got to the auditorium I noticed that it was ham. I couldn't eat it. I thought about it for a long time. I was too embarrassed to go back with it and ask for an exchange, but I couldn't eat it so I threw it away. Later, when I went to college, I stopped being kosher—but I still don't eat ham.*

CHARLIE MOSES: *My parents wanted me to go to college, but I don't think they wanted to me to go so far away [as Cornell]. But I went anyway. And I worked in fraternity houses for a few semesters, and I lived off the campus, where it was cheaper. And for the first time in my life, I ate in a restaurant; I had never before eaten a meal that my mother or one of my aunts hadn't cooked. Had never before eaten any-thing that wasn't kosher. I still wouldn't eat pork, but that was my liberation—eating in restaurants.*

And Phillip Kohn's extraordinary life story explicitly illustrates the transformative power of the American educational system. Kohn was born in 1897 in Lexington, Kentucky, to parents who had just recently immigrated; his father was a carpenter—and poor. Kohn attended the public schools of Lexington, where he excelled: "All of us Kohns stood out. We knew more than the rest of them." In high school, one of his teachers took a particular interest in him, a Mr. White, a gentile. Mr. White had spent a year at Yale.

PHILLIP KOHN: *And then came my turn to go to college and this Mr. White who had this one year at Yale said to me, "What do you want to go to the University of Kentucky for? Why don't you go to Yale?" I didn't know a thing about Yale. He showed me how to write for a catalogue, so I wrote for a catalogue. I told him we were very poor, and he knew that. And he said in the catalogue you will find that Yale has special arrangements for poor students to work their way through.*

In his senior year, Kohn was offered a full tuition scholarship to the University of Cincinnati, but he decided, after conversations with Mr. White, to go to New Haven and take the entrance examinations for Yale:

I'll never forget the conversation with my father about it. He didn't know anything about Yale or Eastern universities or anything like that. And so I said, "Pop [his voice choking], I am going to give it up. I am going to go to Yale. I am going to try and take an exam"—I didn't have any money, I didn't have anything—"but I am going. So Poppy"—I'll never forget his last remark to me [on the subject of college], it was a very wise one: "Varf nisht aroys dos umreyne biz du hast dos reyne vaser. [Don't throw away the unclean water until you have clean water]. You don't have clean water, Sonny. You are not admitted to Yale yet, you are not going, you are not anything, see!" I said, "Poppa I am giving it [the scholarship] up."

And so Kohn set out for Yale ("I cried the whole way") with twenty-five dollars in his pocket and a cardboard suitcase that he carried on his shoulder: "I didn't know that there were other things so much better than what I had." His first few nights in New Haven he stayed in the Yale infirmary; the "self-help department" at Yale had arranged for him to work there, as a janitor, in exchange for room and board:

I had never eaten a nonkosher meal before. I'll never forget my first experience: came lunchtime that first day, he [the supervisor at the infirmary] handed me something like pork chops for lunch. So I said to him, "I can't eat that." I told him that I was an Orthodox Jew and we didn't eat that kind of meat. He said, "Goodness, what can you eat?" I said, "I can eat hard-boiled eggs, and fruit." "By all means." So he boiled some hard-boiled eggs. He couldn't fry them because he fried them in lard. I had hard-boiled eggs and fruit. I did the same thing at dinnertime. I ate a couple of eggs, a bunch of rolls, and a couple of oranges, bananas, and things like that, apples. I was eighteen years old. I weighed ninety-five pounds, and I was so green.

Kohn passed the examinations, entered Yale, and—eventually—stopped being so "green," so Jewish:

Everybody in my class knew I was working my way through, and I am sure most of my classmates knew I was a dumb little Jewish boy who weighed ninety-five pounds. I was unknowing, I was so green. I had never known what the name Vanderbilt means, and I didn't know what the name Whitney means, and I didn't know what the name Morgan means, and Rockefeller: they were all classmates of mine. I would sit down with these boys, eat lunch with them, dinner with them. And I tutored some of them. I worked my way through, and one of the things I did was tutor.

But anyway, I soon learned. We used to go to daily chapel in those days. It was compulsory at Yale in those days. I didn't know that there was a way out of it even, and there wasn't very much of a way out. If you didn't, you had to go to the temple twice a week or something like that. And I didn't know anything about Reform Judaism, about a temple or anything like that, so I went to chapel.

And I used to be invited to debutante parties in New York, because they invited the whole freshman class. I didn't know what a debutante

107

party was. But I borrowed a raccoon coat from a classmate of mine. I didn't have a tuxedo, but I borrowed it. I went to the parties.

I worked at Yale during the summertime. I didn't go home, and my parents did not come and see me, they didn't have the money. I didn't get home in those four years. At the end of my freshman year, I became a tutor for the kids who wanted to go to Yale.

"Yale is what made me," Phillip Kohn asserts, and he is surely right. Yale made him an assimilated American, just as Cornell University did for Charlie Moses, Hunter College for Etta Levine, and hundreds of high schools and elementary schools for thousands of immigrant Jewish children. Knowingly or unknowingly, Jewish parents paid a high price for their children's education; the price of alienation, the loss of Orthodoxy. It was not just lack of funds that kept Phillip Kohn from going home to Kentucky in the summertime. Jewish child-rearing practices had been honed for centuries to produce good scholars. But as the *cheder* and the *yeshiva* had produced good Jews, American schools produced good Americans, and good Americans were not—or at least so it seemed in those days—good Orthodox Jews. Try as they might to please their parents by doing well in school, in America many Jewish children were doomed also to distress their parents by using the schools to break away.

4

THE EVIL EYE, THE X RAY, AND THE PROMISE OF GOOD HEALTH

AMERICANS born in the decades just before and after the turn of the century, our parents—Jews and non-Jews—grew up in the transition from ancient to modern medicine, from traditional to scientific therapies, from medical pessimism to medical optimism. When they were children (between, roughly speaking, 1895 and 1920), cholera still raged, tuberculosis flourished next door, diphtheria was simply to be expected, polio invaded every summer—and mothers routinely recited special prayers in the hopes of fending off diseases. Physicians were helpless (as was everyone else), unable either to cure the most common diseases or to convince their patients that prayer was useless.

The transition period was not brief; indeed it encompassed the entire period of time during which our parents' generation was reaching maturity, roughly between 1905 and 1940. Late in the nineteenth century, Louis Pasteur and Robert Koch had begun to identify some of the microorganisms that cause diseases; and in the early decades of the century, that knowledge was being used to combat them. By the first decade of the twentieth century, progressive city governments were taking responsibility for protecting public health; municipal water supplies were being purified and milk was being pasteurized—thus eliminating some of what had once been the most virulent epidemic diseases. A vaccination against diphtheria had been developed, and a cure for syphilis found. As the result of concerted medical research, each year saw the development of yet another weapon against yet another ancient disease.

The medical revolution of the twentieth century was not completed until after 1940; mass-produced antibiotics still lay in the future, as did hormonal therapies for endocrine diseases (such as diabetes) and vaccines against those caused by viruses (such as polio). But by the time they were starting to become parents themselves, the members of our parents' generation had seen enough to know that pediatricians were more effective than prayers. Mustard plasters, calomel, raspberry tea, and icebaths were replaced by sulfa drugs, X rays, and aspirin; and parents who persisted in preferring religious amulets or camphor necklaces were being brought to court for endangering the lives of their children.

Immigrant youth began to perceive that becoming an American might also mean becoming healthier. Along with learning to speak a strange language and eat unfamiliar foods, the immigrant child was learning how to substitute new, scientifically grounded methods of dealing with disease for older, more traditional therapies. The "old world" came to be seen as a place shadowed by ill health and death; the "new world," as one from which those shadows could be banished—which made speedy assimilation an even more attractive prospect. Small wonder that in the space of that one generation the physician replaced the rabbi as the Jewish cultural hero.

In the Shadow of Death

Those of us born after the medical revolution have a hard time imagining what it must have been like to live in a world where babies routinely died and small children regularly mourned for one or both of their parents. Our parents need not try to imagine it; they need only

110

remember. Max Hirsch, for example, vividly recalls the events of 1914 (he was then fifteen years old) that undoubtedly influenced his subsequent decision to become a doctor:

In 1914 after the war broke out, there was misery, hunger, and worst of all disease: cholera, typhus, typhoid, smallpox, and so on. In three weeks, the following happened, and it began on a Wednesday: my older brother died of cholera (he was taken to the hospital and we never saw him again); a week later, on the next Wednesday, a younger brother died of a cancer of the eye—my brother Esu, he was about six years old—a dangerous thing; and a week later, the third Wednesday, my little sister died, she died of encephalitis.

She was the youngest girl in my family, and she was the favorite, and she died young, she died young. Well, there was a real tragedy. That was the epidemic when the soldiers came in, yes. How did they treat any of this? They didn't. There was no treatment. My sister, the one who took sick, went into a coma so we carried her to the garret so the people shouldn't take her to the hospital. We hid her in the garret on our property. We had a garret on top of the house, and we put her up there. My mother stayed with her, and sometimes I did; we would change. I knew she was going to die. I was fifteen years old. The sickness, the disease. It was so bitter.

Cholera is such a sickness that when you start to make a massage, sometimes you can help—you can save, sometimes, a man or a woman. It is a cramp. It is such a cramp that you can't stand it. So if you, in this minute, if you start to rub it and you have alcohol, rubbing alcohol, maybe you could save him. There was no doctor. The doctors from the town nearby, they were afraid to come. So we organized a squad, a squad of young people, boys and girls, to go and help, and we saved some people.

The village lost almost fifteen percent of the population, and no medical man was available.

In those days, life had no value at all. People used to die. The place was decimated.[1]

And Clara Zinsser, who was born in Odessa, and lived there until she was a teenager, had a family life devastated by disease and death, in time of peace as well as war:

My mother was a sick woman. She got sick when I was probably about six years old. She had a stroke. One arm hung like that, on the right side of her. And I remember taking her to doctors for electric therapy. And then she got a kidney condition, and this is what killed her. She died in 1917, when I was ten years old. My father had been drafted [into the Russian army]; he was never sent overseas but he wasn't home much. Then he came home for my mother's funeral, and then he was discharged, and the [Russian] Revolution started, and he died in 1918 of a heart attack.

I said Kaddish [prayer for the dead] for my mother and father. My father never went to shul, but he knew the Kaddish. So he wrote the Kaddish out for me in Russian and I said Kaddish for my mother. And then when he died I said Kaddish for him. I used to go [to shul] in the morning, before school, and in the evening, too.

We had relatives, of course, and they took care of us. My aunt and my aunt's daughter, they lived with us. And then 1919, 1919 was the worst year for the food supply in Odessa. We saw people, and there was no way of burying them, so families used to take their own dead on pushcarts and take them over to the cemetery and dig a grave and throw them into the grave. There was cholera and typhoid fever and— what do you call it?—influenza.

I remember once, I was sitting in my cousin's shoe store, near the window—no, the door, it was a glass door. And I saw a dog dragging a woman's head, and a couple of boys went over and grabbed the head because they saw gold teeth, and they were pulling the teeth from her mouth. Things like that you saw.

And then both of my sisters got typhoid. And one of them died. The doctor came every day, but it didn't do any good.[2]

Lest we imagine that such tragedies occurred only in Eastern Europe or as the aftermath of war, Aaron Katz (born in Philadelphia in 1903) recalls the death of two of his younger sisters, and Esther Ginsburg the death of her brother.

AARON KATZ: *We happened to be visiting my grandmother, I must have been about four years old, and I remember the baby was ill and someone said, "I don't think she's breathing any more." They took a feather to test her. . . . I can still cry. . . .*

THE PROMISE OF GOOD HEALTH

I never discussed it with my mother. I don't even know what happened. As a kid, there were a lot of questions I should have asked. I don't even recall the funeral; I don't remember sitting shiva [the seven-day mourning period]. I may have been four. The baby was two. I was a youngster. My sister's name was Ruchel—Rachel. The childbirth I don't remember, but this—I had an attachment. The very fact that I remember the name. The other child that died in childbirth, I don't remember the name. I don't remember whether it was a girl or a boy. But my sister I remember. I had an attachment.

ESTHER GINSBURG: *My littlest brother, he died when he was ten and a half, a tragic death, he suffered from appendicitis, this was in 1925. He died of a burst appendix. That was in May 1925, and that was one of the most shattering things that ever happened to me in my life. When Isaac died, the dog would lie on the lawn—the dog would lie there at the end of the lawn looking for Isaac to come home. The dog's name was Baron and he was a collie.*

My brother and I were very close. My mother said she never saw such a close relationship.

And Lillian Winograd, herself a victim of the polio epidemic in New York City in 1916, recounts the shattering experience of her mother's early death:

I died—Freudian slip! My mother died when I was thirteen years old. She died from the flu. It was 1928. She was forty years old. My kid brother was three years old, going on four.

We didn't expect her to die. We called an ambulance. She was in the bedroom I slept in. And it was seven at night. My sister fainted. It was a terrible, terrible time.

My poor father. We were so taken with our own misery as children. He was a young man. He was about forty-two. We were really concerned more with ourselves. And we clung together like glue, the four of us. My kid brother was afraid to sleep by himself, so we used to wrap him in a blanket and put him on the floor in front of the radio, in the living room. He fell asleep.

It is funny. I remember right after shiva the four of us were in the room together. And for some reason as we were talking, we were really a support group for each other, and locked our father out completely, and here my mother was just buried, maybe a week before, and I don't know what we spoke about or what prompted it, but we began to laugh, and he heard us, he came storming out of the bedroom and he screamed at us, "What are you doing? How dare you sit here and laugh? Your mother isn't even cold in the grave yet." He must have felt his isolation, whatever he felt.

Now as an adult myself, I understand what he was, who he was, so I am more generous in my feelings toward him. That I understand why he must have done it. I realize now that he must have resented us shutting him out, clinging together like that, we were even able to laugh. We were a real support group for each other but not for him. We all went through a very bad time.

In the early years of the century, many people had very similar "bad times." Doctors could not offer much comfort—and precious little optimism—to a family struck by disease, for they lacked effective therapies for many of the common illnesses that were fatal or seriously disabling, the diseases that struck down children or adults in the prime of life.

ROSE JANOFSKY: *My younger sister was very susceptible to upper respiratory ailments and used to get pneumonia, or what at that time was diagnosed as pneumonia. My mother would call the doctor to our house, and it was a dollar, he would come to the home for a dollar. And he told her to take the child's temperature every two or three hours and tell him what it was. Well, she didn't want him to come to the house again to do this, because then he would charge a dollar, so he left the thermometer. She couldn't read it, could not read the thermometer, so she would take my sister's temperature and take the thermometer to him several times a day for him to read the temperature to see how the illness was progressing, to save the dollar.*

But the only thing that they could do was to sit around and sponge her all day long. There was really no medication they could give. You sit there with wet cloths and apply them to the kid's head and hope it will drive the temperature down. That was the only thing we could do. It was very frightening. In those days just the word pneumonia could strike terror in your heart. Today they are over it in a few days.

Pneumonia, of course, was not the only terrifying word; there was also *influenza* and *scarlet fever*, *croup* and *tuberculosis*, *polio*, *summer diarrhea*, *childbed fever*, and *measles*—words that frightened our parents and grandparents rather as *cancer* or *AIDS* frightens us today. At worst, each could mean sure death; at best, months, perhaps years, of anguish, frustration, and pain.

And hospitals provided no alternative. In the shtetls, hospitals simply did not exist; but even in the cities—both European and American cities—they were regarded with dread, as places to which were sentenced only the poorest of the poor, and from which only the very luckiest emerged alive. Tess Egrovsky recounted how one of her brothers died around 1920 when still a young man:

He was in college—Cornell, studying agriculture—and he came for a rest for ten days in our house [she was married by this time], and he got the flu and died. We had nurses day and night; he had double pneumonia. We put him in the front room when he got sick. He didn't go to the hospital because I felt home was better. You get better care at home when you have nurses; and I had a doctor coming there three times a day.

And when my son had scarlet fever, I had nurses day and night for the first ten days, and then I had my niece, a nurse, for seven weeks, taking care of him. If he had been in a hospital, he'd be dead. And my doctor would not even let him go to the hospital. When he was sick I didn't neglect him. Some people couldn't care, they send the children to the hospital. I felt that I am capable to take care of my family so I never let him go to the hospital.

And Clara Zinsser recalls what happened in Odessa when one of her sisters contracted diphtheria:

One of my sisters had diphtheria in the summer of 1918. My aunt told him [my father] to put her [the sister] in the hospital. But my father didn't want to do that because if he put her into the hospital she wouldn't survive. So he went to the man who was in charge of the neighborhood—if anyone was sick or something—he was a tailor and he explained to him the whole situation. So all the neighborhood took their children and put them with some relatives; they emptied out the neighborhood so that she could stay home. The doctor came every day and everything, but her heart remained weak. She died of typhoid fever when she was only eleven years old.

Folk Remedies and the Evil Eye

Over the centuries, the Jews, like most traditional peoples, had developed a basic theory of disease and a set of acceptable remedies and rituals aimed at combating it. By modern standards, these theories were not grounded in "good" evidence, and few of the remedies were truly "effective"; but our grandparents believed them to be the only possible armaments human beings could use in the battle against illness, disability, and death. Even the trip across the Atlantic did not disabuse older Jews of this conviction.

Most diseases, according to the ancient Jewish explanation, were the result of invasion: some "foreign agent" overwhelms a weakened body. Thus, persons in a naturally weakened state require special protection. Babies should be kept as warm as possible, protected from blasts of cold, fresh air, wrapped like mummies. Houses, especially in the wintertime, had to be sealed as tight as possible; children were encouraged to play inside, rather than out. Since foreign agents could also enter the body through cuts and bruises, these had to be avoided—even if it meant severely restricting children's activities—and when cuts did occur, they had to be covered up, with special ointments made from animal fats, as a defense against invasion. Food—and the body fat it could produce—was understood to be the ultimate weapon: more fat meant a stronger body, more resistant to invasion. Rebecca Green recalls that that particular folk belief remained potent even after she and her family had immigrated:

I was always so thin that my mother was sure I was going to die of TB. I did have severe coughs. Sometimes, when a cold persisted, she took me to the doctor, but most of the time I was given Maltine [powdered malted milk] with cod liver oil. It was very thick—dark brown and thick; and I had to have tablespoons of it, not teaspoons. And also, when I wasn't sick, I had to drink lots of milk, milk with sweet cream in it. It was so rich it was awful. You can imagine what it was like: three quarters of a glass of milk and one quarter of a glass of heavy sweet cream. All of this to fatten me up. In my mind I called the milk drink "guggle-muggle." It was milk, sweet cream, honey, and a spoonful of cognac.

Jewish housewives also had a ready arsenal of remedies with which to battle disease. All of these folk remedies—many were ointments or herbal teas—were probably ancient, and few were uniquely Jewish. At this remove, it may be impossible to discover how—if at all—these remedies were related to the invasion theory of disease, but no matter—most of our grandparents and some of our parents swore by them:

In general [in the Jewish communities of Eastern Europe] one was treated with domestic methods, which were known to every reputable woman and which were passed on by inheritance from one generation to the next. In case of a throat sickness, for instance, everybody knew that one has to take a long warm sock— of course, a used one, not a washed one, an important factor was the smell of sweat—and one had to roll into it half a candle and put it to the neck for a whole night.

... In various cases of internal ills one put on the navel, steer-gall. If a child got fever one would rub in the mother's or the grandmother's urine ... some even gave the urine to drink. ... On a bleeding wound one used to put a cobweb found in a very dirty place. In case of a nose bleeding one would stick into the nostrils a piece of paper torn from an old prayer book or the Bible. ... In case of convulsions the best method was to break in front of the child's face a plate or a pot. Weak children used to wear on the neck a "mascot," consisting of a small bag which contained a little salt, a small old piece of matzo, a tiny scrap of paper on which a good Jew had written some sayings.

A universal treatment of various ills was to build a tuft of hair on the head. It was mostly practised by women. For a time they would stop washing and combing their hair, thus building the tuft which became infested with insects. The tuft was not supposed to be touched as long as there was the threat of death or of a severe

117

illness. Occasionally a woman would dare to get rid of the filth, but in any case not at once, cutting it gradually.[3]

One of the most enduring of these folk remedies was cupping, the practice of applying several small heated glass cups (*bankes*, in Yiddish) to the surface of someone's body—ostensibly to draw out the foreign, invading substances. Cupping was such a familiar practice in Jewish communities that it spawned an equally enduring Yiddish expression—"*s'vet dir helfn vi a toytn bankes*"—which reminds us that any futile activity "will be about as helpful as applying cups to a dead man." Many an immigrant bundle carried a set of *bankes*, carefully wrapped.

ROSE JANOFSKY: *During the influenza epidemic in 1918, the local barber was putting cups on people—in those days, barbers pulled out teeth, too—and then he caught the influenza and died, and my mother took over the work. She went to houses and she did it. She charged twenty-five cents for doing it.*

These little glass cups are put into a basin of hot water so that they are clean. The cups are about three fourths of an inch at the bottom and then they belly out to maybe an inch and a half and they get small again at the opening. As you take them out of the hot water, you put a light to a wick, it slips into the cup, you put the flame in for about five seconds to consume the oxygen, consume the air. As it uses up the oxygen, there is a vacuum in the cup, and immediately you put it on a person's flesh, usually the back. And it sticks. The vacuum keeps it in place. You have about a dozen, or nine or ten, depending on the size of the person.

The cups are near the lungs on the back, and it clears up the inflammation that is in the lungs; by making the flesh pucker into the cup, it has a pulling effect; it pulls out the foreign matter that is causing the problem. The Jewish people and the Italian people have faith in this; they believed in this business.

I remember this lady begged her once to come to her house. I think she had a child who was very sick and I think she begged my mother to come and do this to the child in an effort to save it. I think this child did survive. Yes, absolutely, she went, and went to lots of people in the building, and lots of them did not survive. But I remember this one survived, so this lady was really very grateful to my mother, because she thought this is what cured her child.

Ultimately, however, traditional Jews believed that the the "Evil Eye"—a malevolent, metaphysical being, an anti-god—was the source of all disease. While neither the Old Testament nor the Talmud makes mention of such a being, pious Jews—most especially Jewish women—nonetheless believed in it; and even those who didn't completely believe saw no harm in acting as if they did. When a baby became ill, a pious mother would change its name—or "sell" its name to someone else—so that the Evil Eye could not find it. If one child had died in a family, then the next one might be called *di Elte* (the oldest one) so as to fool the Evil Eye. Children were not supposed to be praised too much lest they attract the attention of the Evil Eye. Over the centuries, numerous special prayers had been composed for invoking God's assistance in the battle against His opposite; numerous rituals had developed as protection against the anti-god:

> One of the very popular treatments used to be the conjuration of spells. This used to be practised by old teachers, sages and wise women. The conjurer did not have to see the patient; it was sufficient for him to have some item of his wearing apparel, as for instance a shirt, a scarf, etc., the patient's and his mother's names. The conjuration used to be done in a very low voice, by whispering all kinds of mysterious words, spinning around on one spot.[4]

Childbirth was a particularly precarious time, ripe for the Evil Eye. Women were not supposed to engage in public preparations for an infant—no knitting of tiny garments, no fussing over health—so that the Evil Eye would not be apprised of their susceptibility. Newborn infants were supposed to wear red ribbons on their wrists or on their cradles, because red repelled the Eye. The bed on which a woman was to deliver had to be surrounded by sheets and drapes—no windows, no air, no breezes—with written or printed incantations pinned to them. Not infrequently a conjurer might be called in to "assist" at the delivery:

> Through the parted curtain he sees a strange and wild looking person holding a black rooster. Incense is burning in the room and

this wild looking man is making strange movements. The man hits the rooster on the head while he pronounces some mystic words of incantation, which do not have any meaning. He is constantly repeating one word to repel the evil spirits. Then he stamps his feet and gesticulates with his hands as if he is fighting with somebody. He is constantly repeating the word *mpspts* to repel the evil spirits from the mother. Each time he pronounces *mpspts* he hits the rooster and the rooster cries and makes a terrible sound. . . . The wild person continues to shake and throw himself in wild incantations. He seizes the rooster at his neck and spins it around as in the ceremony of *kaporis* [the swinging of a rooster over a person's head in order to absorb his or her sins; performed on the day before Yom Kippur]. The rooster should be the sacrifice for the mother and the baby. The rooster is then thrown into a little hole that has been previously dug by the side of the bed and covered with soil. A bench which has been removed from this spot is placed over the soil. The ceremony is now finished and everything in the room is restored in its usual place.[5]

There were similar mystical rituals intended especially to deal with epidemics, especially terrifying visits from the Evil Eye:

There were also measures against epidemics, however different from today's. Believing that they came as a punishment, there used to start a persecution of unbelievers, punishing them as far as it was possible to do so. Other old and proven measures were used, such as pouring wax, measuring fields, and arranging weddings of cripples at cemeteries. While I was in Roumania during World War I I saw a town ravaged by typhoid. The following signs were written on houses: "typhoid was here already;" "nobody here," "everybody left." On some of the houses one could see on the door a big padlock; it should look as if no one was there. All these measures were taken to mislead the evil spirits who spread typhoid.[6]

Max Hirsch rembers vividly how, when he was a child, a cholera epidemic ravaged his town:

During one cholera epidemic, the people of the town decided to do something for the Deity, for God. They chose a very poor couple, to marry them off. The poorest girl in town, who had no parents, and the poorest man in town, who had no occupation or parents. And they married them off on a day when a rabbi died. It so happened that a certain day a rabbi died, so there was a procession. First came a rabbi; then they carried the dead rabbi in the casket; behind him went the mourners; after that came the couple: the chassen [bride] and the kalleh [groom], the bride and the groom and the wedding party and the people—the citizens of the community—then a band playing klezmer music [Ashkenazic folk music; usually improvised]. There must have been at least one hundred people from the community. Notices had been posted telling the community about this ceremony.

We get up to the cemetery, there was a grave, it had already been dug. The casket is placed on top of the grave. Kaddish is spoken, for the dead rabbi. Then the marriage took place. Then when the rabbi said, "Haray et m'kudeshet li, be thou consecrated unto me according to the law of Moses and Israel," the bride had a lock—a key lock—and she put it on the casket, before they lowered the casket into the ground. She locks the lock and puts it on the casket, with the key in the lock. That was the marriage ceremony. The mythology in this was: to lock the epidemic.

Then after the music played, people danced on the grave. I was there; I was fifteen years old; I was part of the citizens' group. I marched in front of the band playing the klezmer music. There was dancing and so forth.

And then what happened? The epidemic went on like hell, people were dying. In other words, the gods were not at peace, the Deity was not at peace. People were dying. It was merciless.

Belief in the Evil Eye, or in the medical value of prayer, or in the healing power of words, did not dissipate on this side of the Atlantic for those Jews who had immigrated as adults.

SAM SMILOWITZ: *My mother had a child that died when it was six months old. It died of an infection which was not uncommon in those days in the crowded East Side of New York. There was no treatment for any infection in those days. After that baby died, my mother had* another child, and at the age of six months that child died. I don't remember either their names or their sexes.

In any event my mother, who came from a small town in Austria, began to think that maybe a curse had fallen upon the family. And she had a lot of faith in the rabbi of the small town from which she had come. He had a reputation of being able to perform miracles. My mother had a twin sister, and she had her sister go back to Europe and speak to this rabbi in Austria and tell him the story of my mother's life: how she had two children who were perfectly well, and she had subsequently given birth to two children and that they both died at the age of six months. My aunt spoke to the rabbi, he listened very intently, and he told her to go home and tell her sister that as long as she lives no child of hers will ever die again. And that was the message that was delivered to my mother.

Then I was born. At the age of six months, I took sick with what was diagnosed as erysipelas. It's an inflammation of the skin and high temperature and usually is fatal within two or three days. And, lo and behold! I made a complete recovery!

And from that time on, my mother's faith in the rabbi was unshakeable. Despite anything that happened to her family in subsequent years, she had no fears about any dire outcome.

Indeed, even some of those who immigrated as teenagers (Esther Ginsburg was thirteen when her family left Lithuania for the United States in 1911) continued to adhere to the old-fashioned notions.

ESTHER GINSBURG: My father gave his life for me. In 1926, I got very sick; the doctor said I had a fifty-fifty chance. It was erev [the evening or time just before a holiday] Yom Kippur. My parents called the hospital and they said I am still lingering, but it didn't look good. My father said, "Whatever happens to Esther, it should happen to me better first."

The day after Yom Kippur, he said to my mother, "I am going into Boston, to the landslayt [people who came from the same village or town]. They should all pray for me." But before he went he got a headache. So my mother said, "Go lay down and take a rest. You'll go an hour later." He never got up.

And it happened. And I fell asleep and I had a dream. I saw a cemetery with stones and every one had the words saved, saved, saved, and it *meant that I was saved, that I was alive: everyone of those tombstones had the word "saved." And he was gone. He never got up afterward. I had this dream in the hospital the same day my father died; then I woke up from the dream and I took a turn for the better.*

The Old Medical World and the New: The Polio Epidemic of 1916

People like Sam Smilowitz and Esther Ginsburg were caught in the transition between the old medical world and the new. They were born in the years in which bacteriology was in its infancy and scientific medicine was just beginning to feel its oats. Today they may know that CAT scans and insulin are much more effective than cupping and incantations; but when they were young, between 1910 and 1940, that end result was not yet clear. Modern medicine was full of promise, but the promise had not been fulfilled. The tubercle bacillus had been identified, but no cure for tuberculosis had been found; diphtheria antitoxin had eliminated one scourge of childhood, but dozens of others remained—measles, scarlet fever, whooping cough, pneumonia; a reliable test was available that could determine whether someone had syphilis, but syphilis therapy (with salversan) was only partially successful. The shadow of death and disease had been lifted, but only just a little; in a pinch (and the pinches tended to be frequent in those days), cups and incantations—their value having been tested over many centuries—were likely to reappear.

Nothing illustrates the character of this transition better than the polio epidemic in New York City in 1916. In some ways polio was the most terrifying of all the diseases that parents had to fear; a child happily playing in the yard or the street might one day show signs of a slight fever. The next morning one leg, or maybe both, might be limp (an early name for the disease was "morning paralysis"), and within a week the child would either be dead or condemned to life as a cripple.

Polio also seemed to be a particularly twentieth-century scourge; only a few cases were described during the nineteenth century, and no epidemics were reported until the 1890s. During most of that time, no one really knew what caused the disease or how to react to it. Some physicians attributed it to teething; others, to "inflammations" or "effusions of serous fluid" in the sheaths of the nerves. Some recommended bleeding the patient as an effective form of treatment (depleting the supply of serous fluid); others suggested creating a running sore by the use of red-hot irons over the infected spot, so as to encourage the dispersal of the contaminated fluids.

Around 1885, however, a physician discovered that paralytic polio was the result of damage to cells in the spinal cord, which is why, once contracted, the paralysis was unlikely to disappear entirely. Once having learned this, physicians became nihilistic; recognizing that nothing in their bag of remedies could repair damaged nerve cells, they advised parents to make children as comfortable as possible when the paralysis began—and pray for the best.

Then, in the summer of 1893, a minor epidemic of polio—23 reported cases—occurred in Boston. A year later, again in the summer, Rutland, Vermont, was hit: 132 cases. In each succeeding summer, another city succumbed. In 1907, at least 1,000 children were stricken in New York City. Public officials became panic-stricken, slowly acknowledging that the disease appeared to be contagious. Rudimentary forms of household quarantine—confining stricken children and their siblings at home—were attempted; quarantine notices were posted on the front doors of houses and apartment buildings.

In 1908, two Austrian pathologists discovered that polio (which had also been ravaging European cities) was caused by a microorganism. Panic turned to hysteria: how could an epidemic disease caused by an invisible, omnipresent agent—not unlike the Evil Eye—ever be controlled? Mason City, Iowa, was hit in 1910; Cincinnati in 1911; Buffalo, New York, in 1912. Every summer the number of reported cases increased (the U.S. Public Health Service designated polio as a reportable and quarantinable disease in 1910); and as the epidemics became more virulent, adolescents and adults also succumbed; small children were no longer the only victims. Some patients came down with a fever and temporary minor paralysis that dissipated in a few days; many others died or were paralyzed for life. And nothing seemed to work; parents, doctors, nurses, and public officials were helpless.

Helpless, that is, until the summer of 1916, when the most progressive health officials of the most Progressive city in the nation—New

*"One morning I got up with a raging fever and I couldn't walk.
And somebody called the Police Department, because there was
hysteria all over the entire city, mass hysteria."
Seattle policemen outfitted to enforce the quarantine
during the flu epidemic of 1918.*

York—decided that they could show the nation and the world how best to slay the beast of polio. In their proud efforts to record and report on what they did, and in the memories of those of our parents who, as children, lived through that particularly famous epidemic, we can find a particularly frightening account of what it meant to live on the borderline between ancient and modern medicine.

The first six cases were reported in one Brooklyn neighborhood, early in June. Nurses and social workers were assigned to search, from house to house, for additional cases: twenty-three were discovered, despite the fact that many parents were unwilling to admit to having a paralyzed child, fearing what might ensue. Physicians at the Baby Health Station in the afflicted neighborhood reported that mothers were bringing sick infants to the station: one child could no longer hold his bottle; another, no longer raise his leg.

Officials at the Department of Health, fairly certain that an epidemic was building, began to take action. Additional nurses were hired to search for cases. As domesticated animals were suspected carriers of the virus, the ASPCA was asked to round up and kill stray cats and dogs; the *New York Times* reported, on 26 July, that 72,000 cats and 8,000 dogs had been destroyed in a "lethal chamber" since the first of the month. (Later in the summer, as the epidemic increased in intensity, people started killing their own pets.) The Department of Street Cleaning hired extra sweepers to flush the streets with water once a day; the sweepers were not allowed to use burlap bags for garbage, lest liquids and dust sift through them. Children carried notices home from school, warning parents that the disease could be spread by discharges from the nose and throat—and that antiseptic gargles and nose sprays were ineffective.

On 28 June, quarantine regulations were issued. Every person who contracted polio had to be hospitalized—not because hospitals could cure the disease, but because they could isolate patients from the community. Parents could not accompany children, no matter how young, in ambulances and could visit only twice in the hospital, and then only if the child was desperately ill. Janet Sommers remembers when public health officials came to her home:

My mother was the mother to the whole building. If somebody became ill, it was my mother to whom they went to cry about it. I remember the ambulances stopping in front of the house. There were three tiers of stretchers on each side of the ambulance, and this is the way they took the people—the children—away. I see that picture in my head, and I knew that it was a horrible thing. People cried constantly.

And then as luck would have it, my brother was afflicted with it. I remember the pounding on the door of the doctors and the nurses. "Mrs. Grossman! Open the door!" And my mother said, "No! Go away!" "Mrs. Grossman, we have to take the little one!" And she said, "Cut off your little finger!" She would not let them into the house.

She didn't want him in the hospital because they were dying like flies in the hospital. If he were going to die, he would die at home, not in the hospital with the others. But after they left, another nurse came to the door and knocked on the door and spoke to my mother through the door. "Mrs. Grossman," she said, "I understand. I understand. Dr. Berger is going to open a private hospital nearby soon and maybe you'll be able to get your little boy in there." And that is what she did.

As the summer wore on, health officials discovered that the nurses were too lenient with mothers, so police officers were sent to do the work instead. Lillian Winograd, who was born in 1915 and got polio in the 1916 epidemic, does not remember the epidemic at all, but her parents told her about it:

One morning I got up with a raging fever and I couldn't walk. And somebody called the Police Department, because there was hysteria all over the entire city, mass hysteria, and they came and my mother wouldn't let me go, held on to me, and they were pulling me from her arms because I had to be quarantined, and they finally pulled me from her arms and in the hysteria forgot to tell her where they were taking me. I got to be in one of the hospitals where they were taking contagious children, and she finally found me after going to a few hospitals, looking through all the wards for children that had come down with polio. She found me.

I don't remember her finding me; I was a year old. But I used to fantasize that maybe I wasn't her daughter, maybe she thought I was and I belonged to somebody else, and she found me and took me—you know. That was the story they used to tell me.

Imagine grabbing a child out of the mother's arms and not telling

*her! One policeman holding her and the other running out to the am-
bulance with me. And then letting her go. And her running. It is like
a grade-B movie. She tried to run after the ambulance. Of course the
neighbors were not sympathetic and they probably resented her for not
calling and saying "Come take my child" to begin with. They were so
hysterical. Then my mother sent my sister and brother into the country
with my grandmother to get away from the city. It took her something
like five or six days to find me. And she said when she found me they
had shaved my head; I had no hair and she found me. I don't remember
a thing, I was sixteen months old.*

In the scorching heat of a New York summer, play streets, theaters,
and movie houses were closed to children under the age of sixteen.
Street carnivals, parades, picnics, and excursions were forbidden. Special guards were posted at playgrounds and swimming pools, and children had to present certificates attesting that their households were
free of polio before they were allowed to enter. Mothers who were
obtaining purified milk for their babies from public milk stations had
to arrive early in the morning, before all other clients, if there was a
quarantine in the building in which they lived. Those quarantines,
which were announced with placards on front doors and daily lists in
newspapers, affected all the children in a family in which one child had
already had polio; siblings had to remain indoors until two weeks after
the afflicted child had either died, been removed from the house, or
recovered. The superintendents of multiple dwellings were charged
with enforcing the regulations, and people who were caught violating
them were subjected to arrest, fines, and—occasionally—short terms
in prison.

JANET SOMMERS: *And I remember being quarantined. We were not
allowed to go out. Food was passed into us through the window, and
about eleven or twelve at night my mother did sneak us out just to
walk in the street and back again. And, of course, we wore the camphor
things.*

The "camphor things" were bags of aromatic materials that one
wore around the neck, a medieval practice imported into the twentieth

century. By midsummer so many herbal practitioners were producing various charms—amulets of camphor, red pepper, garlic, asafoetida, and inscribed prayers—that the Department of Health felt obliged to undertake "the prosecution of unscrupulous persons engaged in the despicable practise of selling worthless preparations and preventions as cures for poliomyelitis to the gullible public."[7] Six persons were brought to trial and sentenced, with considerable attendant publicity. Each got thirty days in jail and a fine of $250—none of which put a stop to the sale of the bags.

Desperately searching for a remedy, doctors were willing to try almost anything. Some, still immersed in nineteenth-century forms of practice, favored cupping, mustard plasters, strychnine pills (to kill the microorganism), and massage. Others, aware of recent successes against diphtheria, tried injecting serum from recovered patients into as yet unaffected children, in the hope of conferring immunity; still others tried removing fluid from the spinal cord of afflicted children, with the intention of then injecting it into the child's bloodstream, in the hope—futile as it turned out—of stimulating antibodies.

Unimpressed by the "experts'" performance, the citizens of New York sent more than 230 suggestions to the Department of Health over the summer. Some people thought that ice cream (it chilled the stomach), soft drinks, candy, and summer fruits were the cause of the epidemic; others implicated cold cereals and canned foods. Commercial laundries were blamed (they spread the germs), as were poisonous gases from the European war (an enemy plot), gasoline fumes, excessive tickling of children, and the "increasing amount of radio calls and wireless electricity in the air."[8]

By early July, the epidemic had spread from Brooklyn to Manhattan and out of the tenements into the wealthier sections of the city. An average of fifty new cases were being reported every day; the mortality rate climbed to 20 percent, four times greater than in 1907. Parents were sending their children out of the city if they could possibly find a way to do so; most summer camps had, by then, closed their doors to New York City children, but relatives in nearby communities were implored to help. Janet Sommers remembered that later in that summer, when she was five or six, her mother farmed her out to some relatives: "And I went and stayed there until the neighbors found out why I was there, and then they made me go home." For as fast as children were being sent out of the city, so too were they being sent back. Blockades were posted on roads, and policemen examined passengers at railroad stations. In Huntington, Long Island, the *New York Times* reported on 9 July, five hundred people (of whom two hundred were Boy Scouts) engaged in a house-to-house search for New York City children, who, when discovered, were promptly driven back to the city line.

In the end, the Department of Health had to admit failure. The city had spent over $300,000 on its "hospital quarantine"—2,000 cribs for city hospitals; 33,000 diapers; 8,000 children's nightgowns; 211 oxygen tanks—to little avail. The rules and regulations, advocated by prestigious physicians and public health experts, based upon the "latest" scientific evidence, enforced at enormous expense both in money and in anguish, had turned out to be about as effective as the camphor bags. Between June and November 1916, 6,000 people died of polio in New York City and 27,000 people were paralyzed by it. One of those people was Lillian Winograd:

My earliest recollections are from the age of three. We lived in Bedford-Stuyvesant [in Brooklyn]; my father had bought a home because it was too difficult for my mother and my father to carry me up five flights of stairs. We had the ground floor and the basement, and we had one tenant. My mother used to sit me outside in a chair because I didn't have crutches and braces so I couldn't walk, and she'd sit me out, and I would watch the people go by. There was a little space in front. And she would peek her head out, I remember very well, peeking her head out and asking me—she use to call me Lillie—"Are you all right? Is everything O.K.? Do you want something? Do you need something?"

But I was, believe it or not, I was the happiest kid on the block because everybody passing by spoke with me. There were no cars running by, and I had a little girlfriend across the street, and her mother used to watch her when she crossed over and kept me company. All I remember is that if I wasn't outside she would knock on the front door, shouting, "Lillie's mother! Open the door!" I was very happy because I constantly had people giving me attention.

My grandmother, my bubbe, she was my mother's mother, and gave up her own house when I came down with polio to move in and help

130

my mother with me. And she was all mine. She belonged to me com-
pletely. I don't remember her real name besides "Bubbe." She belonged
to me. My sister and brother resented her because she belonged to me;
she gave me her undivided attention.

My grandmother lived with us until she died, when I was nine. I
had her a long time. I have wonderful memories with her. Every Satur-
day she would put me in a carriage and take me to the neighborhood
movie—every Saturday—and leave the carriage in the manager's
office. And I learned to read at a very early age because she couldn't
read and they didn't have talkies then so I used to read the subtitles to
her. They were silent movies. And my grandmother used to buy me a
lollipop every Saturday—lime.

They used to operate on me in the summertime—to get me to walk,
I guess; it was my time to be operated on. And then they put casts on.
I used to wake up in the middle of the night. Those were the days
when they put very heavy casts on you. They wrapped your feet in
cotton first, so you itched like crazy, all summer long. I used to take
rulers to scratch myself. Sometimes I would take a pencil, and I would
put it down so deep I couldn't get it out, so when they took the cast
off, they would find pencils. So it used to itch, so I would start calling
for my mother, and my grandmother would run out of bed and come
to me because my mother and father slept in a bedroom that was pretty
much removed from the rest of the bedrooms, so I would have to call
her real loud for her to hear me through the wall. So my grandmother
heard me first. And she would come to my bedside and I can still hear
her: "Lillie, don't wake Momma. She's tired. She worked hard all day.
Come, I will play cards with you." And we used to play cards: one
o'clock in the morning, two o'clock—pisha paysha [a card game]. I
would say, "Bubbe, it itches me, it itches me." She would say, "You'll
forget it. Come, let's play cards." And I did. And I still remember her
so well, I feel warm when I think of her.

A valiant woman, Lillian Winograd explained how she came to
terms with her disability:

I slept in a room with an older brother and sister. The three of us was
born within four years, and we all slept in the same bedroom. There

131

was just three of us in the same room, and I came down with it. They didn't. I came to the conclusion that I probably could handle it better than the other two—polio.

"Happenstance" Medicine: Diabetes and Tuberculosis

Physicians were also caught between the old medical world and the new. Charlie Moses and Max Hirsch were both trained in medicine during the years when medical therapy had not yet benefited from medical science, the years in which bacteriology, chemistry, and even physics had provided physicians with excellent new tools for diagnosis but none (or close to none) for cures. Moses, who trained in Brooklyn, refers to the years he was in medical school and just beginning his practice (the mid-1920s to the early 1940s) as "the dim days of medicine; not dark, but dim." Hirsch, who trained in Vienna, refers to therapy as "a happenstance experience": you tried anything that might work, and then crossed your fingers—and perhaps you prayed.

MAX HIRSCH: *When I was in medical school in the early twenties, we always had measles and the usual sore throats and infections, and in those days a physician couldn't do very much about it. There were no antibiotics. We treated those diseases just symptomatically. We gave them some perandum, which is the equivalent of aspirin, and let them gargle if they had a bad throat. We also used chamomile; this is used as a gargle, and it is supposed to have good healing power. And if you have nothing better, you use it.*

It was a happenstance experience. When we had pneumonias, we treated them with compresses on the chest. Nowadays we look at this and say we did really nothing. And I would agree; we did very little. We had no facilities to do anything better. For measles we couldn't do very much. If they developed pneumonia, we treated them like other cases of pneumonia. Encephalitis was common in those days too. We treated them as best we could. Mumps, when it affected the testicles, we treated purely with packs, cool compresses—ice was too dangerous—aspirin, and codeine. We did the best we could do—whatever we could learn from the literature.

*"I spent probably the happiest eleven months of my life in that
sanatorium. . . . They had a complete recreational program."*
Patients exercising at Riverside Hospital Sanatorium.

CHARLIE MOSES: *Medicine, between the years of 1926 and 1930 when I went to medical school, could be described maybe not as the dark days of medicine but as the dim days of medicine. We had made practically no strides in medicine therapeutically. For this reason: there were no antibiotics in those days, so the treatment of pneumonia, scarlet fever, measles, blood poisoning, and a dozen other serious diseases— well, there was no treatment. The antibiotics that have meant the difference between life and death in many diseases, we didn't have them. So, for example, a person having pneumonia, when I went to medical school, the treatment was fresh air. I think possibly oxygen by means either of a nasal catheter or later on by means of an oxygen tent, over his head and later on over the entire body, but nothing like penicillin which can overcome pneumonia in one day.*

Meningitis—also no treatment. We did nothing. We did nothing. We had a serum maybe which was valueless. When I say nothing, I really mean nothing. Occasionally the patient would get better, and we would think that maybe the serum did it, but who could tell? If you saw a medical book that was written in 1926, and read the therapeutics of the various diseases, you would see that the therapeutics is the same, in most instances, as it was in 1900—or maybe even 1850.

Here's another example. When I was an intern in 1930, they discovered a vaccine for pneumonia. But then they discovered there was something like twenty-eight different types of pneumonia, so we had to type the sputum to see if we could differentiate the sputum into one of the twenty-eight types of pneumonia, to classify this particular disease that we were dealing with. Then we would have to run to the Board of Health to get the particular vaccine for pneumonia #28 and the vaccine was valueless anyhow. Now all you have to do is to give them penicillin and they are better.

My wife had meningitis twenty-five years ago. And in the hospital they did a spinal tap and it indicated a meningitis and they put her on an infusion of penicillin; and by twelve midnight that evening, she was out of the woods. The first case of meningitis that I saw in practice was a three-month-old child, a house call. The mother called me and I went there, and I just happened to notice that the kid was holding his head a little stiff and his fontanelles [the soft spots on an infant's head] were bulging a little bit; that indicates increased pressure inside the brain. I gave the kid a sulfa drug, because that was all I had; it had a

slight salutary effect in some cases. The kid survived, but when he was
about eighteen months old, his mother noticed that he couldn't hear.
The kid survived, as I said, but was deaf—and the mother blamed me.
I emerged with a black eye. But what could I do?

Two of the diseases that were very familiar to our parents when they
were young—diabetes and tuberculosis—are good examples of what it
could be like not to practice but to experience happenstance medicine.
Diabetes, we now know, results from an inborn metabolic deficiency:
the pancreas does not secrete enough of the hormone insulin; and, as a
result, there are excessive amounts of sugar in the blood. By the 1880s,
organic chemistry had progressed far enough to allow every physician
to test for sugar in a patient's urine or blood. By the turn of the century,
physicians were aware that the disease was probably hereditary, and
that certain ethnic groups—among them Eastern European Jews—
suffered from it inordinately: one expert estimated, in 1941, that since
1900 the mortality rate from diabetes was 50 percent to 75 percent
higher for Jews than for non-Jews in New York City.[9]

Despite their success in diagnosing diabetes, however, physicians
were unable to come up with a particularly successful therapy, other
than restricting, insofar as it was possible to do so, a patient's diet. Most
physicians who regarded themselves as experts on the disease agreed
that it was necessary to eliminate carbohydrates (starches and sugars)
in order to keep diabetes under control; but all agreed that, in practice,
this was difficult to do (as one of the symptoms of the disease was both
inordinate hunger and inordinate thirst). "There is the need for super-
vision of the diet by a second person," one expert explained,

> because the craving of diabetic patients often attains an ascendancy
> over their will power and habits of truthfulness; in fact, a lack of
> mental force and even imbecility are quite characteristic of the
> advanced disease. . . . I have known hospital patients to steal bread
> and potatoes and consume them surreptitiously in spite of repeated
> warnings, and also to acquire such a craving for fluid as induced
> them to drink their own urine.[10]

Diabetic children usually died before reaching adulthood. Adults
who developed the disease later in their lives were usually blessed with

milder cases, but everyone knew that eventually the condition would be fatal, either directly because of a diabetic coma, or indirectly because the gradual weakening of the body would permit infection to run riot. Until insulin was discovered (in 1923) and made widely available (a few years later), there were many children who observed their parents becoming progressively weaker, and the observation—not surprisingly—frightened them.

HANNAH TOPEROFF: *My mother had diabetes. It was a difficult thing to live with, frightening. To cope with it, she used to stay in bed one day a week and not eat. She could drink—tea, water, coffee—but not food. That was the way she lowered the amount of sugar in her system. She used to stay in bed every Wednesday; in the middle of the week she had her fast. Of course she was also on a strict diet. She ate a special bread. It was called "gluten" bread and it is still on the market; she ate things that would not give her too much starch. No sweetening of any kind ever entered her mouth at that time.*

I was in high school then. My mother would eat her food after we ate ours; her food was different from ours. It was prepared differently. It never occurred to us to discuss her illness with her. Not with my father either. I knew what it was, how it affected her. Each one of us knew she was ill with diabetes, it was explained to us, but we never discussed it.

Sometimes my mother would make a joke, though. When she would be served a cup of coffee, and it would be put down, she would say if I wanted it sweet, all I had to do was to stick my finger in it. Stir the coffee with my finger and that would sweeten it—that was the joke.

Toward the end she spent a lot of time in the hospital [this was in 1923]; the last year and a half she was alive, she was in the hospital more than she was out. And when she came out of the hospital the last time, and they brought down her bed into the living room, we had nurses around the clock. One of my brothers was married at her bedside. Finally she went into a coma and just never came out.

The regimen that Hannah Toperoff's mother followed well illustrates what Max Hirsch meant by "happenstance." Some late nineteenth- and early twentieth-century physicians advised that their patients (if strong enough to sustain such treatment) attempt to starve themselves for one or two days out of the week because the condition of a few Parisian diabetics had improved somewhat during the seige of 1871, when a blockade had severely limited food supplies; on theoretical grounds, no one understood quite why starvation should have lowered a patient's sugar level, but it did, so they advised it.

The sanatorium treatment for tuberculosis is yet another good example of happenstance. TB has gone by many names over the years—*consumption* and *phythsis* were two nineteenth-century appellations—but whatever the name, the symptoms have not been difficult to discern. In the early stages of the disease, the patient hardly notices that anything is wrong. "The trouble with tuberculosis," Sol Meyrowitz—who was a victim—reports, "is that when you are finally feeling sick, you are in trouble, real trouble. Before that you feel O.K; but you are really just wasting away. You feel good, but you know something is wrong and you don't quite feel it." At the next stage, the patient may begin to cough violently, and to cough up blood; breath is short; the patient is exhausted. Later on the coughing becomes unremitting, the patient loses weight, and eventually dies when the lungs, incapacitated and filled with fluid that cannot be expelled, become incapable of absorbing enough air to sustain life.

The bacillus that causes TB was discovered by Robert Koch in 1882; but the German bacteriologist's announcement, a few years later, that he had also discovered a cure turned out to be premature. Early in the twentieth century, when X rays had been discovered and the equipment for taking pictures with them was widely available, TB could be diagnosed in its early stages; but no cure—no way of destroying the bacteria before it destroyed the patient—was discovered until after the Second World War. During most of the nineteenth century and a good part of the twentieth, both in Europe and in the United States, tuberculosis was probably second only to pneumonia as a killer of people over the age of eighteen. In 1900, for example, out of every one thousand Americans, two died of tuberculosis and twenty were ill with the disease.[11] Tuberculosis was particularly prevalent in the poorest neighborhoods of the most crowded cities, precisely the places where many immigrants and their children were living.

Knowing that the disease was caused by a bacterium, physicians developed a sensible list of prophylactic measures: diseased patients should be isolated from healthy people; spitting should be forbidden; discharges from the nose and throat should be disposed of carefully. These measures were difficult to carry out if patients were poor: occupying a three-room apartment with five or six other people, sleeping four or five to a bed, washing pillowcases at best once a month, working in filthy factories.

Lacking a cure but desperate for some way of dealing with the disease, some physicians seized upon the sanatorium as a solution, almost by happenstance. Not long after the tubercle bacillus was isolated, an American physician, Edward Trudeau, injected some into an experimental population of rabbits. The rabbits that were kept in damp, dark, crowded pens succumbed to the disease; the ones that were allowed to run wild in the sunlight recovered, showing only slight lesions on their lungs. On the basis of this skimpy evidence, Trudeau proceeded to open a hospital on Saranac Lake, in the Adirondacks, in New York State, especially for the care of tuberculosis patients; and the sanatorium movement was born. Over a span of more than fifty years, roughly from the 1890s to the 1940s, thousands upon thousands of tubercular patients were removed to the mountains, often for years on end, in the hope that dry air, sunshine, good food, and complete rest would result in a recovery. For some it did; for many it did not. The sanatorium cure may have kept afflicted people from infecting their friends and relations, but there is no way to know whether it modified the pandemic character of the disease, since TB continued to be a serious health problem in the West until penicillin was mass-produced in the late 1940s.

Sanatorium treatment was expensive: too expensive for the poorest—and hence, the most susceptible—members of the population. Thus, as tuberculosis became an increasingly severe health problem, some city and state governments were galvanized into action. Special rooftop wards—the closest they could come to mountains—were established for tubercular patients in city-owned hospitals. A few states—New York and Pennsylvania among them—built public sanatoriums in the far reaches of the countryside. Members of our grandparents' generation rarely made use of these facilities, because the "fresh air cure" took many months, if not years; and few poor families could withstand foregoing an adult's wages for that long.

Young people, however, were in a different situation. If they contracted TB before they were married or had dependents (precisely what happened to both Charlie Moses and Sol Meyrowitz), and if the disease was caught early enough (which X rays, available by 1910, could do), the sanatorium became a possibility. Thus, while our grandparents struggled with TB—the shortness of breath, the unremitting coughing—over their workbenches and sewing machines, our parents went—of all places—to the mountains. Charlie Moses and Sol Meyrowitz both spent many months in Ray Brook Hospital, a publicly funded sanatorium near Lake Placid, New York; and the experience, in addition to helping them recuperate from TB, was transformative in other ways.

CHARLIE MOSES: *When I was seventeen years old, I had been feeling perfectly well and we had a public municipal bath in the neighborhood, and every week I would go there and swim in their pool. And on this occasion I had dived into the pool and had swum the width of the pool, which was twenty feet, and when I got to the other side I spit—and lo and behold! what I spit was pure blood!*

By then I had completed about a year and half of college. After a complete examination and X ray, they discovered that I was afflicted with tuberculosis. I was immediately sent to a hospital for a preliminary four to six weeks, while preparations were being made to send me to Ray Brook sanatorium, which was a sanatorium for incipient, which means "early," cases of tuberculosis. I felt fine. I had no symptoms. I had no cough. Outside of the fact that I spit blood, I had no symptoms at all.

I remained there for eleven months, and I spent probably the happiest eleven months of my life in that sanatorium. It was a place which opened my eyes to the world. I had spent my life previously in an insular situation. I had gone to school with children whose outlooks were very constricted. In Ray Brook, I spent my time with young people mostly, not of my Jewish faith, mostly Christian, mostly people who were attending private colleges in the state of New York: things which I never would have seen, things which I never would have done, if I had been in the city. My life was a restricted one; when I left home I left home with my books.

My parents didn't come up for eleven months. Nobody, nobody came up because it was supposed to have been a secret. In those days,

139

tuberculosis was a disease which you were supposed to conceal. It was disease almost like a venereal disease is now. And when my mother used to send me "care" packages of food and gifts and she would meet one of her sisters living in the area, and they would see her, they would ask, "Where are you taking this?" "I am taking this to Charlie," she would say, "he is in college." My mother had told them that I had transferred college. I had told her to tell them that I was in Union College [Schenectady, New York], of all places. I made up a fable that I was in Union College. So she would tell them that I was in college, and she was sending me packages. No one ever knew that I had tuberculosis.

They had a complete recreational program, so that we had parties, and we went to the movies, and we had plays. New York State paid for this; it was all paid by the Department of Health. I had a girlfriend up there; she was a Polish girl from near Buffalo, a Catholic girl; her name was Mary. Our contact was on a very innocent level; there was no sex involved except for kissing and "necking," as we called it then. I broke up with her, though, while we were still in Ray Brook.

And as I say we had picnics; we had outings; we had an hour or two hours each day which were put aside for regulated walks to the village; we had rest periods after lunch. And the Polish girls helped. In those days there were no drugs in the treatment of tuberculosis. The treatment consisted of fresh air and good food and rest.

When they told me that my eleven months were finished and it was time for me to go home, I was very unhappy. I was going back to reality.

SOL MEYROWITZ: *The chances are that I picked up TB from my father. He had it. He died from it. The last few months he just stayed home, didn't go to work, never left the house. My brother got it, and so did my sister—although we never knew she had it until some doctor, many years later, took an X ray and found the scars.*

I was twenty-three when I got TB. I was working in a tie house— we made ties—on my way to a pretty good job there. One day I was on a trolley car, with a friend; we were going out—and I spit up blood. The next day I went to see a doctor—he was my brother's friend—and he took one look at me and said, "The old man really helped you," or words to that effect. I spit up enough blood to scare the hell out of me.

I had became assistant manager of the whole goddamn thing, the tie house, and a couple of months after I had to quit, the manager went into business for himself, and I wasn't there to take the job. They called me at home, before I went to the sanatorium, to tell me that they got a job for me. It was awful; I felt worse about that than about being sick.

Then I went up to Ray Brook. I took the cure. No one was aware of where I was going. I went alone. Pop didn't come up, he was very sick at the time. But when he died, Mom came up, and it was a chore for her. It was a hospital for incipient tuberculosis; they keep you a year, and after that, whatever you need, they transfer you.

At Ray Brook, I stayed in bed most of the time—in bed, strictly in bed. They used bring us trays. I got out of bed for toilet: that was it. When the weather was beautiful, they moved your bed out onto a porch. We didn't lie in the sun, the sun is murder, just fresh air. They don't take you out unless you want to go out. You read if you want to. There is physical therapy, where you make things out of leather, beads, stuff like that if you want to. People come in and talk, bullshit around, those who can. It is never crowded; they have x amounts of patients and that is it: one to a room, two to a room, some rooms. Those that are very ill are one to a room. The first Passover I was there, they served us matzos and roast pork.

But I wasn't bored. It is different; they work on you psychologically; they want you to relax. If you are bored, you are not relaxed and your mind is going: count the leaves; count the cracks in the ceiling; think of things that don't mean a goddamn thing. There was one doctor, Paul Bogart, he would always leave you with a question. When he would see you down in the dumps, he would pull up a chair and sit by your bed. He was a great guy. He was a very ugly man, but when he opened his mouth: beautiful, so soft, and you got to take confidence in him, in what he did. "Read the clouds," he would say, "you will see magnificient figures." Or he would drop a poser on you: "Why do we have Labor Day?" And he would run. By the time he came around, he would say: "Do you have the answer?" When I relax, I still count the leaves and the cracks in the ceiling. It is a wonderful thing.

As with Charlie Moses, Sol Meyrowitz's horizons expanded considerably when he was at Ray Brook. The patients may have been ill, but their illnesses did not curtail some of their activities:

While I was at Ray Brook, I was raped. There was this married woman and she raped me. We had rooms across the hall and we were the only bed patients; the rest were ambulatory. I used her porch for "day curing," as we called it. Laying in bed out there, we were alone out there, and she got into bed with me. Nobody could see; we were up too high. We didn't have clothes on; we are wearing pajamas. First time for me. Yes, it went on for a while and that's why I was getting worse: two, three times a night. At night she came into my room. She was a nymphoma-niac; I didn't understand it at the time. She was beautiful, Jewish, and she came into my room, and she was married to the nicest guy. I felt like the biggest shitheel that ever lived. And it wasn't my fault. This guy, her husband, that is the only guilty feeling I have; I did wrong to him. It went on for months, and I wasn't getting well fast, and that's when she moved out to a cottage down the street, a cure cottage.

I spent thirteen months, and I didn't go crazy because everybody else was doing the same thing. Then some friends got me into a cure cot-tage on Saranac Lake where another organization footed the bill—I don't even remember the name of the organization.

Altogether I was away for about three years, but I came home able to go back to work. I continued to go for pleuro-thorax treatments once a week once I got back, and I did have a recurrence, right after the war [the Second World War], which sent me back to Ray Brook for a few months, but I'm alive to tell the tale and I'm grateful.

Sol Meyrowitz's life was disrupted by tuberculosis, but he did not die from it; his father did. The sanatorium, though a happenstance cure for TB, was at least partially effective—and that effect was crucial. In the early decades of the twentieth century, when our parents were growing up and the sanatoriums were being built, just the promise itself was enough to weaken the hold of the Evil Eye, of traditional medicine. Asked to choose between the world of the Evil Eye and the world of the sanatorium, most immigrant youths (and their contemporaries) opted for the latter and all it symbolized: modernity, optimism, pragmatism, America. In Eastern Europe, young people were still dying of tuberculo-sis; in America, they were being sent to sanatoriums for free.

Recent critics of the modern medical establishment often wonder how that earlier generation was "duped," as they put it, into adherence to what now appear to be the self-serving opinions of medical experts.

How, for example, could so many young men and women have agreed to having their lives interrupted for such long periods in the hope, backed by little evidence, that their tuberculosis would be cured by a rest in the country? The answer appears to lie not just in the beauty of the mountains but also in some of the small miracles medical experts were by then able to perform: tuberculosis, polio, and pneumonia were still dangerous in our parents' youth; but diphtheria, cholera, tetanus, and typhoid had already largely disappeared, at least in the United States. In Eastern Europe, of course, they were still killers, as every immigrant with relatives in the old country well understood.

Our parents also knew from sad experience just how ineffective traditional Eastern European forms of medical care had been. They had lost brothers and sisters, parents and cousins to the prayers and the ointments, to the cups and the plasters. In the space of the first twenty years of the century, modern physicians, especially in America, had managed to amass—even if the amassing had been a bit happenstance—more potent weapons against the Evil Eye than the traditional mystics had developed over two millennia. In the battle against disease and death, success may have been hard to measure, and only partial, but failure could be counted on the tombstones of the cemetery. Small wonder that our parents, and the society of which they were a part, chose the path to "medicalization"; small wonder too, that many of the immigrants came to regard the promise of good health as part of the promise of America.

5

"OF COURSE I WAS A VIRGIN WHEN I MARRIED": CHANGING SEXUAL MORES

THE SHTETL was a small, ramshackle, rural community—about as different from the great commercial cities of the West—London and Boston, Paris and New York—as it is possible for a place to be. Yet, odd as it may seem, the sexual mores of the shtetl residents bear an uncanny resemblance to the sexual mores of middle-class Victorian urbanites. In both places, standards of sexual behavior were clearly delineated and—whether based on the Old Testament or the New, whether articulated by talmudists or by ministers—very similar. This similarity, as we shall see, hastened the process of assimilation for Jewish immigrants in the United States.

Separate Spheres: Men and Women in the Old World

Jewish residents of nineteenth-century shtetls believed that men and women were biologically different, almost opposite, creatures: one dominated by his head; the other, by her body. From this fundamental biological difference different sex roles were thought to emerge: a Jewish man was supposed to study, earn a living, and—if necessary—fight; a woman was supposed to care for babies and run a household, earning a secondary living only if her husband's was not adequate—as was frequently the case in the last decades of the nineteenth century. The male role was thought to be culturally defining (a Jew is a man) and controlling (women must be subservient to men). In order for society to function properly, it was thought, there must be complete, or nearly complete, separation between those domains defined as "male" and those defined as "female"—just as the laws of *kashrut* specify the need to separate meat from milk.

All of which sounds very much like the "doctrine of separate spheres" adhered to, historians tell us, by many middle-class urban people of the West during the second half of the nineteenth century. Morris Hochstadt has a clear memory that makes his father, who was a shtetl carpenter in Poland, sound very "Victorian":

My father never talked to me about sex, except for one thing, his idea of manliness: a man should be tough, should assert himself. I don't know what prompted this, but I remember that once, when I got up after dinner to help my mother with the dishes, he would say, "No! Not a job for a man!"

When I was about twenty, I took out a young lady whose father was a rabbi. This young lady lived across town. By the time I said goodnight to her and left and traveled home, it was early in the morning. And there was my father waiting for me. And always he said not a word, but I knew what he was thinking—"Not manly enough."

At the age of three or four, young boys in the shtetl were removed (sometimes forcibly) from the female domain in order to enter the male. From that time forward, a boy was not supposed to touch, or even look at, a girl his own age:

145

The woman is considered so potent a source of attraction that a man must avert his eyes in order to protect them both.

Some men will not even speak directly to a woman. Most would avoid passing between two of them. . . . The constant danger of confronting or touching a woman has developed in some extremely pious men an almost furtive manner. They enter a room sideways with averted glance, so that people say of a very shy person, "He comes in like a yeshiva boy."[1]

Pious parents raised their daughters in accordance with these same prohibitions. A married woman was expected to shave her hair and wear a wig instead—so as not to be attractive to men. Women and girls were not supposed to appear in public with their arms or legs exposed. "An unusually loving couple," the anthropologists Mark Zborowski and Elizabeth Herzog report, "had their only quarrel when the wife became addicted to advanced ideas and made for their two-year-old daughter some tiny shirts with short sleeves. 'I'd die if she wears them!' bellowed the outraged husband"—reflecting the same sentiment that led Victorian ladies to put skirts around the legs of their furniture.[2]

Both boys and girls were expected to remain modest and virginal (both in thought and in deed) until they married. Jenny Grossman, who emigrated from Poland when she was eight or nine, recalls:

I was a little girl in Europe and I was on a swing. I remember I fell off the swing and one leg was hanging separate. I bled a little bit, and my mother was worried why I bled because she thought I broke my hymen. And she went to her father, who was a rabbi, and he said to her, "I think you should have some kind of written certificate, what had happened to her, because when she gets married she may not bleed and the husband may be in doubt." I don't know what happened to the certificate, if she ever got it or not.

My mother asked me about my first [wedding] night. She asked me if I had bled and I said, "Yes." She was still worried about that swing.

Once married, a couple was expected to engage in intercourse in moderation and only for the purposes of fulfilling God's commandment "to be fruitful and multiply." Both partners to the enterprise were supposed to enjoy intercourse (on this point the Victorians apparently begged to differ), and both had the right to enjoy it:

> A person must not be unduly familiar with his wife, excepting at the regular time appointed for the performance of his marital duty, as it is written (Exodus 21:10): "And her conjugal rights shall he not diminish." Men of a strong constitution, who enjoy the pleasure of life, having profitable pursuits at home and are tax exempt, should perform their marital duty nightly. Laborers who work in the town where they reside, should perform their marital duty twice weekly; but if they are employed in another town, only once a week.... The time appointed for learned men is from Sabbath-eve to Sabbath-eve. One must fulfill his marital duty even when his wife is pregnant or nursing. One must not deprive his wife of her conjugal rights, unless she consents to it, and when he has already fulfilled the obligation of propagation. If he deprives his wife thereof, in order to afflict her, he violates the Divine Command: "And her conjugal rights shall he not diminish."[3]

During intercourse, each partner was to indulge only in the purest of thoughts. As the Code of Jewish Law puts it, "A man should accustom himself to be in a mood of supreme holiness and to have pure thoughts, when having intercourse. He should not indulge in levity with his wife, nor defile his mouth with indecent jests, even in private conversation with her."[4] In any event, the ultimate goal of intercourse was not enjoyment but propagation, not the orgasm but the baby. God had made intercourse pleasurable, shtetl residents asserted, so that people would be induced to help Him fulfill His covenant with Abraham: that the children of Israel should become as numerous as the stars in the sky (Genesis 15:5). Any attempt to enjoy the sensation without realizing that goal was, by definition, a perversion of God's intent, which meant, of course, that fornication, masturbation, birth control (as in coitus interruptus—spilling of the seed), and homosexuality were strictly forbidden.

Traditional shtetl marriages were understood to have been, literally, "made in Heaven"; but God's agents on earth were thought to be not the couple themselves but the parents of the couple and the *shadchen*, the marriage broker. Arranged marriages were not uncommon during the latter decades of the nineteenth century, although the practice was already falling into disuse, especially among the poorest members of the community, those least likely to attract the interest of either a *shadkhn* or potential in-laws. The arranged marriage was another aspect of shtetl sexual mores that was distinctively different from those we call Victorian; a Victorian father expected to be asked for his daughter's hand in marriage, but only after she had already consented to the betrothal.

Some of these sexual rules were honored more in the breach than in the observance, most particularly the rule that enjoined celibacy on unmarried men. Both in the shtetl and in the centers of Victorianism, a young man who had sown some wild oats was generally forgiven his excesses, especially if he had had the good sense to scatter his oats on fields belonging to strangers or at least been able to keep his behavior clandestine. Irving Farber learned the virtues of discretion when he was a *yeshiva* student, boarding, as many students did, in someone else's home; a brief romance with his landlady's daughter helped persuade him to emigrate:

She was so beautiful! Her eyes were such that—I tell you now, as old as I am—she is a statue, a bronze statue! And gradually, being there, first she ignored me and I ignored her and gradually we began to see each other: the younger daughter, Sarah.

We first held hands and gradually pet each other and finally I began to get the idea I liked her. To make a long story short, about a week before Purim [a holiday that usually occurs in March] her mother was away, I was alone in the house, and we forgot to pull the window shade down—the window shade open to the street. One jerk, a student from the yeshiva, was walking along at four o'clock in the afternoon. It was dark outside, and you could see what was going on inside, and he saw I was holding hands with her.

We all went to the same yeshiva, and the next morning my grandfather [who taught in the yeshiva]—whack!—he took a stick and hit me, in the middle of the street, with a piece of wood. I said, "What is that?" He said, "For letting people see you, what you do!" In other words, I don't mind your doing it so long as you keep it a secret.

I didn't say a word. I never cried because I knew I deserved it. I decided that I was going to leave the yeshiva and go to America. I told

148

him, and he said maybe I should stay until the end of the term—it was four weeks more. And I said, "No! I don't want it! That is the end, your dreams are over, grandpa. I am not going to be a rabbi. I don't want to be a rabbi. I don't want to suffer like you."

And Morris Hochstadt, who emigrated with his father and brothers when he was about sixteen, recalls that his first sexual experience involved a Polish servant girl, repeating the pattern so distressing to the Polish priest quoted earlier:

I was twelve, thirteen years old; she was fifteen, sixteen, seventeen. She was a servant who worked in a rich house but she always met me: "Morris, come on and stay with me." To tell you the truth, I was anxious to go with her. When I was thirteen, I was very mature, like twenty. I used to go out with girls, but the anti-semiten [he means non-Jewish] girls were the ones I used to lay. I knew all the girls; the shiksas [gentile girls] I used to have in the country, picking hay, and I used to have a good time with them in the hay.

When Morris married (about a decade later, in the United States, a Jewish woman), both he and his wife had similar, traditional attitudes toward his earlier profligacy. "When I got married, my wife was a virgin," he reports. "She never asked me questions about what I had done before; she just kept quiet on the subject. 'What you did before, I don't care.' "

For girls, as well as for boys, there were some violations of the rules that the shtetl community was willing to ignore—although not without exacting a price. Strictly speaking, the community did not approve of abortion, but many women—overburdened with offspring—tried to find ways to end their pregnancies. Although the community did not condone premarital sexual relations either, it had over the years contrived ways to deal with the inevitable. If no pregnancy resulted, the whole business could be ignored (which is why secrecy was so important); an unmarried girl who was known not to be a virgin could eventually marry, but she could not hope to make as advantageous a marriage as her unsullied sisters. If a pregnancy did result and both offenders were Jewish and unmarried, a speedy wedding could be arranged without much threatening anyone's status:

149

Unmarried cohabitation of the latter kind [between those who are engaged to be married or who have married] in their view [the Talmudic authorities] does not constitute a violation of biblical command; the man, the girl and her father, if he consented to it, suffer no penalities on the basis of the biblical injunction against prostitution, although they may be penalized by local communal authorities for immoral conduct. This peculiarly lenient view of the Talmud toward unmarried sex relations between lovers has never been challenged by post-Talmudic teachers on any legal ground.[5]

Pregnant girls who could not marry (because they had been seduced by a married man or by a Christian) were in a more difficult, unenviable, position: strictly speaking, their children were not bastards (according to Jewish law, a bastard is the child who results from incest or union between a married woman and a man not her husband); but in practice, a girl who bore such a child was doomed—just as her non-Jewish contemporaries were—to life as a social pariah.

Some of the children of the shtetl, most especially those who had been born and raised there, carried this set of ideas about sex and gender as part of their cultural baggage when they crossed the ocean to America. Tess Egrovsky emigrated alone when she was in her teens, but her mother's injunctions stayed with her:

My mother always told me that for women promiscuity is wrong because we are the carriers of children and we have to be kept pure. She used to give me an idea of how my father imposed it on her, actually. This is what I got from her and I used to wonder why she was making me privy to this. I didn't want to be too intimate, too private.

There were certain lines drawn for behavior. My mother said that young people are like a couple of towels—they wipe their hands on each other. That made a great deal of sense. I could appreciate that.

Tess Egrovsky was essentially on her own in the United States. She lived first with an aunt and then with an uncle; but within a few days of arriving, she had a factory job, was earning her keep. She hoped eventually to marry and discovered that, in the United States, courtship involved going out on "dates," a practice with which she was never completely comfortable:

It wasn't a happy situation, but my time with these guys was always simple. I used to neck with them, sure—but they were just as afraid as I was.

I resented it [dating] to a certain extent. I thought that girls had to wait for some dumb cluck to call us for a date. He arranged the whole thing, never asked you what you wanted to do or anything; it was all arranged for you when he picked you up. Some of them were so—I can't tell you. Ordeals for me, the part was being a girl. Your only alternative was to say no, but you didn't do that because your mother felt you ought to go out [in order to get married]. I was very much controlled by what I thought my mother wanted, I know that.

Jennie Grossman also learned about dating when she came to the United States; her mother gave her firm rules about how she should conduct herself:

My first impression of Sol [her future husband] was "a nice boy." And then he asked me out and we went to the movies. You know what my mother would say, in Yiddish? "A feel and a kiss, and don't touch any farther. That is O.K., but that is all!" He was a gentleman. He paid for me. He was very nice. He respected me. I don't know how many dates we had before he kissed me. And after that kiss I knew that was it.

Her mother also insisted that certain of the traditional formalities be observed before the wedding:

My mother called the mikve to make the arrangements, to keep it open. My mother went with me. It was a nice experience. You take a bath and in spite of what people say, dirty smirty it is not.* It is clean, it's sanitary, and they make you feel very comfortable, not to be nervous. Wash your hair, cut your nails. Each bathtub is in a separate room,

---

* In the 1920s, many young, assimilating immigrants believed, following the notions then common among middle-class Americans, that any public bathing facilities were, by definition, unsanitary, because one could not know what diseases the previous occupants were carrying. For more discussion on this point, see chapter 8.

private. They cut your toenails. Actually in the Jewish religion, when a bride gets married she is clean and that is what she is supposed to be. Really clean. I even planned the date of my wedding that I shouldn't have my period.

So you are clean when you go to the pool. So you take the sheet off, what you are wrapped around with, and you go down the steps and you submerge, and she [the attendant] puts a towel over your head, and you make a prayer [a special blessing for women using the mikveh]. And that is the whole thing. And you come out of the pool and dry yourself. My mother was with me but she didn't even watch, she wasn't even in the room there. It is all private. The lady attendant wishes you well and mazeltov [congratulations], and that is it.

"We Mustn't Talk about Things like That": Sexual Ignorance

Some of the immigrant youth raised in families governed by these traditional practices developed a detached attitude about their own sexuality; many speak of their spouses, intimate companions of thirty and forty years, with a tone of estrangement.

SOL MEYROWITZ: *In those days it wasn't like today. The attitude between men and women is not the same. We were old-fashioned and I liked it that way. I walked into my French class and saw her and fell in love immediately. I took one look at her. Instantly. She was the first girl I ever took out. It took me four years before I kissed her at all. I bought her a complete set of Charles Dickens, and she was so thankful that she gave me a kiss on the cheek. I remember once I picked her up at the train and said to myself beforehand, "This time I will kiss her," and when she got off the train I just couldn't. The honeymoon was uneventful.*

I never in my life saw my wife nude. Never saw her undress in my entire life. I don't know where she undressed. I never saw her nude for thirty-five years. And she wouldn't let me walk around with my shorts on. She told me to get dressed. And as soon as we were able to, we always had separate rooms. Our married life was not too sexy at all. In fact, in thirty-five years in some times an entire month would pass without my even coming near her.

When I married her, I married her in the purest way a man could ever marry a woman. I never pictured her as a bed partner, but I always pictured her as someone who would entertain my political friends. To me she was my friend. Absolutely.

She said to me, and I thought that it was a great little piece of wisdom, "Sexual relations is an overrated pastime." I agreed with that. My wife never had an orgasm, not that I would know. No, no, who knew of those things? I would never know the difference. She performed her duties, they were duties. She performed her duties. That's all.

MAX HIRSCH: When I decided that I wanted to marry my wife, she had gone away on a vacation in the mountains with one of her friends. I decided to join them. I had one room, and she and her friend had another room. I took it for granted that I wasn't married to her yet, and that's it. I don't really remember proposing to her, but we decided to get married, and I found a justice of the peace willing to perform the ceremony. I bought her a corsage, and we got married over a bar and grill.

So we got back to the hotel that night, my wife said to me, "You know I am sharing a room down the end of the hall. It will be very embarrassing for me to leave that room and go to sleep in your room even though we are married." I said, "So stay there. I am not going to make a big fuss about love." So she stayed with her friends as usual, and the following day her friend went off and we went off by ourselves. It didn't bother me that on my wedding night I slept alone. You have to be sensitive about these things; she said she would be embarrassed to leave that room and go to the room with me just because we are married. I did not want to embarrass her so I let her have her way, that's all.

The last three days of the vacation we took a room by ourselves, but she was a very difficult woman. She said, "Please don't touch me until we get back to the city." I looked at her: "Are you crazy? What kind of nonsense is this?" She said, "I just prefer that we not go to bed until we get back to the city." She was a pretty shrewd lady. She knew that

153

*she was a virgin and she was worried about discomfort. She told me
that she was not feeling too well and that she had to go and see a doctor.*

*She went to a gynecologist—I found out about it later—she went to
the gynecologist and told him that she was married and a virgin and
she wanted to have as little discomfort as possible so she asked him to
dilate her with an instrument to some extent, which he did. Eventually
entrance was made, and there came a time when she really enjoyed
sex, I guess.*

Etta Levine acknowledged the depths of her youthful ignorance:
"Once at a party a boy came over to me and held my hand and I
got hysterical. I thought I would get pregnant because he held my
hand. That was what I was taught at home," and then went on
tacitly to admit that that ignorance eventually led to both fear and
detachment:

*My husband was a very handsome man. He was a very, very good-
looking man. When I first met him, I was scared to death of him. I
didn't know what he expected, what he would do, what he wanted.
He was so much more sophisticated than I, he was so much older than
I. I was eight, nine years younger. Then when he asked me to marry
him, I was too scared to marry him. I was scared. Kids in my day, girls,
were just scared all the time. We never knew what we were in for.*

*After I was engaged, I necked with him. Of course, no one did that
before, no one did that. Maybe he hugged me, kissed me—nothing,
nothing, nothing, I am serious, nothing. He lived with his married
brother who liked me very much. But I never went to their house. No
I wouldn't—never in a million years. He knew we were going to get
married, then so what? So you wait this long, you wait a little longer,
that's my feeling.*

*I don't even know where we spent our wedding night—I swear to
you I don't remember. Where we went from there, I don't know, I
don't really know. It's a blank. Probably I was so scared, you know.
We took a train and we came back by boat. It takes a long time to stop
being shy. Our honeymoon was pretty good, it was pretty good. I had
a very good time, except my husband thought I was spending too much
money.*

*My husband practiced birth control and I didn't know anything
about that, thank God. Who would want to be bothered with what*

those women have to wear, swallow, and do things? I had no problems that way. We never knew any different; that was how it was. The first baby, that happened; not an accident, just happened. At that time he wasn't practicing birth control. He practiced after the baby was born. I didn't tell him. He just did it on his own, he knew.

Many native-born American contemporaries of these immigrants sounded precisely the same way when they talked about intimate matters. In 1924, Katherine Bement Davis, who was the general secretary of the Bureau of Social Hygiene (an organization funded by John D. Rockefeller and dedicated to the fight against venereal disease), sent out a questionnaire to several thousand American women, inquiring about various aspects of their sex lives. These women were, as the report put it, "of good standing in the community, with no known physical, mental or moral handicap, of sufficient intelligence and education to understand and answer in writing a rather exhaustive set of questions."[6]

Most of the women queried had been born before the turn of the century. Only 71 of the roughly 1,200 married women who replied had experienced intercourse before they married, and 926 of the 1,000 single women were still virgins. The vast majority of the women polled expressed repugnance about touching members of the opposite sex ("Once a boy kissed me and I nearly brained him; always made a point of being extremely unsentimental"), and slightly more than half of those who were married found "marital relations" either neutral or distasteful.[7] These "leaders of the community"—many of them graduates of the nation's most prestigious women's colleges—apparently had much in common with the Meyrowitzes, Hirsches, and Levines, a commonality that might have surprised them all.

Katherine Davis, however, would not have been surprised. Along with many other students of sexual behavior, she believed that much of the sexual prudery of her day derived from the kind of sexual ignorance that is manifest, for example, in Etta Levine's account. Davis knew that in her own day many young people (and many older ones as well) were woefully uninformed even about basic sexual physiology—a topic that the educational systems of the country resolutely ignored. She also knew—and decried the fact—that American parents were generally unwilling to discuss sex with their children. In the

155

course of our interviews, we discovered that what was true for native-born American parents in the early decades of this century was true for Jewish immigrant parents as well. "When my breasts began to develop," Esther Ginsburg recalls, "I was scared stiff. I thought I was sick. I had no idea where they came from." Rose Janofsky and Rebecca Green were equally ill informed.

ROSE JANOFSKY: *I reached puberty when I was nine. My mother never said a word. No one did. I was scared to death, 'cause I was afraid I was bleeding to death. I was riding my bike, and I had taken a tumble about fifteen minutes before, and all of a sudden I thought I was dying and I rushed into the house. My mother was there and I told her, and she started to cry. My mother started to cry, and then I was certain that something dreadful, dreadful had occurred.*

And I remember her calling up one of my aunts—Lucille, who was quite young and had just gotten married—and she came rushing over and she slapped my face—so the blood stays in your face even though you're bleeding. Aunt Lucille did, yes. And then my mother told me what to do. She told me to wear a pad or something or other, you know, and that this wouldn't last long. And I really thought that this would last for about a week and would never happen again.

I was frightened the second time it happened. I told my mother and she said, "That's nothing. It is going to happen a lot of times." I think it was something you don't talk about. I never talked to my father about it. My mother said, "Don't tell your father. Don't talk about things like that."

I think at that time the people around me didn't talk about things like that. It was something that was secret, very secret. My mother was in certain kinds of ways very secret, and I guess that she was simply embarrassed. In those days you didn't even say "pregnant"; you said "in a family way." As a matter of fact, I remember that when my Aunt Lucille got pregnant, my mother asked her not to come to the house because she didn't want my brothers to see her. My mother, who had had her own children, didn't want her sister-in-law to come to the house and have her sons see her! I guess she was just that way.

REBECCA GREEN: *I knew nothing. I was a naïve thing. It was just another world. It was not even conceivable that I could go to my parents* and ask them about it, no. I picked up enough to know that it would be inappropriate. It would be unthinkable. One gets messages, one learns from parents. A kid asks you something and the kind of response you give—"I'll tell you later. We will talk about it later"—and later never comes. And this happens again and again and you know that "later" doesn't mean "in time"; it means "forget."

I remember once, I must have been about sixteen, I come into my house, it must have been around eleven P.M.—I wouldn't dare stay out much later. As I went up the stairs, the bannister allowed me to see into my mother's and father's room. I saw the door was open and I could see that my father was in my mother's bed. I could see that. The lights were out, you know. So I said, "Is anything the matter, Ma?" "No." "Then, why is Poppa in your bed?" Neither one of them moved. They must have been absolutely flipped, and they didn't answer at all, and I just went to my room.

Since neither parents nor schools would address the topic of sex, young people—whether immigrant or native born—turned to two other sources of information: people, often kids, in the neighborhood, and books. Rose Janofsky, for example, finally learned from some of her friends what it was her parents were doing in bed.

It was my second year in high school. We had a pattern which I am sure most girls use. You are invited to the girl's house to do homework. Then comes the time the homework is out of the way, and it is time to go home, and you begin to walk each other back and forth, and then you tell stories to each other. About boyfriends, girlfriends, family fights, everything—and this is where you communicate with each other. And this girl—I remember her name and face, it is clear to me now, she is a beautiful sharp girl, Jenny Brown—she told me.

I remember this because I remember the effect—shock, shock, unbelievable—because she was telling me about intercourse, which I obviously knew nothing about. It took me many weeks to reconcile the fact that it can't be so terrible because my mother and father were doing it, my teachers were doing it, because the whole world was doing it, but it took a long time.

157

Max Weiner, who was born and raised in Chicago, learned some of what he needed to know, when he was eleven or twelve, from an Italian security guard who patrolled a burned-out factory near his parents' apartment, but some he had learned earlier, in a time-honored anatomy lesson:

The kids next door we were very friendly with, they were Jewish, they had three kids. Now the boy was about my age, and the girl was a year older than he was, and the younger one was in there, too. Now when no one was home, we would play doctor. We would also examine each other carefully. We were younger than thirteen; the girl had not reached puberty yet. We were just examining and we were more interested in looking at her behind than looking at her front. It was a funny business. I think that what ended that business is that her mother snuck in on me and caught us without any pants on—all of us. She was the only girl but we examined her carefully. How does this thing look?

You learned everything in that area not from the school books—on the street.

And Sam Reiss, who emigrated from Poland to Providence, Rhode Island, when he was ten years old, also acquired at least some of his sexual education in yet another time-honored fashion:

There were a lot of Jews there [in Providence], and some of us boys had a club. The boys that I hung around with at that time, we were all easily aroused, we decided to go to a brothel. What actually happened was we had one of these houses—one of my cousins was the son of the black sheep of my mother's family—he was a gambler, and he ran around with the crowd that gambled and he went to whorehouses and things like that. And he dared us to go to the brothel with him. So, of course, we couldn't say no.

Anyhow, we went to this place. You parked down a couple of blocks away and you walked around the corner; you didn't want to be seen. We walked in, and the madam, who was the wife of the black-sheep son of a doctor in town, greeted us at the door. They had disowned him; his father was a pillar of the community—chairman of the Hebrew school.

Our hearts were in our mouths and we walked in and tried very,

very hard to look nonchalant. We were led into a parlor—I think there were maybe six davenports there—and we sat down. And a few minutes later, two girls came in, and they would come over and sit on your lap. "Come on, do you want a drink?" The whole idea is to get body contact. They sit on your lap, dance, drink if you wanted a drink— whiskey if you wanted whiskey—it didn't matter. And then after a while you saw somebody you liked, like on a social basis. They were wearing evening gowns that showed as much as possible without being too obvious, showing off their figures in low-cut gowns. Local girls of course, nicely coiffed, and they were attractive looking.

I remember I saw one that looked nice, she looked like a high school girl. And we went upstairs, and I got undressed, and she inspected my instrument to make sure there was no discharge—that is standard procedure. She took me to a wash basin and washed everything off, and then she took off everything except her rolled-up stockings. You see what they did with these evening gowns: with one or two buttons you could take everything off. And that was it. They were ready for action except for the rolled-up stockings. But she kept the rolled-up stockings on and lay on the bed and—uh—and I didn't want her to think I was unexperienced, and I got on and almost immediately came to a climax. And she was very unhappy about that and wanted to know if I wanted a second round. So we sat there and talked about that. She was probably twenty-two or twenty-four, maybe twenty-five. She was a very pleasant person, and that was my first experience.

And would you like to know where I got the three dollars from? I stole it from the club! I was the treasurer!

Many of the people we interviewed can also recall books about sex they read when they were young; and, indeed, there were many such books on the market, at very low prices, in the first decades of this century. They bore such titles as *Clean and Strong* (1909), *Instead of Wild Oats* (1912), *The Story of Life for Children* (1914), and *What to Tell Your Boy* (1918). The authors of these books were principally worried (as John D. Rockefeller and Katherine Bement Davis had been) about the growing incidence of venereal disease and had come to the conclusion that syphilis and gonorrhea could be squelched only if adolescents understood how their own bodies functioned (this, indeed, was one of the educational goals that Rockefeller hoped the Bureau of Social Hygiene would achieve).

These books usually favored the "birds and bees" approach to sex education: first the child was taught how plants, birds, and bunny rabbits "do it"; then the parts of the human reproductive system were carefully described and named; and then the "wondrous" changes of adolescence were described. Sexual intercourse was always alluded to, but never described. Masturbation was universally condemned—as wasting valuable bodily fluids and leading to impure thoughts; and virginity universally extolled (for both sexes). Healthy babies were always born to dutifully married couples who understood that sex—only in moderation and only for the purposes of reproduction—was really part of God's plan for the universe:

> Then, when a man and woman have chosen each other because they can trust and honor and love and believe in one another, they promise to take care of each other and help each other as long as they both live. We call that "wedding" or "marrying" because they are joined together both in words by the minister of God, and, later in that physical union which is to bring forth others of their kind just as all creatures of lower orders are—only without marrying. . . . Where men and women join together and bring children into the world without the sanction of the wedding ceremony, they belong to the lower orders of life even though they are in the form of men and women, and they are not loved and respected by other men and women.
>
> . . . And now we will go back and "remember" a few things. You remember about the ovary in the flower body and that I told you there were also *ovaries*—egg-nests—in the female fish, the female frog, the bird, the rabbit, and all living things, while in the male of all species were the fertilizing sacs. And you remember that when we came to Bunny Cottontail we found a new order of things—the egg lying inside the mother's body in its nest or *womb* until the tiny creature was fully and perfectly formed before it came out into the world.
>
> Now we find that the little baby brother is formed in exactly the same way as baby rabbit.[8]

Given such inadequate guides to their own bodies and their own feelings, it seems small wonder that so many of the people we interviewed—and, apparently, so many members of the generations who came to maturity in the early decades of this century—adopt a tone both of detachment and of estrangement when they talk about sex, essentially agreeing with Mrs. Meyrowitz's judgment that sexual relations are "an overrated pastime." Rebecca Green recalls the connection between sexual ignorance and marital estrangement:

The women were taught that sex was a no-no. Ladies don't even cross their legs, ladies don't do a lot of things that men do. With the girls, everything was hidden down there, and it is hidden, always hidden, and it always remains in the dark. So you never talk about that. The point is that it ruins your whole concept. The gentle and loving side is now shifted under the table. The things are so deeply ingrained that they don't realize that what they are responding to is something in their past, deeply ingrained.

I don't think members of my generation allowed themselves passion. The women were not expected to, so that when they want to be sexual they first had to shed all the things they learned. The so-called honeymoon period is a disaster for most couples. The woman is dying of anxiety, what is expected of her, and he doesn't know what he has got to do, how to get along. They don't know where to go. Honestly. They don't know the mechanics.

My father talked to my husband, but what could he say to him, in the way of enlightening him? He [her father] couldn't tell him [her husband]. My husband didn't know. He didn't ask my father; he would rather spare the embarrassment. I didn't know what to ask my mother. The first night, oh! It was certainly not anything you would write up, you know.

For many it is a dismal failure. We are talking about coming to love and affection. If that works, then you have something; otherwise, it is a nothing. And this is the sadness, and this is why many marriages don't work. They knew nothing, the members of my generation. And it takes a long time to get over the pain, the shock, the embarrassment.

161

"I Was . . . No, I Wasn't": Changing Sexual Mores

While many members of the immigrant generation were sexually
naïve, not all were. The times were changing, and some youths—devo-
tees of the movies and the pulp magazines—were keeping abreast of
the changes. The era of the flapper had begun. By the 1920s, many
Jewish-American girls had stopped dressing modestly: sleeves got
shorter; necklines lower; hems higher. Some girls whose mothers had
never even held hands with a man began to go out on dates and allow
kisses. Some girls were willing to allow considerably more than that.

In the 1920s and 1930s, many immigrant young people took their
vacations at what would now be called "singles' resorts" in the mountains or by the shore: "There were men's bungalows and women's bungalows," Hannah Toperoff reports. "Two of my cousins [female] were
so anxious to get married that it was unbelievable to live with. On
occasion we would find men in one of the beds. Anything that wore
pants was acceptable." A few women, like Janet Sommers, now have a
bit of difficulty recalling their own "deviant" behavior ("When I got
married I was a virgin," she averred when asked. "No! Wait a minute—I wasn't. I really wasn't"); but others have no difficulty at all.

ROSE JANOFSKY: *I slept with Jack before I was married. I had friends
who slept with boys well before they were married. Some of them
married the guys they slept with; some of them didn't. It was not that
unique. We tend to think of it that in our day nobody ever did things,
but it is not true. I went off on a weekend with Jack before we were
married, and he wasn't the first one either. I had gone off on a weekend
with another boy before I was married; it was not the invention they
think it is.*

*I had one serious boyfriend and had met him through a friend at a
concert where I had gone to hear Toscanini play Beethoven's First and
Ninth symphonies. After the concert, I went for coffee and met a
young man who had just returned from attending medical school in
Switzerland, I was introduced to him and really fell for him, bang. I
met him and had an affair, a really close relationship for about a year.
He did not want to get married. He had a long career ahead of him and
was about to go into the service. We had an ongoing romance until*

162

MOTHERS!

Can you afford to have a large family?
Do you want any more children?
If not, why do you have them?

DO NOT KILL, DO NOT TAKE LIFE, BUT PREVENT

Safe, Harmless Information can be obtained of trained

Nurses at

46 AMBOY STREET
NEAR PITKIN AVE. — BROOKLYN.

Tell Your Friends and Neighbors.   All Mothers Welcome
A registration fee of 10 cents entitles any mother to this information.

מוטערס!

זייט איהר פערמעגליך צו האבען א גרויסע פאמיליע?
ווילט איהר האבען נאך קינדער?
אויב ניט, וואָרום האט איהר זיי?

מערדערט ניט, נעהמט ניט קיין לעבען, נור פערהיט זיך.

זיכערע, אונשעדליכע אויסקינפטט קענט איהר בעקומען פון ערפארענע נוירסעס אין

46 אמבאַי סטרים ניער פיטקין עוועניו׳ ברוקלין

מאכם דאס בעקאנט צו אייערע פריינד און שכנות.   ידער מוטער איז וויהלקאמען

פיר 10 סענט איינשרייב־געלד זיינט איהר בערעכטיגט צו ריעזע אינפאָרמייששאָן.

MADRI!

Potete permettervi il lusso d'avere altri bambini?
Ne volete ancora?
Se non ne volete piu', perche' continuate a metterli al mondo?

NON UCCIDETE MA PREVENITE!

Informazioni sicure ed innocue saranno fornite da infermiere autorizzate a

46 AMBOY STREET   Near Pitkin Ave. Brooklyn

a cominciare dal 12 Ottobre. Avvertite le vostre amiche e vicine.
Tutte le madri sono ben accette. La tassa d'iscrizione di 10 cents da diritto
a qualunque madre di ricevere consigli ed informazioni gratis.

"I went to Margaret Sanger's assistant.
The girls at work took me there. . . .
She [the physician at the clinic] told me all the things
I should know, and she fitted me for a diaphragm."
Handbill advertising Sanger's clinic in Brooklyn, 1916.

the middle of 1936 when he suddenly decided that that was it and hurt me very much. I was twenty-one when I went off with him for a weekend for the first time. I was no innocent babe; I knew exactly what was happening. We went off and enjoyed a very great relationship. It ended and that was it. I was sorry—but maybe after a while I decided that I was not so sorry.

At least two out of all of the women we interviewed regarded themselves not just as free with their affections in their youth but as completely profligate.

SADIE REHSTOCK: *I always had a boyfriend. Don't ask me about the first time I had intercourse, I don't even remember. I was available, it was part of my life. A newspaper kid, maybe—he was the most attractive kid around. Then I met another. I was about thirteen, fourteen. We met in somebody's parlor probably, certainly not in my house.*

My grandfather didn't permit me out of the house, and so I would climb out of the window. I would put all of the dressers against the door so that he could not get in, and I would be gone. Don't ask me how I got back into the house, that I don't remember.

Sadie Rehstock's role model was, as she says, her own older sister:

My older sister went out a great deal. There was always men. There were always men around the house, she was always being called. She was always dressed up. She always went out. It had an aura around it. And she was in with the action. She went to the beach. It was a fancy beach to go to. She took a bathhouse, paid for a bathhouse. And they had a group of friends that were very jazzy, very much with it, all wealthy, all young men who were making it, wherever they were making it. And so they were the élite, the yuppies. She was a swinger, very active sexually, and very attractive.

When Sadie finally married she settled down into what would now be called a conventional relationship; yet sixty years after the fact she is still trying to make sense out of the fifteen years (roughly 1915 to 1930) during which she lived flagrantly on the edge of convention, or even beyond it:

For six years I was always active sexually, but I was never promiscuous in a way of each night I had another guy. Each night I was going out. I had a boyfriend, it lasted for six months. It lasted for two years. It lasted for eight months. It had a depth to it, it had a meaning to it, it had a caring to it. And a love to it. And that I think is absolutely true. And in two instances, I had every intention of marrying them. In both instances, they paid a good deal of attention to me. Real personal attention. I had a need for love that was so great, so intense, that other things didn't seem to matter. And I found myself pregnant again. Now, in all honesty, I knew that both the first time and the second time my boyfriends used contraceptives but once they didn't and we got caught. My friend, my boyfriend had a friend who was a doctor—actually, he had just graduated medical school—and he arranged for me to have an abortion.

I left each one of them, I left each one of them. I outgrew them. I plainly outgrew them. I realized that this was not a life style that I wanted. A young man who I met, who lived with a sister and brother-in-law and were very kind to him, they gave him a bed to sleep on in the living room. They were glad for me to come and visit so we could mind the two kids. And they thought I was a nice child. To get married and go into that same setting, I didn't want it. I knew that there were other horizons. Certainly I had been exposed to them just reading novels.

I also had an affair with my boss. He was a great guy; he was a lot of fun; he would do everything; he was curious about everything. He would go dancing at twelve o'clock at night at the finest hotels. We knew we were seen; we had to be seen. He was well known in town. We were not playing publicly around, but we did send up a flag. We didn't run into people often. On occasion we did run into friends who were also playing around at twelve o'clock at night. And the other people would mind their own business, and so did we. I mean, really, who goes out at twelve o'clock at night and has young children? You do it maybe as an occasion on a Saturday night. And I am sure at some point it was a gamble that we were taking. And I loved him enormously. We did this for seven years.

Sadie Rehstock is not alone in her effort to make sense out of her behavior; other people have tried both to describe the changes of the

165

flapper era and to explain them. Neither Sadie Rehstock nor Janet Sommers nor Rose Janofsky was alone in being willing to break the mold of sexual tradition; other American young women, both native-born and immigrant, were doing the same thing. In 1938, two pioneer sexologists, Dorothy Dunbar Bromley and Florence Haxton Britten, published a study of thirteen hundred American college students, both male and female, the vast majority non-Jewish.[9] They found that half of the men and one quarter of the women had already had premarital intercourse, and that 64 percent of the women who were still "continent" were prepared to lose their virginity in a love relationship that might lead to marriage. Katherine Bement Davis's study, conducted a dozen years earlier, had revealed that at that time only 7 percent of the married women sampled had had premarital sex, and only 19 percent of the unmarried women approved of it. The times were indeed changing.

The authors of the famous Kinsey report on the sex lives of American women subsequently reconfirmed those changes in 1953. The flappers, whether Christian or Jewish, had been doing something more than just bobbing their hair:

> Among the females in the sample [roughly 6,000 white women, from all major religious, social and geographic groups] who were born before 1900, less than half as many had had premarital coitus as among the females born in any subsequent generation. . . . This increase in the incidence of pre-marital coitus, and the similar increase in the incidence of premarital petting, constitute the greatest changes which we have found between the patterns of sexual behavior in the older and younger generations of American females. . . .
>
> Practically all of this increase had occurred in the generation that was born in the first decade of the present century and, therefore, in the generation that had had most of its pre-marital experience in the late teens and in the 1920's following the first World War. The later generations appear to have accepted the new pattern and maintained or extended it.[10]

Dozens of explanations have been offered for the change in sexual mores that began in the second decade of this century. No doubt many,

166

or perhaps all, are valid, since such a complex, profound, and deeply rooted change must have had more than one cause. In the course of our interviews we uncovered supporting evidence for several of these hypotheses. In the 1920s, for example, many people placed part of the blame—if *blame* is the right word—on the First World War. So many young women were working alongside men in factories and offices, so many others were being allowed to meet young men unchaperoned in soldiers' canteens, so many young men were going off to foreign countries (where sexual standards were looser) so many needed comfort and consolation after experiencing the senseless devastation of the war that, contemporaries argued, sexual behavior was bound to change. Aaron Katz would certainly agree with this notion: he was drafted into the American Expeditionary Force in 1917; and, as he told us, he remained in France for about a year after peace was declared, enrolled in a university, and had an affair with another Jewish student (in 1985 he could still locate her photo in his desk)—something he never would have considered doing at home.

Urbanization, some would argue, was also partly responsible for changing patterns of adolescent behavior. In times past, it was said, when most people lived in small towns—whether Galician shtetls or American villages—adults had had little difficulty keeping adolescent boys and girls strictly segregated. In crowded twentieth-century cities, however, parents were too overworked to act as chaperones; immigrant parents, in particular, were too distracted by poverty and by cultural malaise to pay much attention to their children; schools were coeducational (as were workplaces); and young people (both male and female) were sometimes earning salaries that made them relatively independent of their parents. All of this meant that young people had the freedom to follow the dictates of their hormones, a freedom few mothers and fathers had ever dreamed possible, or could even understand. Certainly, as we noticed in the course of these interviews, the young people who were profligate in their youth had some characteristics in common: all were the victims, to some extent, of parental indifference; all were angry, to the point of fury, with one or both of their parents; they all craved attention and affection; and the women made almost no effort to protect themselves from pregnancy, to acknowledge, by acting responsibly, that they were aware of what they were doing. Hannah Toperoff's story illustrates this.

My parents put a deposit down on a business school, but they never paid any more than that. They didn't pay my tuition; they only paid for me for three months. I didn't pay it. I got to know the principal. We went out together.

Well, he was my first sex experience, and I look back and I really don't understand myself, in the situation, in his office. Well, it was done this way. I had to go see him, and I said, "My parents can't afford to pay and they don't have any money." And he said, "Well, we can't keep you on without paying." And then he said, "Why don't we talk about it over a cup of coffee?" I said, "All right." And we had a cup of coffee, and he said, "You know, I can make things easier for you"—or some such thing. I was naïve—too naïve, I suppose.

Well, he said that there was a party some place or other: would I go to it? And I said, "Yes." So we went to it. There wasn't any party. It was—you know. I have to say this, I did not give him any fight. I was not—I was acquiescent. I suppose if someone were to say, "Did he rape you?" I would have to say, "No." Psychologically rape, yes—but, you know, you don't fight. You suddenly realize that this is taking place, that this is what he meant all along.

I do know that from that point I hated my mother. Maybe I didn't like her for a lot of things, but never did she say to me, "Haven't they asked you for more money?"—which is my mother's way of doing things, all the time. I mean, she didn't say to me, "Why are they doing this? Why aren't they asking you for more money? How are you going there without our paying?" If she had paid the tuition . . . you know, with my mother, if you don't tell her something, it doesn't exist. Never, never did she want to know. When you don't want to know anything, you don't know it.

I guess he must have used a condom. I certainly didn't use anything. I didn't know anything about it. He must have because nothing happened. I was fortunate. He was very affectionate, very. Well, he had his arm around me while we were in the car; he had kissed me on the cheek after we had finished a cup of coffee. It was very fast or else I blocked it out. I took off my dress. He may have helped me; he did not undress me. I had my shoes on. I remember my shoes, I never took my shoes off—that I remember to this day. Then he drove me home. I think he assumed that I had had sexual relations before. I think he thought I knew what was going to happen because he said something

like, *"Make yourself comfortable." Is that the way you talk to somebody who doesn't know what you are talking about?*

*I slept with him three or four times. I always had my shoes on, al-
ways, never had any sex him while my shoes were off. Even when I
removed my stockings, I would put my shoes back on, I don't know
why. I am very partial to shoes, let me tell you. And I have always
loved shoes.*

*After I graduated from that business school, I was not a very nice
girl for a while. After the experience I had, I was available. I worked
in a department store. My parents moved someplace and I stayed with
my grandparents. During this time I used to go to a bar with one of
the people that I work with and I started having sex with a man there.
Whether he was part owner or not I don't know, but I suspect that he
was because the facilities that we used was back of the bar. There was
a very nice room at the back of the bar. I worked fairly late. My hours
were something like eight to seven, ten dollars a day. I would always
tell my grandmother that I was going to be late, and she would ask me,
"When are you coming in? Is someone bringing you home?" She was
a very old-fashioned lady, not like my mother.*

Although Hannah Toperoff has no recollection of using any form
of birth control herself ("I never used anything; I felt very unthinking
about consequences really"), she was somewhat unusual in that regard
since birth control devices (the diaphragm for women, the condom for
men) were relatively easy to obtain in her day. Indeed, some authorities
believed (both then and now) that it was precisely the easy availability
of birth control (including abortion) that liberated young people from
traditional sexual strictures. In the United States it was illegal to advertise birth control devices in interstate publications and also to ship them
through the mail (a result of the famous Comstock Law, passed by
Congress in 1873; Anthony Comstock was postmaster general at the
time). Manufacturing, however, was perfectly permissible and so was
selling in many states, just as long as the device was accompanied by a
printed message indicating that it was intended for use in the control
of diseases. Condoms were dispensed by pharmacists, and diaphragms
could be obtained from many physicians—for female complaints; indeed, a decision of the Second Circuit Court of Appeals in 1936 made
the dispensing of diaphragms by physicians completely legal. In New

169

York City, in the 1920s and 1930s, the clinics operated by Margaret Sanger allowed a woman, even if unmarried, to obtain a diaphragm without great expense. Many of the women we interviewed recall visiting one of those clinics (some before, some after marriage); no one—either male or female—could recall any difficulty in obtaining a birth control device when one was wanted.

ROSE JANOFSKY: *I went to Margaret Sanger's assistant. The girls at work took me there. Actually, they took me there before I was married. She [a physician] told me all about it because I didn't know. Oh no! Who was supposed to know? Not my parents, don't be ridiculous.*

When I was going to be married, my friends said, "Now you have to have two appointments. First, you have to go and find out all about it." She [the physician at the clinic] told me all the things I should know, and she fitted me for a diaphragm.

Neither could anyone who wanted one recall difficulty in locating an abortionist. The practice of abortion was illegal in all the states in the early decades of this century, and was not condoned by Jewish law either—but neither form of community disapproval deterred some of our parents. Every doctor who "didn't" knew a doctor who "did," and many a neighbor knew somebody who knew somebody who "would." In the days before antibiotics, abortions were considerably riskier than they are today, but many a young woman (and older ones, too) considered the risks preferable to an unwanted pregnancy. The diaphragm with which Rose Janofsky was fitted just before her marriage apparently did not work; she knew precisely what she wanted to do: "I certainly got pregnant and I was very much against it. I went to have an abortion." Lillian Winograd's mother had an abortion at the age of forty, just before she died of the flu: "In those days to have a child at forty was a *shonda* [embarrassment]. I mean, you admit that at forty you had sex, your children would know. When you have a seventeen-year-old daughter, you just don't have a baby. There were a lot of abortions going on."

Locating an abortionist was readily done: everyone we spoke with who had an abortion had it performed in a doctor's office. Irving Farber, for example, who first ran afoul of sexual tradition when he was sixteen and holding hands with his landlady's daughter, continued

170

to be a sexual gambler long after he was out of the range of his father's and grandfather's ire; he eventually had to seek three separate abortions for three separate girlfriends:

I paid for three abortions. It cost very little. A doctor did it, he saved me a lot of trouble. I found out about him through a head nurse in a hospital; her husband was in the dress business with me. I didn't use condoms all the time.

The first time I went to this doctor, I went into a room. It was very quiet. I was sitting in the living room. Not a sound did I hear—not a sound. I was dying. I said, "Please God, if this guy is a butcher, and if she is dead, what will I do with her?" I always thought that I would take her, put her in a car, and dump her some place. Nobody would ever know it, nobody would ever know. That is the thought that ran through my mind. Maybe they would. Maybe they wouldn't. She [the fetus] came out, a little bambino; it was a girl. He [the doctor] said, "Now take her [the girlfriend] over to that bar over there and buy her a good whiskey, a good hooker of whiskey." We sat around and chatted, and I took her home.

Sadie Rehstock, who had three abortions before she was married, remarked in describing them that "most of my friends were like me. Their great concern was not pregnancy, but that somebody would blabber about their sexuality. They were not virgins when they got married, even though that was the family standard, posted on the wall." Pregnancy, in Sadie's day, could easily be prevented or remedied.

When asked how they first learned about birth control, many of the people we interviewed answered, "From my friends"; not a single one reported learning anything on the subject from a parent. A few, however, recalled reading a book: Jenny Grossman took books out of the library and read them with her fiancé; Charlie Moses recalls buying several when he was in his twenties. Books that discussed birth control were not like the ones, mentioned earlier, that were intended to keep young boys and girls continent. There were no "Bunny Cottontails" in their pages, and no discussion of the horrors of "self-pollution"; their authors believed that sex is meant to be enjoyed—without procreation. Some even argued that it is meant to be enjoyed by people who

171

are not married to each other. In these liberated books, "marrying" was replaced by "loving"; "God's plan" gave way to "scientific prevention"; and two new words appeared in print—*orgasm* and *erection*. In the early decades of this century, many people believed (probably with good reason) that the very existence of these books was itself causing an increase in the frequency of the real phenomena.

The first of the liberated books were the monumental scholarly tomes of Richard von Krafft-Ebing (*Psychopathia Sexualis*, 1886) and Havelock Ellis (*Studies in the Psychology of Sex*, 1896–1910), which attempted to describe, almost taxonomically, all possible varieties of human sexual experience. Most of our parents, however, were not reading Ellis or Krafft-Ebing; popular tracts were cheaper and easier to locate. Many of these were written by people who advocated a new approach to sex (sometimes called in its day "free love"), an approach that depends upon birth control. Marie Stopes may have been the first such popularizer; her justly famous *Wise Parenthood* was published in England and then blackmarketed to the United States in 1910. Stopes was followed by Ellen Keys's *Love and Marriage* (1911)—which argued that premarital sex was the best possible foundation for a happy marriage; and by Edward Carpenter's *Love's Coming of Age* (also 1911)—which argued that humans had evolved beyond the need for restrictive sexuality. In *The Renaissance of Motherhood* (1914), Ellen Keys maintained that parents ought to plan their fertility in the interests of good parenting; and in *Married Love* (1918), Marie Stopes argued that women deserved to enjoy the sexual act as much as men, and suggested various ways in which the female orgasm could be stimulated: 241,000 copies of *Married Love* had been printed by 1923. Close on the heels of Stopes came Margaret Sanger—dear to many of our mothers' hearts—with *Woman and the New Race* (1920), *Happiness in Marriage* (1926), and *What Every Girl and Boy Should Know* (1927), as well as scores of American and British physician-eugenicists, all of them convinced that sex education and birth control were the keys to ending the scourge of venereal disease and the decline of the "civilized" races.

Occasionally clinical, but more often romantic to a swoon (Freud's name was never mentioned, nor had his theories of infantile sexuality yet had any influence), all of these liberated books dispensed precisely the kinds of information that the "birds and bees" books avoided (particularly about intercourse), and at the same time argued—often passionately—that sexual activity (even premarital and extramarital) is natural, clean, and healthy—as long as it does not produce unwanted children:

> If I look at sex right out of my own soul, it seems like something which God didn't fail with, but succeeded with. Like something not polluted, but purified. Like something having everything, instead of only an occasional thing, to do with life. But the world shakes its head. The world is nasty. The world has eaten. But the world says it's best to starve. . . . Sex is like eating. Who would eat if he didn't have to. To say you enjoy a meal is carnal. To say that you derive some sense of ecstasy from paternal and maternal desires is a confession of depravity. Sex at the best is a sin. Sex at the best is like stepping down. That sex might be an ascent. That sex might be the only means of growth and expansion. You never suppose that! You only assume perdition. You are afraid to assume heaven.
>
> . . . So it goes. . . . The more you look at the mess we've got sex into the worse it seems. *Someone's got to peach.* Someone's got to tell the truth. *You can't give spirit its due until you give sex its due.* You can't accept one and cast aside one. They go together. They are inseparable.
>
> You parents. You professors. You prudes. This is addressed to you.[11]

The professors and the prudes may not have been listening, but some of our parents clearly were. But our parents, both Jews and Christians, both immigrant and native born, tend to forget that, on the long road to sexual liberation, some members of their own generation were the first revolutionaries: tentative revolutionaries perhaps, but revolutionaries nonetheless, destroying some of the barricades that had kept their parents and some of their contemporaries estranged from each other and detached from their own emotional needs. Janet Sommers now may have trouble acknowledging that she slept with her husband before they were married, but her mother would have remained a virgin until she became a bride. Jennie Grossman may have visited a *mikve* the evening before she was married, but she had also read birth control manuals and unlike her mother, who had six children, had taken their lesson not just to heart but to bed. Whatever may have caused the change in sexual mores that began in the second decade of this century, there can be little doubt that it occurred and that at least some of our parents participated in it, with delight sometimes, with ambivalence at others.

In some ways, the change was more significant for the daughters of Jewish immigrants than for their sons. The unwritten sexual code of the shtetl had always permitted more leeway to men than to women, just as long as the men "played around" with Christian girls, with *shiksas*. In America, young Jewish men (some older ones, too) continued to play around—but their partners, remarkably, were Jewish.

IRVING FARBER: *The first time I was, I guess, nineteen. There were a lot around, I had a lot of women. I was managing a store at the time. Married women used to come into the store. There were two women, Jewish women, who with their husbands had a coffee shop. I used to go up there and bang one of them practically every day—not in the coffee shop, in their home, a block away from the store—on my lunch hour. Every other day, one or the other. Their husbands were knocked out working in the store, they couldn't give them sex. They would go by with their baby carriages and you would make friends. I was a young guy full of life. I used to eat in the coffee shop, too. I am telling you it knocked me out.*

I had more girls come into the store and get laid than you have hair on your head. Where? In the back of the store, for Christ's sake. We had a big store. We had a basement with merchandise in it; it was clean; we put a cot down there. I had a girl, a girl come in, a Jewish girl, by the name of Lee. She came into the store, and I sold her four wooden chairs and a table and took them up to her parents' apartment. The most gorgeous thing you ever saw—she was beautiful, too, she really was. I introduced her to my friends, and they said get rid of her, she looked like a trollop. I used to take her in the basement and give her the business. I still think about her.

CHARLIE MOSES: *I had the usual pattern of older women being flattered by a younger man. I remember, when I was in medical school, I paid for a lunch in this woman's house. After a while when the child would go back to school, somehow or other I had the feeling that this was going to be an available woman, and it proved to be available and several times a week after lunch I would copulate with her. And that was that. She was married and she hated her husband. She and her husband were not getting along, and she was getting even with the S.O.B. by cheating. It didn't interfere with my studies. I was young, I had strength, and I screwed her and walked back to school as if nothing happened. That's it.*

It went on for a while, even after I graduated. I took her out once for lunch and I was scared stiff of my being observed. She used to come up to my home. I would tell my mother, "I am going to have company," and my mother understood and she would go out and do her shopping and this lady would come and we would have a morning session. Eventually she and my mother became very friendly. Her husband didn't find out. As a matter of fact, he and I went to an amusement park together, just the two guys. It went on a number of years. It was very convenient; it was damned nice. I had no responsibilities. She was a clean person. Anyway, she was Jewish.

Apparently, for some Jewish women, the process of assimilation meant more than just being liberated from poverty.

Sexual Myth and Sexual Reality

Many of our parents, both Christian and Jewish, like to paint their generation abstemiously, especially when comparing themselves to us and to our children: "Things were different in our day," they say. "Good girls just didn't. We knew how to control ourselves." In a sense they are right. Many more people followed traditional dictates in their day than in ours; in their day sex was not explicitly discussed at dinner parties or graphically displayed in every movie; young men and young women did not hop into bed with each other as quickly or as early as they do today, nor did they live with each other openly or frequently.

Yet two remarkable things emerged from our interviews. The first is the fact that some of our parents, particularly some of the women, were not as abstemious as we have thought and as they have liked to pretend. The second is that, in this regard, the Jews and the Christians of their generation were similar, or at least the middle-class Christians and the much poorer Jews were. Both started, around the turn of the century, from a traditional base that could equally well be described either as Talmudic or Victorian—and both began departing from that base during the second and third decades of the century.

Somehow, on matters of sex, Jewish youth managed to assimilate quickly to the patterns their Christian contemporaries were just beginning to establish. In the flapper generation, there were both Christians and Jews, both native-born young people and immigrants. With truly incredible speed—in the space of just a decade, or at most two—Eastern European Jews learned to behave precisely in the same fashion as their middle-class, native-born Christian contemporaries—affluent contemporaries, the children of people who might have lived by the dictates of the doctrine of separate spheres, students at the best colleges whom Bromley and Britten might have interviewed.

Can it be entirely a coincidence that the Jewish immigrant youth who learned to imitate the sexual practices of their more affluent contemporaries were also, at the same time, learning to fight their way out of poverty? No one, to our knowledge, has ever implicated sexual mores in the process of Jewish assimilation; and yet there they are, unquestionably embedded in many of the immigrant life stories we heard. Americanization, sexual liberation, and financial success seem to be linked by having happened at the same time to many of the people we interviewed. The nature of those linkages is by no means clear, but the coincidence suggests a hypothesis worth pursuing: the Jews may have won the prize of general affluence faster than other immigrant groups because they started from the same sexual starting gate as their largely Protestant, native-born competitors. Middle-class status, after all, has something to do with learning to control fertility, as well as learning to control profits.

6

"TRAPPED IN THE BOOK": CHILDBIRTH AND CHILD CARE

MOST OF THE immigrant Jewish youth became parents some time between 1920 and 1945—years when, for all Americans, initial prosperity turned to depression and then to war. Among the many social changes of those years was the rise of the child-rearing experts, people who—along with the health experts and the sex experts—were destined to have a profound effect upon this generation, and the next.

Earlier in the century, in the shtetls of Lithuania, the ghettos of Warsaw, or even the tenements of Chicago, a pregnant Jewish woman might, if she had a question or a problem, consult her mother or her sister, or perhaps a midwife, a rabbi, or a neighbor. By the second decade of the century, such a woman, if she were living in the United States, would be more likely to consult a "professional"—an outsider, someone who was neither Jewish nor a member of the community. The midwives, rabbis, and relatives had been replaced by specialists—physicians, nurses, psychologists, social workers, and home economists—all of them anxious to tell American parents how to raise American children properly.

The specialists were assisted by a small army of philanthropists, bureaucrats, and entrepreneurs—all allied, like the housing experts, under the banner of Progressive reform. In 1909, the *Ladies' Home Journal*, under its campaigning editor Edward J. Bok, created a Babies Registry so that mothers could receive the most up-to-date child-rearing advice through the mail. That same year, President Theodore Roosevelt (who happened to be a friend of Bok's) convened the White House Conference on the Care of Dependent Children (reconvened in 1919 and 1930). As publishing companies grasped the size of the potential market of new parents, hundreds of preaching physicians were soon clamoring for attention in print. (All of these doctor-experts are now lumped together, in our parent's memories, under the name of one of them who was actually a very late—1946—entrant in the field: Dr. Benjamin Spock.) The Children's Bureau of the U.S. Department of Labor was created in 1913; and within a few months, it, too, began to publish. Over a million copies of its booklets on prenatal and infant care were distributed between 1914 and 1921 (by 1981, the figure was up to sixty million); and by 1929, bureau officials estimated that half the mothers in the United States had been influenced by these booklets. Revised editions were circulated every several years, even during the depths of the Depression and the turmoil of the Second World War. *Parents' Magazine*, which first appeared in 1929, astounded its original publisher by selling 100,000 copies a month within a year after it hit the newsstands.

During the 1920s and 1930s, philanthropists also became involved in the child-rearing business. The Laura Spelman Rockefeller Memorial (created by John D. Rockefeller in 1918) and the Commonwealth Fund were the first of the major foundations to devote themselves in earnest to the welfare of children and mothers. Together, the memorial and the fund financed research institutes devoted to child psychology (at Columbia, Yale, and the universities of California at Berkeley, Minnesota, and Iowa), child guidance clinics (in St. Louis, Dallas, Los Angeles, Cleveland, and Philadelphia), demonstration nursery schools (in Albany and Buffalo, New York, for example), and a host of local and national conferences (such as the First National Conference on Child Development, co-sponsored by the National Research Council in 1935).

"I never discussed it [child rearing] with my parents. No, not with
my husband's parents either. They thought we were crazy."
Basic equipment required for raising a child the American way
in the early 1940s: bathinette, high chair, potty chair,
stroller, and tricycle.

Perhaps most significant of all, the Rockefeller Memorial was interested in parent education, in finding innovative ways to bring the message of the experts to the ears of the practitioners. In 1930, for example, the memorial purchased most of the stock in *Parents' Magazine* and gave it to a consortium of universities so that the profits from popularization might endow the research on which the advice was based. The memorial also poured thousands of dollars into the treasury of the Child Study Association, an organization devoted to parent education; it had been founded in 1888 by a group of reform-minded German Jews, intent upon a program of assimilation not only for themselves but also for their more recently arrived brethern. With its newly acquired largesse and an expanded sense of its mission, the Child Study Association began to publish a series of booklets that formed an entire curriculum devoted to "modern" child rearing. Through the auspices of organizations such as the Parent-Teacher Association and the American Association of University Women, that curriculum became the basis for short courses offered in communities all over the country.

The motives of these experts and reformers were easy to discern: they wanted to save the lives of mothers and babies—American mothers and babies. In the early part of this century, infant and maternal mortality rates in this country were high. In 1916, for example, roughly 16,000 women died in childbirth in the United States: twice as many (in proportion to the population) as had died of the same causes in the same year in Norway and Italy. The infant mortality rate in the United States was even more horrifying: 1 out of every 10 babies who was born alive died before the end of its first year (by way of comparison, the current infant mortality rate in the United States—still high by international standards—is 1 out of every 100). The reformers believed that modern medicine and modern chemistry could be used to reverse those trends.

Secondarily, the reformers also hoped to alter the child-rearing practices of the nation's most recent immigrants. Spanking, whipping, cuffing, punching, and slapping were the principle techniques by which Italians, Jews, and Slavs seemed to be disciplining their children. These practices were by no means limited to immigrant groups, as the reformers well knew; Progressives hoped to stamp out physical abuse, wherever it was directed against children, for they believed that children treated in this way grow up to be submissive and angry adults, not

180

the best type of citizen for a democratic republic. Since the people who regularly whipped their children were the same people who had the highest infant and maternal mortality rates—the poor, both immigrant and native—the obvious course of action was to establish a national standard for the care of mothers and infants and persuade parents across the land to adhere to it.

The reformers set to work with religious zeal. The gospel of "modern" prenatal and infant care was carried to schools, churches, newspapers, settlement houses, extension courses, outpatient clinics—and occasionally even in the health parades organized by various public health groups. Women were told—straight out and none too subtly—that if they wanted to save their own lives and the lives of their babies, and to raise strong, upstanding, successful Americans, they had to change their ways, to give up the traditions their parents and grandparents had carried across the seas.

Among the many young Jews who were no longer immersed in the culture of Yiddish, the message fell on willing ears. Possibly having lost their own mothers in childbirth, certainly having experienced the death of a brother or a sister or a cousin, unwilling to tolerate the same future for themselves, unwilling also to remain outside the mainstream of their adopted country—many young Jewish couples turned away from the traditions of Europe and opted for the experts of America. This change was difficult for immigrant parents to accept, as Rebecca Green testified:

I never discussed it [child rearing] with my parents. No, not with my husband's parents either. They thought we were crazy. The strain in our relationship, if it was that, was the difference between two ideologies. The way they behaved! Because I would boil materials, and I would cook all the vegetables in paper, some kind of paper that did not make the water seep through.* My father, one time, he said to me, "If you are boiling cereal, is it all right to pass through the kitchen when you are boiling the cereal?" It was that kind of thing.

And I know they thought I was crazy, but they let me be crazy. Besides, we never talked about things like that—never personal things,

---

* This was a heavily waxed paper recommended by nutritional experts; food was wrapped in it, prior to steaming, so as to preserve its vitamin content.

181

not with our parents. Maybe they talked about it when I wasn't there, but they never talked to me about it. And I never asked them.

As hard as it is for us (and sometimes for them) to believe, our reasonably well educated, sometimes unconventional, almost always argumentative parents did not argue with the experts. If *Good Housekeeping* suggested cod-liver oil once a day, many a child was forced to swallow the vile-smelling stuff. If some nutritionist discovered that baked potatoes were a rich source of B vitamins, our mothers raced home from the playground to pop them in the oven for our lunches and our dinners. If S. Josephine Baker (a prominent physician, director of the New York City Bureau of Child Hygiene, and regular contributor to the *Ladies' Home Journal*) advised that babies be fed every four hours by the clock, our fathers were dispatched to the hardware store to purchase a special clock for the nursery. Those of our parents who departed from "expert practice" were regarded by their contemporaries as hopelessly barbaric.

Conception, Pregnancy, and Birth

At the moment of conception, the youngest generation of Jews was already unusual; not only the first wholly American generation but also the first both to be "planned" and to be born in a hospital. One birth control technique or another was used by every man and woman we interviewed; even those who had remained sexually naïve before marriage did not hesitate long when a doctor or a friend pointed out the advantages of birth control. Each couple had their own reasons for wanting to control both the advent and the spacing of offspring. Many young women were happily and securely employed; "I really preferred going to business," is the way Janet Sommers put it. Many young men—especially in the 1930s—were struggling to make ends meet: "He was not working steady," was the reason Jennie Grossman gave for delaying her first pregnancy. Later, many men and women did not want to risk bearing children in the midst of a world war. Whatever the reasons, most of the people we interviewed were aware that, within certain limits, they had significantly more control over pregnancy than their parents, and virtually all had fewer children than their parents.

182

CHILDBIRTH AND CHILD CARE

Sol Meyrowitz's experience illustrates the transition between older and newer forms of birth control, and also illustrates how much difficulty some couples may still have had—despite all that they may have known or read on the subject—in discussing their plans and desires.

At first we didn't use any birth control, no, but when I felt that I was going to eject, I pulled it out of her. That's all. One night we were making love to each other, she made the remark to me: "Would you like to have a nice baby, like Marion?" Marion was my wife's brother's baby. "Well," I thought to myself, "my wife wants a baby! I guess we go at it." So that's how it happened, our first baby came along. Then I stayed inside of my wife.

Later on she went to New York, to Margaret Sanger, and she got a diaphragm. So she used the diaphragm. She went to put that goddamn diaphragm in, it took her an hour. She had to make sure it was right. Crawled in the bathtub, for Christ's sake, and make sure it was right.

Sol Levine's children were planned in more or less the same way. The Levines used a condom for birth control and managed, although they did not discuss their intentions explicitly, to space their three children each four years apart:

When my wife decided that she wanted to have a family, I remember the night in question, she said to me—we had separate beds—she said, "Come into my bed and forget the rubber." Well, of course I knew what that meant. So we copulated that night, for the first time without my wearing anything.

In those days, the recommended course of action, once a pregnancy was suspected, was to begin consulting experts, as Rebecca Green recalls:

When I became a mother, that was where I began to move into a whole new part of my life. I began to feel, to read a lot, to try to understand children. To deal with them, I began extension courses in preparation. I enjoyed that, I really enjoyed it. Instincts, those are no good. You must read, you must know. You shouldn't rely on instincts.

183

Some women were so anxious to contact a physician that they rushed the matter somewhat. Sol Levine recalls that the morning after the night he didn't use a "rubber," his wife called their doctor to confess that she was having morning sickness: "The doctor told me later that he burst out laughing, but she couldn't understand what he was laughing about." Some women consulted specialists—gynecology and obstetrics had become a medical speciality for some physicians by the first decade of the twentieth century—believing that a general practitioner would not suffice for their needs. Pregnant mothers became especially conscious of the nutritional value of what they were eating, and most expected (and were counseled) to gain a considerable amount of weight:

> As soon as a woman thinks she may be pregnant she should choose her doctor and go to him at once for a complete physical examination and for advice as to the hygiene of pregnancy. . . . The doctor will tell her when he himself wishes to see her—at least once a month during the first six months, every two weeks or oftener in the next two months, and every week in the last month. . . . If she cannot afford to go to a private physician, she should go at once to a prenatal center or clinic. She should report to the clinic as required and should follow absolutely the directions given to her at the clinic just as she would the instructions of a private physician.[1]

Yet try as they might to be modern, some women could not lay tradition entirely aside; many were still beset by the ancient notion—not unique to the Jews by any means—that the fetus can be seriously affected by what a woman does during pregnancy. Even Rebecca Green, with all her books and extension courses, confessed, "For nine months, everything you see, on the streets, if it is frightening you think it will happen." Hannah Toperoff, a high school graduate, nonetheless retained several superstitious notions:

Going back and forth to the doctor, inadvertently I ran into a boy about twelve years old who had a harelip. The doctor was nearby. I used to walk to the office. I had to go back once a month, every two weeks. I changed my route so that I would not run into this child—and he would be on that route, too. Haunting me. I just made myself sick from it. I had read somewhere, I forget what the percentage was, but some number of children were always born with a cleft palate or a harelip. And this drove me crazy. I would not mention to anyone this mishegoss [craziness] with a cleft palate, and a harelip; I wouldn't mention it to my husband, my sisters, to no one, because I was afraid that if I mentioned it, it would become a known fact. And when she was born, I remember the doctor saying, "Oh look!" I thought he was going to say that she got it. I said, "I must see the baby!" He said, "But, Hannah, she is dirty." "I have got to see the baby!" She was not completely out. All I wanted to do is take a look, to see, and I remember falling back to sleep again. But I had to see for myself that she was normal.

And Rose Janofsky, a college graduate, believed that she could influence the personality of her children by her conduct during pregnancy. During her first pregnancy, she recalls, "I went to every concert and opera that I could possibly go to. Not because I was particularly musical but because I felt that if it was going to influence his childhood in any way I was going to do it that way. I didn't know whether this child was a boy or girl, but I wanted this child to be musical." And during her second: "I went to every art gallery existing. I went to all the art things that I could find. I don't know whether there is any influence or not but I felt as long as I was having one aspect of creativity I would have another aspect of it."

In the shtetl, men were traditionally excluded from the scene of childbirth. Women—midwives, mothers, sisters, even daughters—attended other women when they went into labor; and men—husbands, fathers, brothers—were hustled out of the house. In the New World, under very different conditions, this tradition continued: few Jewish women even expected their husbands to accompany them to the hospital, let alone into the labor or delivery room, from which, in those newly germ-conscious days, everyone other than the woman in labor and her specially trained attendants was excluded. Aaron Katz, for example, recalls that he was not informed, until after the fact, about the birth of each of his children:

When my wife finally went into labor, she didn't tell me she was in labor. All night she went into the bathroom and chewed on a towel.

185

In the morning I got dressed and went to work. And the moment she heard the elevator door slam—my brother heard this, my brother then was living with us and was sleeping in the living room, on the couch— she let out such a scream. She called the doctor, and he told her to get dressed. "I will come over in a little while," he said, "and I will take you to the hospital. There is no rush." And he came over and took her to the hospital.

I wasn't present at the actual birth of any of my children. The doctor took my wife to the hospital in the middle of the night and after my second child was born I got a phone call that a son had been born and I took a cab to the hospital. Saw my wife, saw my child, and took my wife's coat home.

Hannah Toperoff's experience was akin to Mrs. Katz's:

I went into labor alone. My husband was at the office. My sister lived around the corner, and I told her, "I think I am going into labor." I called the doctor and told him my symptoms and he said, "Meet me at the hospital." Men are always in the way when it comes to things like that; they are overprotective. I didn't want anyone there, I wanted to be alone. If I wanted to scream, I didn't want to stifle a scream [shtetl practice encouraged women to scream as much as they wanted in labor]. And I feel much better when I scream. I am one of these people who likes to scream, but you can't scream when your husband is around.

With the first child it is a long labor, a really long labor. Really a long one. I got in there it was about eleven thirty or twelve midnight, and I had the baby about five in the morning. By then he [her husband] knew about it. I called him and told him that he was not to come with me. When the baby was born, I called him on the telephone. I had my nurse or whoever call him and they woke him up. He was fast asleep.

And the very first thing he did—and he talks about this so much and so often that his son has done it with his three children—he goes to a delicatessen and has a sturgeon sandwich.

By 1920, anesthesia was also available for labor and delivery, and most Jewish women chose to use it, to spare themselves unnecessary suffering. The availability of anesthesia was, in fact, one of the prime reasons so many women preferred hospital delivery. Doctors advised women to give birth in hospitals because it was safer (childbed fever had, by then, been conquered), and reinforced that advice by charging lower fees for hospital deliveries. Such deliveries had the additional (though oft-unstated) advantage of being considerably more convenient for the doctor. All of the fifty or so women we interviewed delivered their babies in hospitals. Rose Janofsky, for example, had helped her mother deliver at home in 1922: "I must have been about eleven or twelve at the time. [It was] my brother, my youngest brother." While she wasn't put off, she says, by the experience ("the noise and the groaning and the blood and all of that") she was determined to have something different for herself: "I didn't want it at home, there was no special reason. In a hospital I would have the attention of people who could help me and were trained for it. Both of my children were born in hospitals."

The Physician as Expert: Bed Rest and Baby Bottles

By the 1920s, physicians had replaced mothers and midwives as the experts on whom women relied when they gave birth. Many of the women we interviewed confessed that they could not, in any event, discuss such emotional subjects with their mothers. Hannah Toperoff believes this lack of discussion was the result of her mother's inhibitions: "That kind of relationship did not exist in my life. I simply didn't talk to my mother about anything that had to do with sex or with bodies." Rose Janofsky believes that her mother was too distracted by her own household to care very much about what was happening to her daughter: "I didn't talk to my mother about things like that. Who could talk to my mother? You have no idea what it was like, with all those people around, and everybody sick all the time."

In hospital confinements, the physician's word was law. Doctors believed that one way to curtail maternal mortality was to provide extensive bedrest for mothers, under sterile and supervised conditions. Hence, in those days, women spent from one to two weeks in the hospital after giving birth—more frequently the longer rather than the shorter period. During that time, the critical first weeks in an infant's life, physicians supervised every aspect of maternal and child care; their authority was paramount. The following passage is from *Congratulations*, a magazine given to every new mother confined in Beth-El Hospital, Brooklyn, New York:

> You are at home in your hospital, the home in which your baby first opened astonished eyes on this perplexing world. Very likely you have never thought of a hospital as a home, but that's precisely what it is—a place of refuge and solace for those in need of medical and surgical aid, where they may be assured of scientific care. What a comfort to think that your baby, and you too, have available such medical skill and modern nursing technique!
>
> . . . So here you are comfortably propped up in bed, in a homelike room, with a smiling nurse in attendance. . . . Then there's the doctor whose visits are presaged by everyone bustling about to have things in readiness. Could there ever be another man so kind and understanding! You can tell the goodlooking young intern is as devoted to him as you are. . . . Then one fine day, your nurse comes in and says, "The doctor is letting you sit up for ten minutes today!"[2]

Few of the women we interviewed can recall ever defying their physician's instructions, not even to the extent of struggling out of bed to visit their newborn infants in the nursery. We heard only one childbirth story that involved such defiance, and in that case—Hannah Toperoff's second child, born just at the end of the Second World War—the defiance was thought to be justified only by special conditions:

When I went into labor the second time I did not want to disturb him [the doctor] because it was in the wee hours of the morning. When I did call him, he came to the house and said, "Why did you wait so long! You are practically halfway through!" He took me to the hospital. My husband was already at work, and the doctor called him at work and he came to the hospital.

The second delivery was absolutely unbelievable. I got into the labor room, and my doctor is standing next to me and said, "Hannah, you're not quite ready yet. I will be in the hospital and will see you some time this afternoon." I am on the table and I had very, very severe pains. I called for the nurse, and she comes in. I say to her, "My doctor said he would see me this afternoon. With the kind of pain I have I will not last until this afternoon." And she looked at me as if to say, "Lady, what can I do for you?" And she proceeded to walk out, at which point I screamed, "The baby is out!" Suddenly everybody is running around, and they are wheeling me from the room I was in, the labor room, to the delivery room, and they are paging my doctor, and they are yelling at me, "Keep your legs crossed! Keep your legs crossed!" The house doctor was there and then they are telling me to bear down but I didn't have any idea what they were talking about because the first time I was knocked out—what did I know from bearing down? When my doctor finally showed up, the baby was already born, and I was really mad.

Every day after that, he came to see me in my room, and every day he discovers that I am someplace else. After all, I gave birth on V-J Day! The doctor doesn't understand this. "You're supposed to stay in bed," he tells me. But I am visiting other people on the floor. Anybody can have a baby, but when a war ends, that is something to celebrate!

The first generation of babies to be planned and to be born in a hospital was also the first to receive most of its nourishment from a bottle. Breast feeding was yet another matter on which a woman's behavior was largely governed by her physician's attitude and by hospital regulations. In order to control disease, to minimize inconvenience for the nursing staff, and to ensure bed rest for mothers, most hospital regulations dictated that babies should be housed in nurseries, separated from their mothers (and also from their fathers), to be brought out at regular four-hour intervals for feeding. Under such conditions, breast feeding, as any mother who has tried it knows, is very difficult to establish. As it happens, only a small percentage of the women who gave birth in hospitals during the years between 1920 and 1945 were particularly interested in trying.

Some experts, especially those who wrote magazine articles and child-care manuals, held the belief generally held today that breast feeding is best for the baby:

> The privilege of nursing one's own baby is a heaven-sent gift, second only in importance to the coming of the baby itself. If we

189

place the matter on a purely utilitarian basis, there are so many arguments in favor of nursing and so few arguments against it that it would seem as though it ought to be adopted as a universal custom. From the point of view of the mother, the advantages are many. She can set her mind at rest regarding the possibility of her baby having an upset digestion. The summer diseases need not worry her. She has no need to depend upon an erratic milk supply.

From the point of view of the baby the advantages are just as striking. The breast-fed baby is always stronger than the bottle-fed baby, he has better teeth, firmer muscles, is less apt to have any diseases, his gain in weight is more even and regular; he is usually well nourished, strong and vigorous, and his advantage holds good not only during the first year, but it also gives him a certain sturdy preparation for life that is absolutely invaluable and cannot be gained in any other way.[3]

The authors of handbooks for hospital administrators also favored breast feeding, even during wartime, when hospital staffs were particularly hard-pressed:

It is recommended that efforts be made to have every mother of a full-term infant nurse him. The efforts should include encouraging the mother's cooperation, withholding artificial feeding even in the presence of early weight loss (provided this is not excessive), giving only water until the mother's milk begins to come or until it is evident that the mother is not going to supply an adequate amount of breast milk.[4]

But popular opinion, insofar as it was expressed in the behavior of women who had any choice in the matter, was opposed to breast feeding. No one knows quite why, in this one domain, American women apparently were willing to contradict the recommendations of experts. Some students of the question believe that the culprits were physicians in regular practice (as opposed to those who wrote advice columns) who preferred bottle over breast so that mothers could get more rest in the hospital; not perhaps coincidentally, bottle feeding gave these doctors more control over their patients (as babies grew, mothers depended on doctors to make changes in the formula and in the recommended number of bottles per day)—and substantially higher fees. Yet others lay the blame on the advertising men who wrote copy for the manufacturers of milk supplements, bottles, sterilizers, and nipples. These men were determined to convince parents that bottle feeding was simultaneously more convenient, more modern, and more likely to produce healthy babies.

Contemporary observers, such as Dr. S. Josephine Baker, believed that the blame should be placed squarely on the mothers:

> Every once in a while someone brings forward the idea that women are becoming less and less able to feed their babies nature's way. I have never been able to determine that this was true. There is undoubtedly some basis for the belief that women in some walks of life are less *willing* [italics added] to nurse their babies than they used to be, and that the amount of natural nursing that goes on among our foreign population and the more primitive groups of people far exceeds that which is found among the more socialized or even the so-called more intelligent classes. In nine cases out of ten, a woman's inability to feed her baby the proper way is due to her lack of willingness to make herself fit to do so rather than to any inherent inability in this line.[5]

In some respects, Baker may have been right. Many young Jewish women may have been reluctant to breast-feed because they associated the practice with the "foreign population." None of the women we interviewed, however, were willing (or even able) to make that connection. Some are convinced that they failed to breast-feed because they simply had no milk—a physiological condition that appears to have been endemic in this, and only this, generation.

JENNIE GROSSMAN: *I didn't nurse my babies. There just was no milk. I wasn't made for that. My sister-in-law, the flat-chested one, she had milk. Cream she produced. But me, I didn't have enough.*

I was given the pills to dry it up. The doctor decided to do that.

Other women believed that hospital practices were at fault. Sadie Rehstock, for example, believes that the nurses who attended her were particularly unhelpful, showing no interest at all in helping her learn how to breast-feed:

I started nursing, but I wasn't sure how it would work out at home because I wanted to go back to work. It wasn't explained that way to me. The nurses said, "You nurse your baby or you don't nurse your baby, some do and some don't. Whichever you feel most comfortable with."

They brought the child to me, and they got me prepared for the nursing, and it was very early, I guess I wasn't producing yet, but they didn't tell me that you don't produce milk or much milk in the first few days. Nope. I only found that out later. Just that I had to make up my mind whether I wanted to nurse or not nurse. The nurses weren't putting pressure, but they had to make a decision what to do, too. The nurses didn't say you must make up your mind. They put it differently. "What are you doing? Are you going to nurse the baby or are you not going to?" They kept asking me, every couple of hours, until I made up my mind.

Certainly, some aspects of hospital practice must have made it difficult, if not downright unpleasant, for mothers who were trying to breast-feed:

> It is recommended that the nursing mother wear a nightgown that is open in front; that her hands be washed with soap and water before nursing and her breast be washed before and after nursing; that the baby lie on a clean paper or cotton towel during nursing; that all visitors, even members of the family, be excluded while the mother is nursing the infant.[6]

And since some experts preferred boric acid to soap and water for complete sterilization of the nipples, the experience could not have been pleasant for the babies either. Etta Levine recalls, for example, that "breast feeding was torture for my child. She screamed and screamed and wrinkled her face." Debbie Levine ended up with a bottle.

On the subject of breast feeding, expert advice was, in any event, something of a double-edged sword: while the experts insisted, on the one hand, that natural nursing was best for babies, they also insisted

192

that babies needed to gain regular amounts of weight every week in order to ensure good health. Thus, breast-feeding mothers were at a disadvantage; they could neither know nor brag to their neighbors about how much their babies were imbibing; some nursing mothers, in order to quiet their own fears, terminated each feeding with a bottle. Advertisements in magazines also led mothers to notice that breast milk was thin and almost bluish, while cow's milk (and especially evaporated cow's milk) was thick, white, creamy—in a word, "rich."

Certainly, no one had a vested interest in placing ads for breast feeding. The periodicals that campaigned against infant and maternal mortality were the same ones that advertised milk supplements and baby foods, sterilizers, nipples, and bottles, assuring their readers all the while that their pages advertised nothing but the most reputable and reliable products. In all their profusely illustrated pages, neither the *Ladies' Home Journal* nor *Good Housekeeping*, neither *Parents' Magazine* nor the *Saturday Evening Post* ever carried one photograph or drawing of a mother with a child at the breast—even to illustrate the articles that advocated feeding at the breast.

Mothers could not have helped concluding that the best interests of the child were met by bottle rather than by breast. Thus, this advertisement for a milk supplement:

> Avoid Summer Diarrhea!
> Eliminate summer diarrhea and you eliminate almost every other danger to your baby. . . . Summer diarrhea is usually caused by milk which has undergone fermentative changes due to the presence of bacteria. . . . Milk in every form (mother's as well) must be stopped. As a temporary substitute doctors recommend: Nestlé's Milk Food, one teaspoonful. Rice water, three ounces.
> But why not avoid all rush and go to Nestlé's Milk Food at once? There will be no danger from fermented milk, no changes of food made necessary by travelling. Baby goes steadily on, storing up strength, building bone and muscle.[7]

And another advertisement, this one for rubber nipples:

> Your Baby Beautiful!
> It's so important to give that baby of yours every possible advantage, right from the start. You'll want baby to have the best of

193

everything. The softest woolies. The gentlest bath things. The things that will help that tiny body develop and grow in a normal, healthy way.

Infant feeding, authorities declare, can have much to do with the proper development of the tiny jaw and palate. Davol "Anti-Colic" brand "Sani-Tab" nipples are scientifically designed to act as nearly like natural feeding as possible.[8]

Esther Ginsburg was one of many mothers who opted for the bottle. Born in Lithuania, an immigrant at thirteen, Ginsburg had learned enough, from magazines she says, to reject breast feeding as the appropriate insurance of her child's health:

I was a terribly nervous mother, constantly worried about my children's health. I didn't nurse my first baby, didn't try, didn't want to. I know it would have been easier. You had to do everything yourself in those days—make the formula, sterilize the bottles. It was very complicated. If I nursed, I would have to weigh her before I fed her and after I fed her to know how much she had taken.

Even such brave souls as Rebecca Green, who did breast-feed, learned to handle their babies in a manner that was as germ-free and "scientific" as possible:

I loved nursing my babies. I nursed all the way. I nursed for nine months each kid. I get to know them this way. But that was the time when you didn't lift the baby and nurse him in your arms. You lay down and you put him on a little blanket at your side and you nursed him on one side and then you turned and nursed him on the other side. I conditioned him to turn from one side to the other. He learned quickly where the milk is coming from. I was with him all the time. It was rewarding, it was very, very rewarding to do this.

Teaching "Good Habits": The Baby's Schedule

Once babies emerged from the hospital, they were left almost entirely in the hands of their mothers: in this, shtetl and mainstream American practice did not conflict. Some parents, those who could afford it, hired

The Baby's Nursery Clock

By Emelyn Lincoln Coolidge, M. D.

THE HOUR

Cut Out This White Space

REGULARITY in taking care of a baby means everything to him and to the entire household. From the first day of his birth a regular system should be maintained. As the baby grows older this system may have to be changed from time to time; but always have some regular plan to follow for the baby's day and night. If this plan is followed the baby will soon wake on the exact, scheduled time for his meals, his bath and for everything else that is done for him, and he will just as regularly be willing to sleep at the correct hours.

When a baby has not been started by a regular system it will no doubt be hard to train him at first, but it is well worth the trouble. He will have to be gently waked at feeding time, for a few days at least, until he grows used to the idea of a schedule, and he will have to be allowed to cry a few times if he has not been made to take his naps or to go to bed at regular hours. But this crying will not harm the baby if he is a normal child. If he is a sick child the doctor must decide what is best for him.

Nursing or feeding a baby whenever he happens to cry for it, frequent night meals, keeping the baby up so that the parents may exhibit him to friends, or taking him out calling in the evening, are all exceedingly bad things to allow. It is never too early to begin the regular training.

Best Schedule for Average Babies

SOME babies will have to be started on a two-hour schedule for the first month of life, then on two hours and a half for the second month and on the three-hour time at two months of age, but it has lately been found that the average baby can do with three-hour intervals for food almost from the beginning of life; therefore this schedule has been made with the three-hour food interval as the basis.

If for any special reason the shorter feeding interval is necessary, or it is found that a longer interval of four hours between meals is desirable, the bath, exercise, outing and sleep should be changed accordingly; but keep the general relation of the

other events to the food the same. A bath, for instance, should be given before a meal and not right after one. At least one hour should elapse after the baby is fed before he has a bath. As bathing usually makes the baby sleepy and comfortable, it is best to plan the bath, then the feeding and then the nap, one after the other.

The water mentioned is to be boiled and then cooled to tepid in the winter, or it may be given cool in summer, but it should never be given ice cold, as this is apt to cause colic. It is best to give this water from a bottle, but if one prefers it may be given from a teaspoon, a cup or a medicine dropper. If the baby refuses to take it do not give up but keep right on trying it. The water should not be sweetened, but it may be flavored with a little orange juice, if necessary, as this takes away the flat taste of boiled water.

The Proper Exercise

THE exercise mentioned is simply natural exercise that the baby will take himself. Pulling him up by letting him grasp the fingers, working the delicate little arms and legs about by manipulation, tossing him about, etc., should not be allowed. A strong grown person does not realize how very delicate a little baby's ligaments and muscles are. The baby should be undressed, except for his band, shirt and diaper, and placed in a warm room on a wide bed for a few minutes at a time, when it is the correct time for exercising, and then left alone to kick and play with his hands and toes by himself.

When the baby is older an exercise pen on legs, so that there will be no danger of drafts from the floor, is the correct thing for the baby to exercise in. This pen should be made at home or by a carpenter, as it is seldom possible to buy just the right thing. The pen may be used when the baby is five or six months old, and he will learn to creep and walk in it as he develops. Do not urge him to do these things.

The fresh air will have to be regulated a little according to the different seasons, but give all the air possible without taking foolish risks.

Cut Out the Chart Illustrated Above Along the Outside Black Line and Mount on Bristol Board or Very Thin Cardboard

Then Cut Out the Disk Below Along the Outside of the Black Line, and Mount This on a Piece of Thin Cardboard

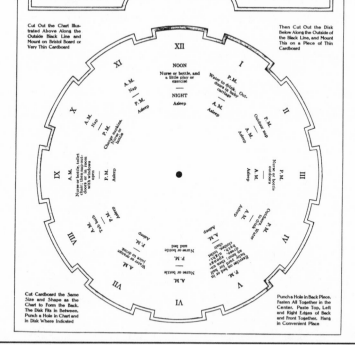

Cut Cardboard the Same Size and Shape as the Chart to Form the Back. The Disk Fits In Between. Punch a Hole in Chart and in Disk Where Indicated

Punch a Hole in Back Piece. Fasten All Together in the Center. Paste Top, Left and Right Edges of Back and Front Together. Hang in Convenient Place baby nurses for short periods; but with this single exception, the generation born between 1920 and 1945 was raised—as generations in the shtetl had been—almost entirely by mothers. While fathers might occasionally play with children, they did not get involved in the day-to-day details of child care. Sol Meyrowitz remembers his own father as having been quite distant, taciturn, removed:

He was a dutiful father, but he never kissed me, never talked to me and had conversations with me. He never hugged me—he never hugged anybody. He could play solitaire for five, six hours. He had affection but he never showed it. He must have loved me because he took me to see Wild Bill Cody—Buffalo Bill. I remember I saw the Atlantic Fleet—my father took me to see that. He was probably a good man, but he was a loner.

When I went to high school, I played on the varsity baseball and soccer teams, but my father never attended a single game. He never spoke to me. I never knew from his family how many brothers and sisters he had. He never talked. He had one brother whom he hadn't seen in twenty-seven years, and I never knew that. I was raised that way and I thought that's the way it is supposed to be. I wouldn't dare have fights with him. Oh no! I was afraid of him, never rebelled against him.

I could never talk to my father. I couldn't talk to him about anything. He never told me any of the things about his life. I never knew that he had sisters. They were on the outside. Twenty years I lived with him and he never mentioned them. They lived for twenty years in the same town and he never spoke with them.

When his own turn came, Sol Meyrowitz repeated his father's pattern:

She [his wife] loved her children; she loved all of her children. Every child is different, every child is born different. I loved her children, too. I was a good father in one way: I never stopped giving. I wanted them to have an education, the best education I could give them. I worked hard for that more than anything else. I wasn't a good father in the point I didn't spend the time I wish I could have, should have spent. Because all I had in my mind was that I had to go out and work.

There was a number of years that Sunday was my most important day to work. I used to tell my wife, "Everything is a challenge."

It is a challenge in life to get along in life. It is a challenge to do business, to outsmart the next fellow. And that's what the hell life is. I never changed the baby. In some ways I enjoyed being a father, but changing the baby is women's work. At that time I wouldn't know how. I was working and very busy, and my wife's work was in the home. I happened to believe in that philosophy, and the division of labor.

Rose Janofsky's experience must have been similar to Mrs. Meyrowitz's. Jack Janofsky must have wanted children very much. He persuaded his wife not to have the abortion she would have preferred when she was pregnant with their first child. But, as she says, when it came to spending time with them or paying attention to them, his mind was elsewhere, unless education was at issue:

Jack is very tough, very tough. If he had his way he would do nothing but go to meetings, to work, and it has been difficult. My children now tell stories about how every time we went off some place, after I had packed the car to the top, with three kids and all the stuff, and he got in to drive, he would always say, "We have to stop at the office for a few minutes, I have to do something." And the kids remember this very well. An hour, two—while all these kids are sitting in the car with the mattresses up to the top. That was his way of living.

He was afraid to touch the babies—he waited until the babies were big enough to handle—he was really afraid to touch them. He did not know what to do. He would say, "I don't understand this, I don't understand that." He just felt very awkward, uneasy, detached—not good for a father from where I stand. He didn't hug them and kiss them—no, I don't think so. He was physically remote from them while they were growing up. Yes, I am afraid that is true. He is good-natured. He never spanked them. But he never walked them. He never took the baby carriage out. Never dawned on me to even ask him.

I remember Bob [her son] came to me and said, "What does he want?" He [Bob] brought home a report card, maybe he had an A— and Bob came to me and said, "What does he want?" Jack didn't stress A's; it was his peculiar sense of humor. He thought he was being funny

197

*when he would say, when he saw a report card with all A's, he would
say, "Is that the best you could do?"*

And Charlie Moses, also devoted to his profession (he is a physician),
plainly regarded his children primarily as a burden. "I never learned
how to diaper the babies," he confesses.

*Of course having a child, a son, changed my life because we are now
obligated to take care of an infant. As free as we had been, we couldn't
take a trip to Nova Scotia as we had a year or two before, that was out.
I had a baby to take care of. We didn't think of taking a baby on a trip
of that kind. It never occurred to us to do it.*

*There were times I played with them. I did not want more than two
[children], and she insisted on a third child and I suspect—I don't
know, I never asked her—that she was hoping for a daughter the third
time around. After my last child [it was a girl] was born, I accepted my
child, I accepted her and that was that.*

*There was a lot of responsibility of having children. There were
times when it was fun and times when it was a chore. I was very realis-
tic; children like everything else have their pluses and minuses, and so
I went along with it and did what I had to do. When they did well in
school, I enjoyed it and so on, and when they did poorly and were pains
in the neck, in that respect I was uncomfortable.*

The babies who were the first to be fed by a bottle were also the first
to be reared on a schedule. On this issue, American Jewish parents
diverged markedly from their European forebears, who had believed
that parents should respond immediately to any indication of a child's
distress, up to the age of three or four.

With regard to scheduling, American experts spoke to parents in
one voice, and parents listened as if they were of one mind. Children
need discipline, the experts said, and they need it from the moment
they are born: not the immigrant discipline of the fist, of course, but
the American discipline of a schedule. Dispense with physical punishment, the authorities counseled, and instead withdraw affection, for
this is the only way in which you will succeed in raising a child who
is both happy and responsible. Feed your children by the clock. Put
them to bed by the clock. Do not listen to their entreaties, do not capit-

ulate to their demands—lest your children be "spoiled." In the effort to avoid spoiling children, parents apparently were convinced that if they surrendered control for even one minute of one day—in a moment of weakness, cuddling a crying baby—the child would be transformed instantly into a juvenile delinquent.

Many historians have erred in attributing the vogue for schedules to J. B. Watson, the father of behaviorist psychology. In fact, Watson, whose *Psychological Care of Infant and Child* was published in 1928, was a late arrival; the Progressive women of the Children's Bureau had begun advocating schedules a decade and a half earlier. By 1930, they had even learned how to convey the message to mothers who were almost illiterate:

LESSON NO. 1—ARE YOU TRAINING YOUR CHILD TO BE HAPPY?

We can help you to make your baby happy, but you must help, too. You must try very hard.

You must never stop trying.

You are tired and busy some day. Your baby is crying. You say, "This one time does not matter. I will pick him up. Then he will stop crying."

Then your smart little baby says to himself, "Hurrah, I was the boss that time! I can be boss next time."

Before you know it, he will cry again. Will you pick him up again?

Do you always give him what he wants?

Then he will not be happy long.

Read this little book. It will help you to keep your baby happy and good.

LESSON NO 2.—HOW YOU CAN HELP YOUR CHILD TO FORM GOOD HABITS

Do you want your child to form good habits?

The first time you do something new it is hard.

Next time it is easier.

Next time it is very easy.

Soon you can do it and not think about it at all.

Then we call it a *habit*.

Your child is learning everything that way.

He is *forming habits.*
He can learn a *good* way to do things.
But he can learn a *bad* way instead.
He learns the way *you* teach him.
Do you want to teach him the good way or the bad way?
Do you want him to form good habits or bad habits?
This lesson will tell you how to teach him good habits.
Begin when he is born.
Feed him at exactly the same hours every day.
Do not feed him at any other time.
Let him sleep after every feeding.
Do not feed him just because he cries.
Let him wait until the right time.
If you make him wait, his stomach will learn to wait.
His mind will learn that he cannot get things by crying.
You do two things for your baby at the same time. You teach his body good habits and you teach his mind good habits.[9]

And when the experts said, "Feed at exactly the same hours every day," they allowed for no exceptions. Thus, in 1915 the *Ladies' Home Journal* advised mothers:

Regularity in taking care of a baby means everything to him and to the entire household. From the first day of his birth a regular system should be maintained. As the baby grows older this system may have to be changed from time to time; but always have some regular plan to follow for the baby's day and night. If this plan is followed the baby will soon wake on the exact, scheduled time for his meals, his bath and for everything else that is done for him, and he will just as regularly be willing to sleep at the correct hours.

When a baby has not been started by a regular system it will no doubt be hard to train him at first, but it is well worth the trouble. He will have to be gently waked at feeding time, for a few days at least, until he grows used to the idea of a schedule, and he will have to be allowed to cry a few times if he has not been made to take his naps or to go to bed at regular hours. But this crying will not harm the baby if he is a normal child. If he is a sick child the doctor must decide what is best for him.

Nursing or feeding a baby whenever he happens to cry for it, frequent night meals, keeping the baby up so that the parents may exhibit him to friends, or taking him out calling in the evening, are all exceedingly bad things to allow. It is never too early to begin the regular training.[10]

As a result of all these admonitions, many babies of this generation (both Jewish and Christian) were disciplined to a schedule from the very first weeks of life. "People say that babies are 'too young to know,' " a hospital magazine counseled young mothers in 1940,

but that's a trick phrase. It paves the way for many a tiny tyrant's tantrums. Your baby is smarter than even you may think he is.

From the day of his birth a baby begins unconsciously to acquire habits. Whether these will be habits which will tend to make him easy to live with or haphazard habits which will upset him and the household as a whole, depends solely upon the start he gets at home.

In the hospital a time-clock system is established which will work well for babies at home. If this routine is followed after bringing baby back to his abode, it will be easier for everyone concerned.

In his bed the baby should stay until time for his 6:00 A.M. feeding. But *you* must be up before this—say 5:30 A.M. so as to get his meal ready on time. . . . Feed the baby at 6 A.M. sharp. But what if signs and sounds indicate that he is awake at 5:30? Diaper changing is permitted at this hour, if need be, but no peace offering in food form! He must be taught to wait.[11]

Esther Ginsburg, like many mothers we interviewed, now regards herself as having been a fanatic on the subject of schedules:

Everything had to be on schedule. Six o'clock dinner, then a bath. And I would walk around with a book, and I would not deviate from the norm. I used to travel around with Dr. Spock [since Esther Ginsburg's children were born well before Benjamin Spock's book was published, in 1946, she must be referring to some other child-rearing book; many of the people we interviewed made this error]. I took that book with me everywhere. Parents' Magazine, I read. Five minutes off her schedule was catastrophic. By the second one, I was a little more relaxed, but not much.

When the kids went to bed, no one, but no one, not even God Him-self, was allowed to disturb them. My in-laws would want to take a look at them, and I was firm about it. They thought I was crazy.

Apparently Mike Ginsburg, Esther's husband, was just as crazy. He was an engineer, very precise; and Esther recalls once creating a ruse so that he would not discover that she had fed the baby "five minutes off schedule":

Well, we lived in an apartment then and we used to park our car in a garage across the street. And I was feeding the baby one day, and I looked out the window and saw my husband coming, and I looked at the clock and it was ten. So I pushed back the hands of the clock! Yup, that's what I did! I pushed back the hands of the clock so it said nine-fifty instead of ten. I never told my husband. I meant to, but then he died young and I never got to tell him.

Sam Smilowitz recalls that when Daylight Saving Time was insti-tuted, and his wife put their son to bed at his regular time, he (the child) was not sleepy (that bedtime being for him an hour too early). The baby yelled so much that he vomited in his crib, but Mrs. Smilo-witz was afraid to pick him up, for fear that she would spoil him. Jennie Grossman is now sorry that she was, as a new parent, devoted to scheduling:

I remember Stanley [her first-born], we then went by the books, and I remember them saying, "You don't touch the baby. You feed the baby regularly and you don't touch the baby in between." And that baby cried for a very, very long time. We had a sick baby and a baby who really needed to be loved and held. And I remember the first time I really held him because he was sick—he must have been seven or eight months old—and I looked down at him and said, "My God! You are a sick little fellow, aren't you?" or words to that effect. And that is the first I remember rocking him. And after that we walked with him at night and we paid much closer attention. It took that much time for me to relate to this child. We were trapped in the book.

Just after she was married, Janet Sommers learned about scheduling from her sister-in-law who had just given birth.

My sister-in-law had a baby about a year before I did. I guess that she must have felt inadequate, she did not know what she was going to do with a baby. She read books and she adhered to the letter of the books, and whatever was written, she adhered to the letter of the books. She brought Dick up by the numbers.

I had strict orders that if they were to leave the house and the baby cried, I was to guard the door so that my mother would not go in and pick up the baby. "Don't allow your mother to come in!" And I did stand at the door and said, "You may not come in, Mom," and she just pushed me away and went in and picked up the baby. The baby was crying. Ada [her sister-in-law] used to nurse him. She would nurse him and weigh him before and after she nursed him to make sure he had got the allotted amount of milk. Catastrophe when the baby peed in his pants while he was being nursed!

Despite some initial skepticism, Janet Sommers followed the same rules herself when she became a parent—that is, until she had a distressing experience when her baby was about six months old:

But, you know, I did the same thing myself when my turn came. The book said, "Feed the baby at twelve o'clock." I fed the baby at twelve o'clock. The book said, "Don't pick up the baby in between." I didn't pick up the baby in between.

Well, I used the disposable diapers—you inserted a paper lining into a pair of panties, the lining rested in plastic panties; my husband got them wholesale. Anyway, I was giving the baby a bath in a bathinette [a waist-high portable canvas bathtub, very popular in this period]. My doctor told me that the baby had a birthmark on the base of her spine, but not to worry about it. Well, while I was giving her a bath, her father noticed that the birthmark was festering; it was really sore. The *panties must have caused an irritation. We took her to the doctor who said that it had to come off.*

But for days she had been crying in her crib and in her carriage, whenever I put her on her back, and I let her cry when she was crying. And then it turned out that she was really sick. They used dry ice to burn off the infected birthmark, and it was awful, and she cried a lot, and I had to walk her home from the doctor's—it must have been about three miles—just so the carriage ride would calm her down. After that I said, "To hell with the book!"

Ironically, by the late 1930s, expert opinion was beginning to mirror Janet Sommers's experience; in the pages of their professional journals, some of the experts were confessing to each other that scheduling could sometimes have disastrous effects on the parent-child relationship. Demand feeding—which had been, of course, the general practice in previous generations—did not come back into vogue, however, until the publication of Benjamin Spock's *The Common Sense Book of Baby and Child Care* in 1946. Spock asserted, vividly and firmly, that scheduling was a profound mistake. He had been in practice as a pediatrician during the 1930s, when many of our parents were enamored of scheduling; and consequently, he knew precisely how to address an audience of parents who had once been told that scheduling was good character training for their children:

You may be so used to the idea that babies are fed on schedule that you are surprised to hear that it was once very different. Up to sixty years ago ... babies were fed when they seemed to be hungry, even in the most careful homes. And even today most of the mothers all over the world have never heard of a schedule. They would probably think it was pretty funny.

Mothers have sometimes been so scared of the schedule that they did not dare feed a hungry baby one minute early. They have even accepted the idea that a baby would be spoiled if he were fed when he was hungry. What an idea! As if puppies are spoiled by being able to nurse then they are hungry. Why does a baby cry near mealtime? Not to get the better of his mother. He wants some milk. Why does he sleep the next 4 hours: Not because he has learned that his mother is stern. It's because the meal satisfies his system for that long.[12]

Weight gain was as much a source of worry to parents of the inter-war generation as were schedules. During the 1920s and the 1930s, the experts told parents that weight gain was the single best indicator of a baby's health. Thus, some babies, like Janet Sommer's nephew, were weighed after every meal; others, every day; many, at least once a week. Mothers competed with each other to be the first on the block to start solid foods. As part of the first generation to have discovered how important vitamins are to health, many parents (both Christian and Jewish) worried incessantly about how to provide the proper quantity of each in a meal, a balanced diet. "Loss of appetite" was a topic on which the experts discoursed at length, because—overfed and end-lessly hassled at mealtimes—"loss of appetite" was pandemic among babies of this generation. Sam Smilowitz, for example, remembers the way his wife fed the children:

She was very foolish. If they didn't want to eat and wouldn't swallow, she would hold their nose so they would have to swallow. And they would react by regurgitating the food; you had to clean up the mess. I can visualize the high chair right over there in the kitchen where the children would do that. By holding his nose, he had to open his mouth in order to get air. I have no recollection of my reaction or what I did.

Magazines and child-care manuals in those years carried endless de-tailed instructions about how babies and children should be properly fed:

Cod-liver oil—Cod-liver oil should be begun before the end of the first month of the baby's life, preferably by the end of the second week. Begin with one-half teaspoonful twice a day of pure plain cod-liver oil tested for vitamin D (the antirachitic vitamin). . . . In climates where children can not have enough direct sun-light the year around, cod-liver oil should be given regularly twice a day. It should be given throughout the first two years of the child's life.

How to give cod-liver oil to a baby. With the baby lying across her lap, the mother pours out the cod-liver oil in a spoon held in her right hand. With her left hand she opens the baby's mouth by pressing the cheeks together with her thumb and fingers. The oil may then be poured little by little into the baby's mouth. If his mouth is not held open until the oil entirely disappears the baby will spit out what is left. The mother must not let him know by her facial expression that she does not like the smell of the oil because that will teach the baby not to like it. She must take it for granted that he will like it, even if she herself does not.

Rebecca Green recalled, especially, that baked potatoes were particularly recommended: "Wherever a woman was at eleven A.M., she raced home to put up a baked potato." The experts, however, hoped that women would be even more careful than that:

Potatoes—When a baby is 10 months old, baked white potatoes (2 tablespoonfuls) may be given three or four times a week at the 2 P.M. feeding. After a month or so he may have potatoes every day, but they must not take the place of green vegetables. If a child does not eat the green vegetables that are offered him it is wise to withhold potatoes, as many babies like potatoes best and will not eat green vegetables as long as they can get potatoes.[13]

In the shtetls of Poland and Russia, infants were closely swaddled, heavily blanketed, and generally protected, whenever possible, from drafts of fresh air. In the United States, however, experts recommended—in addition to regular schedules and nutritious food—that what a baby needed to stay alive and kicking was fresh air and sunshine, vitamin D. In their rigid adherence to this prescription, American Jewish parents broke from Eastern European tradition.

JENNIE GROSSMAN: *By nine, if you were taking good care of your baby, you were out walking with her in the sunshine. This was absolutely a must. You get your baby out early in the morning so that the baby has plenty of sunshine.*

I was a ridiculous mother, nervous, overly protective, to their health, to their schedule. In the coldest, coldest weather, Susan had to be out at nine in the morning, regardless of how cold it was. At least two or three hours. And I was dying from the cold.

As a result, when Julie [her grandchild] was born, I would call Susan at nine in the morning to see if she had the child out yet. It got to the point when she wouldn't even answer the phone any more because she knew it was I calling!

Above all, the experts impressed upon our parents the notion that babies did not have to die, that even frail children could be saved by careful attention to both food and regimen:

What is meant by a delicate child?
One with feeble vitality; usually much below the average both in height and weight. The rate of growth is very slow; there is but little muscular endurance, little resistance to disease and slow recovery after any form of illness. Such children were often feeble infants, reared with the greatest difficulty; they require constant and intelligent care or they fall ill.

How are such children to be managed?
They must have the simplest and most nourishing diet—fed up to seven or eight years old as carefully as infants. Their habits must be absolutely regular; the slightest variation from the normal routine is often followed by serious upsets. They need two or three more hours in bed than the average child and the midday rest should be continued until they are nine or ten years old. They are often much benefited by spending one entire day each week in bed. They require plenty of sunshine and fresh air, but no coddling. The amount of exercise they can take is limited and one should be careful not to exceed it. They should especially be protected against measles and whooping cough.

What are their chances for improvement as they grow up?
Provided they get through the early years without acquiring any serious disease, the outlook improves with each year. Some take a decided start for the better at seven or eight years, others not until toward puberty; but with proper care it is surprising how many reach adult life in good physical condition.[14]

Sol Meyrowitz, who had struggled with TB, was very frightened when a physician told him that his son was frail and underweight:

All the time, he was so delicate, we were afraid he was going to die. We used to put him out in the backyard to have the sun shine on his body—there is a therapeutic value in having the sun shine on the body—and we fed him a lot of vitamins; that was the doctor's prescription. We wanted to build him up. We were told by the doctor to give him heads of lettuce and malted milks. When I was born, we didn't have all the vitamins. I felt the vitamins had helped sustain him, keep him alive.

Like Sol Meyrowitz, many immigrant parents were determined, sometimes beyond reason and consciousness, that their children not die in infancy or become, in childhood, "familiar with death." The high infant and maternal mortality rates that worried the Progressive reformers had also rent these parents' hearts when they themselves were children. Thus, parents boiled diapers and gave birth in hospitals, forced cod-liver oil down unwilling throats and concocted formulas, paid doctor's bills and insisted that teeth be brushed three times daily—all in the hope of staving off death.

And the hope was realized. These Jewish parents—and other American parents—were the advance troops in one of the most successful public-health campaigns of all time. While the reformers were forcing legislatures to purify milk supplies, parents were sterilizing the bottles that would receive the milk. Before the housing experts had managed to eliminate dank and sunless courtyards, parents were going to parks to sun their children in baby carriages. Hospitals began to enlarge their maternity pavilions because mothers and fathers were willing to pay for the privilege of patronizing them.

And year by year, little by little, infant and maternal mortality rates began to fall. Infant mortality went from 100 out of every 1,000 live births in 1916 to 69 out of 1,000 in 1928, 51 in 1938, and 32 by the end of the Second World War. Maternal mortality declined just as precipitately: from 91 out of every 10,000 pregnancies in 1916, to 69 in 1928, 43 in 1938, and 11 by the end of the war. In the space of thirty years, and well before the mass production of antibiotics, all the bed rest and sterilization, all those baby scales and forced feedings, all that cod-liver oil and sunlight had succeeded in reducing infant mortality by two thirds and maternal mortality by well over three quarters. In 1946, Benjamin Spock could advocate that parents let down their guard a little—and, in so doing, produce a best seller—because, by 1946, the battle had been won.

In this great battle, young Jewish parents could not turn to their elders for assistance. The experience of the Old World was of little value in the New, for the goals had changed. Those who had been born and raised in Eastern Europe were inured to death; infant and maternal mortality were to be endured stoically, accepted as God's will. Rose Janofsky discovered this when she gave birth to her first child, a Down's syndrome baby. The baby died during the first week of life, but before that happened:

My mother-in-law had said to us, "You bring that baby home, and I'll take care of it." What she meant was not that she would take care of the baby but that she would "take care" of it so that we would not have to bring it up. She really meant that—she would have done what had to be done. My mother-in-law said that in Europe this was not uncommon, and it was not uncommon for somebody to do it. Somebody would come in and put a pillow on the baby or turn it over on its face, and that was it. That was it, no questions asked.

But Rose Janofsky and her contemporaries were not similarly inured. The younger generation had been told that science and technology could, just possibly, defeat death; they were determined to try.

To whom else could our parents, children not of the shtetl but of the public school, turn, except to the physicians and the nurses, the psychologists and the teachers—the experts—of America? "What's this?" Jennie Grossman's mother might well have asked. "The fact that I raised seven children in a two-room hut with dirt floors and no running water in Poland—and then in an unheated three-room apartment, up five flights of stairs in America—that doesn't make me an expert?" To which Jennie (and many others) apparently responded, albeit unconsciously, with the memory of the babies who had not grown up and the mothers who had either died or been worn out by the process.

To this second generation of immigrants, bearing and rearing children seemed a treacherous business. They did not want to bury their children and hoped that if they followed the advice of the experts they would not have to. As it happens, they turned out to be right—no matter what we may now think about the wisdom of scheduling, bottle feeding, anesthetized births, and cod-liver oil.

7

YIDDISHKEIT:
THE KEY
TO SUCCESS
IN AMERICA

THE ROAD OUT of poverty into affluence was, as many commentators have noted, particularly short for a large number of Eastern European Jewish immigrants, and traversed in just the time that it took one generation—our parents'—to mature: people who had spent their youth in cold-water flats reared their own children in ranch houses; others who had been forced to leave school so as to earn a living sent their own children to college without benefit of scholarship aid. Even those who, by their own standards, were failures lived longer and more comfortable lives than their own parents could have dreamed possible.

Their success can be attributed—as no one knows better than they— to their own labor. No welfare system, no workmen's compensation, no medical insurance benefits eased their way. Two wars and a depression created additional obstacles. Few were able to inherit worldly goods from their parents. They "made it" on their own. Many observers, in their day and our own, have tried to figure out how.

Their passionate belief in the value of education was no doubt an important factor; and so, too, possibly, was their rapid acceptance of birth control. But there was also *Yiddishkeit*—and although it may be hard to define, it cannot be discounted.

Yiddishkeit is the unique blend of cultural traits that makes the Jews of Eastern Europe (and many of their descendants) different both from their Christian neighbors and from their fellow Jews in other parts of the world. It derives not so much from *halakha*—the set of rules and regulations that govern the lives of pious Jews and have their foundations in the Torah (particularly Deuteronomy) and the Talmud—as from the special historical experience of the Jews of Eastern Europe.

Entrepreneurship in Eastern Europe

For many centuries in Eastern Europe, the Jews had been neither serfs nor aristocrats. At various times in the Middle Ages, the various Christian rulers of the area had refused to allow the Jews to own land, thus denying them access to what was at that time the most immediate source not only of wealth but also of political power. Lacking land to trade for protection, the Jews of Eastern Europe were entirely exempt from the two hereditary conditions that defined virtually everyone else living there at that time. The Jews thus lived on the fringes of a feudal society without ever quite becoming part of it—a marginal existence that eventually would benefit their descendants who became Americans.

In odd but understandable ways, Eastern European Jewish culture—*Yiddishkeit*—developed into the opposite of the culture defining Eastern European Christians. Unable either to own or to till the soil, the Jews of the medieval East earned their livings, however meager or resplendent, in other ways—in the vacuums, the social spaces that neither Christian serfs nor aristocrats, for their own various reasons, could occupy: as peddlers and glaziers, as goldsmiths and tailors, as merchants, moneylenders, and masons.

Serfs were bound to their land; they could not move from place to place. By way of contrast, the Jews could—and did—move about the countryside in relative freedom, searching out economic opportunities: traveling from town to town; buying and selling goose feathers, let's

211

say, when pillows were in great demand; switching to horses or cheeses when the bottom fell out of the pillow market. Jewish traders became skilled, over the centuries, in assessing and satisfying local demands. In addition, all that traveling made habits of hospitality and mutual assistance a cultural necessity (as we have seen in chapter 2).

Gossip was (and still is) also a key ingredient in *Yiddishkeit*. Today we might call it "networking"—the habit of chattering on about the price Moishe paid for the cow he bought from Itzhik, or discussing at length the tactics that might induce Count Esterhazy to reduce his fee for the use of the mill seat just outside of town. Skill in gossip was precisely the skill that enabled the Jews accurately to gauge the needs of the marketplace.

As they were not confined by the hereditary caste systems of Europe, the Jews had long practice in encouraging every boy to "do better" than his father, every girl to "make a match" better than her mother's—in contrast to the Christian peasants who, of necessity, rewarded those children who learned precisely how to follow in their parents' footsteps. Indeed, being neither serfs nor aristocrats, the Jews were not governed by most of the legal system of Eastern Europe (which was largely concerned with the privileges of one caste and the obligations of the other). Many local officials had, over the centuries, permitted Jewish communities the legal autonomy to develop systems of entrepreneurship: the ability to take risks and to innovate and to do both those things in the context of a money economy.

This culture, *Yiddishkeit*, was pervasive, as cultures must be: it governed styles of child rearing, mundane rituals, patterns of daily discourse. Since it was pervasive, it was not easily discarded. Even when the liberal czars of the early nineteenth century rescinded the rules that forbade Jewish ownership of land, the Jews did not give up the habits of centuries, did not immediately buy or rent land and try to farm it; indeed, even toward the end of the century, only 3 percent of the five million Jews then living in Poland and Russia held farm-related jobs.[1] Neither did the Jews shed *Yiddishkeit* when they emigrated. It was part of the baggage they carried with them to America—and there stood them in good stead. Indeed, even some of those Jews who jettisoned much of *halakha*, who ceased keeping kosher or observing the Sabbath, held tight to *Yiddishkeit*, understanding (perhaps unconsciously) that it was part of the key to success in their new home.

From Worker to Owner: One Path to Success

At the turn of the twentieth century, the United States was entering the second phase of its industrialization; it had traveled much farther down the road of modernization than had the countries of Eastern Europe. The frontier had closed; land was no longer cheap; and profitable farming required a capital investment—in plows and harvesters, reapers and milking machines. Few of those who had been farmers in the Old World could afford to become farmers in the New; most former peasants, long accustomed to hard physical labor, became factory workers or miners or laundresses—or the hardworking wives of poor factory workers and miners.

But those, both male and female, who had developed entrepreneurial skills in the Old World were perfectly placed, even if they arrived poor, to profit from the American economy. The people who had sold dry goods from a stall in a village square in Poland could (and did) easily learn to sell them from a pushcart in Manhattan or an apartment in Chicago. Such a business could be started with only a minimal investment—a few bolts of cloth, two dozen pots and pans, perhaps nothing more than some second-hand clothes. Both Jewish men and Jewish women had earned a living in this fashion in Eastern Europe and continued to do so in America. Those who had been craftsmen in Eastern Europe (usually males) could work for someone else in America (often a *lanzman*, a person who had come from the same Old World community) while accumulating enough capital to set out on their own. Those who arrived as teenagers, unskilled, could begin as factory workers, learn a trade, and then progress perhaps to foreman, and from foreman to partner—or could marry a foreman on his way to becoming a partner.

In cities all over the country, in Lowell and Trenton, in Pittsburgh and Durham, in Chicago and New York, immigrant Jews who had started out as factory workers or peddlers, carpenter's assistants or sewing machine operators ended up, a few years later, with retail or wholesale businesses: selling sandwiches and soft drinks, hardware and stockings, upholstered furniture or paper cartons: trading in their own names—as their ancestors had done—rather than laboring for others.

213

"The transition period from the junk peddler to the iron yard owner, from the dry goods peddler to the retail or wholesale dry goods merchant, from the cloak worker to manufacturer," a contemporary observer noted, "is comparatively short."[2]

Jewish immigrant progression "from cloak worker to manufacturer" epitomizes this process. Between 1899 and 1910, roughly 145,000 Jewish tailors entered this country; if the statistics are to be believed, more Jewish tailors emigrated from Eastern Europe than any other occupational group.[3] Those tailors first found employment in the burgeoning clothing factories of the largest American cities—New York, Chicago, Philadelphia, Boston. The ready-made clothing industry was, at the turn of the century, entering a boom period, taking advantage simultaneously of what had been accomplished in an earlier phase of industrialization (the mass production of cotton and woolen cloth) and the still unrealized potential of the current phase (more non-farm workers with more disposable income, ready and able to spend it on factory-made, rather than home-made, clothing). Jobs were so numerous that even those who had never learned tailoring in the old country but did in the new could find employment. Rose Janofsky's mother was one such "Columbus tailor." Her husband died in the flu epidemic of 1918, leaving her with three children to support. "My mother had no training," Mrs. Janofsky recalls. "She was absolutely stricken." In her first attempt to cope, she put her children in an orphan asylum, but the next day

she came back for us and took us home. She decided that she would have to work and tried to support us as best she could. And she learned how to sew on a sewing machine. At that point there were opportunities for women like her, to do what they called piecework. You took home whatever. She took home a batch of stuff, sewed it at home, and then brought it back, and they paid you. You brought a bundle of these cut things home, and all you had to do was learn to put them together, all ready in big bundles. You were paid for as many as you brought back. She managed to do that for a while, and then we were sent to a day nursery.

I guess she must have worked in that front room that had a window out to the street. I don't know how many hours a day she devoted to this. I am not sure how she got the money for the machine—I never

214

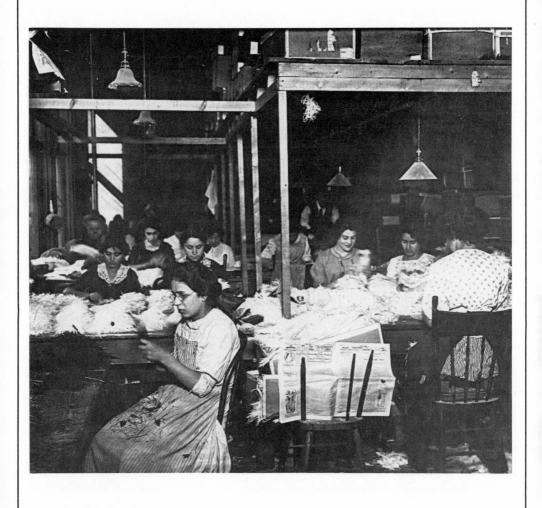

"That factory happened to be considered a nice factory.
Nice—electric light. . . . and people sit in a line and work."
Factory work, preparing decorative feathers, early twentieth century.

questioned it. There was a foot pedal. She may have bought it on the installment plan, she may have been given it by the contractor, or they may have loaned it to her, in which case she had to return it. I seem somehow to remember we always had a machine, although my mother was not a good seamstress.

Newly trained tailors and seamstresses, like Rose Janofsky's mother, were precisely the people who gave more skilled clothing workers the chance to become entrepreneurs:

My first shop was on Hester St. [New York City]. Eighteen men and women were crowded into a small dark room: operators, pressers and finishers. During the season there was no time limit. We started working at dawn and stopped at ten or eleven at night. If a worker happened to be an hour late he was met by the others with ridicule, "Here comes the doctor!" In their conception only a doctor could permit himself the luxury of sleeping so late.

The operators (machine workers) were the best paid. They usually took on learners, young people who had just landed, as their apprentices. The apprentices did not receive any pay for the first six weeks. After that they were promoted *by the operators* to $5.00 per week. In this way one worker profited from the labor of another.[4] [Italics added]

As time went on, many Jews who had started out as workers learned how to profit from the labor of others. An in-house subcontractor could become a "sweating" subcontractor by purchasing one or two sewing machines and setting them up in his own apartment, turning his wife, his children, the boarders, maybe a cousin or two into his employees. If this proved profitable, a "sweater" could, by renting floor space—however minimal—become a manufacturer in his own right. Again, only small capital investments were required—some flat irons, some shears, some thread, some cloth—plus a great deal of hard work, fourteen or fifteen hours a day, six days a week—and a gift for entrepreneurship:

One reason why piece work and high speed have become the frame work of the contractor's shop is probably because the Jewish

216

people are peculiarly eager to earn a big day's wages, no matter at what sacrifice. The Jewish workman is willing to work very hard for this and does not want to have it said that there is a limit to his earning capacity. . . . Usually he is anxious to accumulate money and open up a contractor's shop for himself or go into some kind of business. . . . The Jewish immigrant is peculiar [compared with other immigrant nationalities] only in that he is not by nature a wage earner.[5]

Many immigrant Jews—"not by nature" wage earners, but preferring to be self-employed—went through the transition from worker to subcontractor to manufacturer during the first decades of this century—not only in the ready-made clothing business but in other businesses as well. One of these was Irving Farber, who decided not to pursue religious studies and immigrated, alone, in 1912 at the age of sixteen. Farber had a brother and an uncle who had immigrated earlier:

My uncle asked me: "What do you want to be? Do you want to work in a factory, making luggage?" I said, "I don't like it. It is dirty work." Metal work, you see; the factory was dirty and I don't like it. He said, "Well listen! You learn. Take it. It would be easy for you. I got a little business. It won't take you a long time and you'll get used to it."

I didn't like it. I don't know why I didn't like it. Finally after four weeks, I got settled; I got settled with my aunt. I looked for work, and I found work in a cigarette factory making cigarettes. I walked in and I see women there making cigarettes with the machines. And I become a cutter. They showed me and they told me.

But I didn't like it. I couldn't see my friends. Saturday and Sunday were the only times we used to call each other, I wanted to go out and see, I wanted to see everything. So I worked there at the cigarette place, until I was earning maybe twelve-fifty. I had my own machine there.

Then I met a lanzman *who knew my father already. They used to be neighbors, his father was in the* shul *with my father. He said to me, "That's not for you, twelve dollars a week." I said, "So what can I do?" He said, "So listen! You come with me."*

The *lanzman* took Irving Farber to a hardware store owned by a friend; and for two years, Farber worked there, learning English—as well as a few other things (amply described in the previous chapter). He was earning fifty to sixty dollars a week ("Now that was *money!*") although he had to work on the Sabbath (which did not bother him much); but after a time, even "good money" was not enough. The inbred habits of *Yiddishkeit* spurred Farber to seek something else:

After I was working there two years, I went out to a certain place to meet some people and make my proposition to go into dresses— dresses, I could make dresses. I made my proposition, and they said all right, I should come up and look around the place. I went up and looked around the place. It was beautiful, nice young girls, quiet, six- fifty a day, everybody spoke English. I looked around and said, "Oy! I like it, I like it!" It was like somebody says, "Do it! Do it!"

I had luck. From that time, the minute I stepped into that factory, I must have stepped in with my right foot. The next day I come in there, and they showed me what to do, and I watched. And I do, I do. Well, actually I worked four weeks there at twenty-five dollars a week.

So after four weeks working there, the chairman [probably a work- ing partner in the business] comes over and says, "The boss says that kid works. He knows his business. Why don't you give him piece- work? And if you don't want to give him piecework, give him good wages." So the foreman decided to give me piecework. I worked one week. I made the first week fifty-four dollars. The foreman didn't like that because before I made the same thing for twenty-five dollars. So he goes over to the chairman and says, "I can't afford to do it," and he gives me then a raise to thirty-two-fifty.

I didn't fight for the money at that time because you got to work at least a year, two, in the shop. You get ideas, for four seasons a year, different materials, different handlings, different styles. You got to learn. It is complicated.

I learned. I liked it. They made me foreman. Later I went into busi- ness with partners. It was a good living.

Harry Gitlitz, who was born in Cleveland in 1905, also progressed from worker to owner, even though his original employer was his fa- ther. The Gitlitzs were cattle traders, one of the businesses that Jews had dominated in Eastern Europe. Harry Gitlitz's account of his career is permeated with *Yiddishkeit*, wheeling a bit here, dealing a bit there, *hondling* (bargaining) all the time:

When I finished my junior year in high school I went to work for my father, driving a truck, gradually learning the business. Buy beef cattle, calves, dairy cows. Every week there were shippers from all over who shipped cattle. There were buyers down there [in Kentucky] who bought the cattle. They shipped by train, and we would load everything on Mondays. If we had an extra truck load, we would drive down. Tuesday morning the train would roll in, and we would unload the train.

We had a man that would clean off the dairy cows, milk them out, brush them, wash their tails, and that man is still alive now. We gave him ten cents for every cow that he washed and cleaned off. Make them look as clean and nice as they can look—just like a show, you see. Brush the cow off with a real good brush, a curry comb to get all of the manure off so the cow would look as clean as possible.

Going to the stockyards and selling cows week in and week out was quite a job. Because one week we might bring in a bunch of cows and there would be good buyers, and they would buy the cows quick and fast and give us a good price. When we came home, what would we do? Head for the country—went out and buy cows and pay good prices for them. The next week it would be just the reverse. They didn't show up or they weren't in the mood to buy cows. Anyway, lots of times what we made the week before we lost this week. Or maybe the next week would come in, and there would be a job to get our money back. If in a series of six weeks we broke even, we did well. That's the way it was in the market. This was in the years, the Depression years. There is no question that you had to wiggle and waggle as much as you can.

I can remember one day sitting on a bale of hay down in the stockyards. My father sold a cow for $75 to a man, and then half an hour later another man came along and my father sold that same cow to this other man for $100. It made me mad. I said to my father, "Couldn't you get that $100 from the first man? Made the $25 yourself? You need that $25." My father said, "Don't you worry about that. I made that first man $25 and he didn't have to touch the cow; he made money off me. He is going to come back next week and buy more cows." And

219

that is the way it turned out. A satisfied customer comes back and you can't get away from that fact.

Up until 1937 we had a barn and we would bring dairy cows in there and I would milk them. Of course, we didn't sell milk in those days; we weren't set up for that. We milked the cows only to keep them until we shipped them to market. But we had friends, a fellow by the name of Sam Miller. He couldn't make a living in those days, but he used to come up and help us do chores and he would take home the pails of milk. And he half lived on those pails of milk because he made butter and cottage cheese and sour milk and so on; they lived on that. We never sold any of it; we would give it away if somebody wanted it. Give it away, that's all.

My father used to say, when we had a bad market, "So you wiped your mouth; forget them. Go out and look for others." We would get up the next week and buy accordingly. That was a favorite expression of his and he was one thousand percent right; that's the way business was done. You buy according to market and you sell according to market. Tomorrow is another day and you go out and buy accordingly. Nobody is smart all the time. Things turn. The smartest business men in the world have had things back up on them. You look at The Wall Street Journal and you see how many smart guys are kicked out because they want somebody else.

In 1937, Harry Gitlitz took over his father's business and bought a farm on which to house the cattle he was buying and selling:

We really didn't start making money until we bought the farm here. We bought the farm in 1937 for fifteen thousand dollars. We got a loan. I don't know if we put a dime down. During the war we made good money for the simple reason beef was very scarce. They had the OPA [Office of Price Administration]. Couldn't get much beef at all, the stores couldn't get much beef. I took a few days one time and went around to local area grocery stores and meat markets. Made a proposition to them that I would furnish them with beef. Started ordering cows, beef cows from Chicago, these were not steers, they were just beef cows. We bring these beef cows in. We had a fella, he had a little slaughterhouse up in the woods. These beef cows would come in, these cows were marked for some store. We would charge them the live-

weight price for these cattle. The OPA could not do anything to us because we were not selling dressed weight. And these butchers would have to come and get the cattle at the slaughterhouse. See, this was the way we maneuvered it so we were not doing anything wrong. If we sold them live weight, the OPA could not do anything to us. If we sold them dressed weight, that would be a horse of a different color. So we made money that way. Well, you could call that black market to a certain extent, but we didn't do anything in the real black market.

Forty years later, elderly and quite wealthy, Harry Gitlitz still arises before dawn and gets on the road, buying and selling dairy cows. He remains enthusiastic about his work:

You sure you don't want to stay over and go to the auction with me tomorrow? This auction is under a tent with seats and everything and high-class cattle, and you will hear a real good auctioneer and I don't mean maybe, and you'll get a thrill of a lifetime out of it.

Only a few of the Jewish immigrants who started out as employees, like Irving Farber and Harry Gitlitz, ended their careers in the same position. The small businesses the immigrants created required a great deal of hard work—ten-hour days, seven days a week, no Sabbath; and, not infrequently, that work was shared by husbands and wives, for Jewish women shared equally in the entrepreneurial culture of *Yiddishkeit*. Morris Hochstadt immigrated when he was thirteen. His father had been a carpenter in Poland; with his wife's help, he climbed the ladder from worker to owner in the upholstery business:

My father had a lanzman who had a furniture factory and asked him to take in two boys and teach them a trade. And so we did. We were learners. You shlepped: you go out and bring lunch for the boys; you sweep up the place, all kinds of manual work, before we knew how to become a mechanic. In seven years we made it.

Upholstered furniture we made. Somebody else made the frames; we upholstered. After a while, they [the company] became very big and started to make their own frames up on the fifth floor, and they came down to the third floor to be upholstered. My job was to do the upholstery on the furniture. It was sold to the major department stores.

We were working in this place for quite a while, and we wanted to organize into a union. So we pulled a strike. We were on strike for eighteen weeks. I was single then. We finally lost the strike and came back with our tail behind our legs. Then we worked for about a year and pulled another strike. One morning we come to the shop; we were on picket duty. The whole company had moved out—lock, stock, and barrel. Overnight! We didn't know what happened to it. My father's lanzman, he took a few mechanics with him who he could trust, and we didn't know where they went to. Finally we found out that he went upstate. The town gave him a plant and told him he could have ten years free rent, providing you employ local help.

I said, "No more! It's time to go into business for yourself." By then I was married; I even had a kid. I opened a decorating shop and was in it for twenty-six years. My brother kept working for other people. It was a gift shop—draperies, and all that, and everything that belongs in the home. They called up, and we come up to the house with samples and show them and give them an estimate and send a truck and take it down. I had people working for me who did it [the piece of furniture] over—two people, plus myself, and a [sewing machine] operator.

Right away we started to get busy. I didn't have to travel to work. I was my own boss. If I wanted to work, I worked. I was open on Saturdays. Saturday was the busiest day because husband and wife [came] together.

Of course, my wife brought up [our] children [there], pushing the carriage in the store and talking to a customer at the same time. She helped me; we worked together. She was good because she had more patience. Sample book after sample book after sample book. We used to stay open until eleven o'clock at night, every night. I spent my youth in that store. Did nothing but hang around the store. I had to be open. My competitor was open. I couldn't go out on a Saturday night. I couldn't go out. I was stuck. We brought up our kids in the store.

Many of the people we interviewed can remember such difficult working conditions in the early days, but only a few allow themselves also to remember the difficult personal relations entrepreneurship could create when husbands and wives, brothers and sisters, cousins and *lanzmen* found themselves working long hours in close proximity.

Hannah Toperoff, for example, remembers how her father's dry goods store tainted the relationship between herself and her brothers:

I always worked in my father's store: I did everything that had to be done. My father had to make a living and we all had to work at it. My father and mother opened the store in the morning and I would work in the store when I came home from school, particularly if it was busy. Often we worked until eight at night; that was the way it was. That's what makes me mad about people who get through at five o'clock and think they are doing a big deal. He never closed the store for a vacation; it was open fifty-two weeks a year. It is a gruelling schedule but it was not an uncommon schedule for people of that era.

My brothers worked in the store under duress. I forced them to work there. My father did, too. My father gave vent when they finally came into the store, but I gave vent at home to make them go to the store. I got them out of bed so that they would report, then he would yell at them once they got there. That's the way it was. I have vivid memories of coming into the store at eight o'clock in the morning, maybe it was during summer vacation, and my father had already been open for an hour and he was mad at me because my brothers weren't with me.

In factories, personal relationships became strained when family members found themselves on opposite sides of a worker-management dispute. In the early decades of the century, many of the shops in which immigrants worked were becoming unionized; Jewish immigrants were, many of them, avid union members, often union leaders. Yet many were also becoming foremen, partners, and owners—management. Many historians have commented on the unique character of the old Jewish left: composed of two parts unionism, one part Zionism, and a hefty dose of *Yiddishkeit*. Few have noted—as is implicit, for example, in Tess Egrovsky's account—that ambivalence must also have been part of the brew. As operators and pressers became subcontractors and then owners, union members found themselves sometimes married to some of the "bad men" who had once been foremen, or discovered that they were going out on strike against the "evil capitalists" who were also their fathers, brothers, and cousins. Tess Egrovsky immigrated when she was sixteen, sent out of the Ukraine by her

223

mother, who feared that she might be raped or murdered during a po-grom. She went directly to an aunt's home in Philadelphia, and one of her cousins helped her find a job in a factory:

Not long after I arrived, I went to work in a shop. I didn't know how to sew, but it didn't take long to learn. A waist shop, it was—blouses; we used to call it "waists." I used to sew the sides of the waists, the seams. I didn't know anything. I didn't know anything at all. You just came to the factory, and they showed you, and it was just seams to make. On a machine.

Maybe a hundred worked there—young girls, young men. I started at eight o'clock, and a half-hour dinner, and you worked till six o'clock. You couldn't stop during the day. You could go to the bathroom. That factory happened to be considered a nice factory. Nice—electric light. The machines were at a long table, and people sit in a line and work.

I worked in this shop six months, and then I left. I had an argument with the foreman. Over a little nothing. I made a handkerchief with lace, and you were not allowed to use their merchandise. I made a little handkerchief, maybe six inches. A scrap I picked up off the floor! The lace was scrap! And then he said I am not allowed to have it. And I couldn't work there any more. And he fired me! The son of a bitch! His name was Shulman. The son of a bitch! Otherwise, he couldn't be a foreman; he had to be a bad man. It's a fact: the foreman had to be bad.

They were like slave chasers, you know what I mean? They were no good. They watch how you work, or if you did something wrong or anything. He had authority to do what he wanted. I still remember what he looked liked—tall with glasses, wavy hair. I still remember him. It was my first impression of a bad man. I never liked that man.

We all worked piece goods. Let's say, a dozen bands and a dozen were so much and so much. I used to make, in the beginning, in fact the first week, I made seven dollars. Yeah, and that's why I think he was after me. Because I was a foreigner [a greenhorn] and I made, right away, money. Three dollars, four dollars, at that time was considered good for a foreigner. I made seven dollars the first week, and that was a fortune. And he resented it. "Look a greener, a foreigner, and she already is making money." Well, I happened to be a very fast worker, very fast worker.

And then my brother find it out, and he decided I had to come to him. He had four or five machines; he was like a contractor in a factory, and he took me right there. And I went by train to him, and then I went to live with a cousin.

My brother was a contractor in the shop. He had three or four machines. When I came the first day—I'll never forget—he took a bundle of fabric, and he gave me lace, and he said to me, "Here is a blouse, look at it, and that's the way you have to make it." And I made it. And my brother started me with nine dollars a week.

I met my husband in that shop. He was a real union man, very active. In fact, when the first strike came up with the union [this was about 1921], my husband was one of the leaders. And I worked that time for my brother, and I even went on strike against my brother. Everybody went on strike. In fact, my brother told me to get out of the shop anyway, because everybody went. I was out ten weeks.

That time, when the strike was called, my husband worked for his father. And he striked against his father for ten weeks. We all strike. It was a very long strike.

Some immigrant youths succeeded in turning small ventures into large ones because they were clever manipulators—like their ancestors in Eastern Europe—of the banking system. Aaron Katz, for example, was the first child born to his parents after they immigrated in 1903. His father, a weaver in Lithuania, had succeeded in establishing a small, but fragile business in Philadelphia as a specialized weaver of silk cloth. Katz went into business with his father but, in the early years of the Depression, had both the courage to transfer his base of operations to the South, the foresight to stop weaving and start selling machinery, and the wit to convince some bankers to take a risk on a stranger:

My father had a little silk mill, where he was a commissioned weaver. I went to work for him. Every week was a tragedy because on Monday we would need the money for the payroll on Thursday. On Tuesday he would go to New York to get the money for the payroll. On Wednesday he would call and tell me how bad the goods were: we

225

were asking four cents a yard, and they wanted to cut to three cents a yard because the goods were bad. They were giving us a hard time. We would cut the price and get the money in time for the payroll. It was a very hairy existence. So we started to buy and sell second-hand weaving machinery. In 1931, things were very bad in Philadelphia, and I went down to the South to see what the prospects were. I decided the prospects weren't very good. In the South they wanted to know, "Where you from, boy?" They thought Jews had horns. Catholics had horns, too, but Jews had longer horns. I went back and continued to sell machinery in the North and Northeast, traveling all over.

But then in 1934 I got married. The truth of the matter is that the soup was getting very thin; there was no bone in the soup. So my pregnant wife and I drove to the South because the rayon industry had overtaken the cotton-weaving industry, and we figured that maybe there is a place in the South, either in Greensboro or Spartanville, Greenville or Atlanta. So we drove south.

So I started buying, looking, going from one mill to another, and every place I went I got the same run around. "Who are you? What do you want?" It was during the Depression. Every superintendent, every manager who was fired became a second-hand dealer. They were all members of the same religious and other groups. They were all Christians.

The good Lord was kind to me. The strangest thing happened. I was in Victory, North Carolina, and I see a sign for a hosiery mill, and I go in and, instead of a runaround, they say, "Come in and sit down. What've you got?" And I said, "What do you need?" And they said, "We need so and so and so and so and so." I put that in my little black book, and that night I went to another hosiery mill, and they said the same thing, and I discovered that in hosiery there was a vacuum.

The hosiery industry had moved from Pennsylvania and New England in the 1920s. Then the cotton farmers, the merchants, and the professional people [in the South] suddenly found that they could make hosiery because the yarn was right next door, didn't have to move it up to New England and send it back again. By the 1930s, they were starting to need new machinery. I found myself in an orchard with lots of apples, and I was the only one picking them.

Like many fledgling businessmen, Katz also had the good fortune to have not just a courageous wife, but one who was also possessed of entrepreneurial instincts. When they set out for the South, she was pregnant with their first child:

I didn't have any money. I was down to two thousand dollars, which was rapidly being eaten up. What I didn't know was that my wife had her own little knipl [purse]. She had been making forty-five dollars as a secretary, and every week she saved five dollars. Instead of taking a streetcar or a bus, she walked. She had saved up one thousand dollars. And that one thousand dollars was the difference between me giving up and me going back and continuing.

And then another wonderful thing happened. When I first came down, I went to the bank and borrowed five hundred dollars on my name alone. I didn't use the money. After ninety days, I paid it back and borrowed seven hundred fifty dollars. In the course of a year and a half, I got it up to around fifteen hundred dollars. I never used it because I was waiting for a long-term opportunity to buy surplus equipment from a large mill. And then I heard that there was one for sale in Wisconsin. I don't remember how I heard; I had various sources of information. I took the train and went up there, and there were seven hundred machines, which I could buy for five thousand dollars. They had taken off the cream, but the skim milk was still left.

So I took the train to New York and went to my wife's rich relatives and asked them for five thousand dollars. "If you can lend me five thousand dollars," I said, "I will give you half the profits." The answer: "Well, I'll tell you, right now I am a little tied up for ready cash. Come back in sixty days and I'll see." He was worth maybe eight million dollars at the time; they were in real estate and wallpaper.

Anyway, I come back home and go to the bank and see the president and asked him if he knew anybody who wanted to put up some money in venture capital. I give him the details. And he said, "You don't need any partner. Just sign this note." I almost cried. It was for six percent. I signed it and made twenty-eight thousand dollars on it. That was the first step in my progress as a trader.

Now and since then I am the fair-haired boy among my relatives. That was in 1938. There was a vacuum. I tried to fill it. I kept it filled.

For many years, my wife was my sole employee—stenographer, with a little office in the building. When she was pregnant, she would sit in the office with her shoes off, because her feet swelled. Normally I would be out Monday, Tuesday, Wednesday, Thursday. Come home Friday, stay Saturday, and go back out Monday. I did it all year long. The kids used to wonder who was that man with Mommy.

After a while I learned that in South America—this was after the war—the business, hosiery, was in the hands of Jews and Arabs. So I started to take two trips to South America a year. I learned to speak Spanish, but I also talked to them in mama-loshen [Yiddish; literally, mother tongue].

I brought the company public in the 1960s, because one of my good Christian friends made a remark that stuck in my mind: "There is a time in life when a person should have some sleeping money." Going public gave us some sleeping money. We sold some six hundred thousand shares for around seven million dollars and kept the other twelve million shares. We, my sons and I, owned that twelve million shares. We made a lot of money. That is our sleeping money.

Other immigrant youths succeeded in keeping small ventures afloat because they were clever manipulators—also like their ancestors in Eastern Europe—of the legal system. Irving Farber, for example, was a risk taker par excellence in many facets of his life, including (but not limited to) his business:

I gambled on everything. I went into horses, football, baseball, even gambled in the dress business. The dress business, the business I was in, by 1940 I was a manufacturer. During World War II, I made more money than I could think of in the black market. Lost it all gambling. Piece goods! If you were in the business, you could get the cloth. It was sold to me and I resold it. All cash. I used to carry around fifty thousand dollars in my automobile trunk every day, every single day. I had no government contracts because I was in women's dresses. I would buy a piece for twenty-nine cents and sold it for a dollar. Cotton. A million yards at a time, a million yards at a time. There were other guys in with me at the time. Naturally I had to have others, you couldn't do it alone.

228

In addition to selling cloth on the black market during the Second World War, Farber recounted, unblinkingly, that he used to bribe (*shmir*) buyers for department stores ("one time we gave out fifty thousand dollars at Christmas to all the buyers") as well as pay off the mob (first the Jewish mob, later the Italian mob) in order to sustain a contract with his truckers. He also asserted that certain kinds of "theft" were standard business practice:

I'll tell you something. One Saturday I came down. Snow, hail, wet, rain. I could have got pneumonia, gray. I am looking for fellas to make a game, card game, crap game, anything just to get some action. I am walking up Fifth Avenue and I see a dress in the window. I buy the dress and bring it in Monday morning and with a note on it, "Have the kid [a dress designer] work on this dress. I want him to copy it." So I come back about eleven, and I hear that my partner doesn't like that dress; it has a fish tail in the back. I leave again and come back and I keep missing him. I told the kid to keep working on it. Then a buyer walks in with a guy from Miami. I tell him, "I got a hot dress," and ask the kid to bring it out on a mannequin. She brings it out, and they order five hundred dresses. Five hundred pieces! Another buyer walks in and asks, "What's doing here?" And she sees the dress, and I show the dress. "How soon can it be delivered? Can you make it in navy or black?" And she orders two hundred units!

We delivered, we shipped one hundred thousand dresses at ten seventy-five. A million dollars' worth of business I did on one dress I bought for twenty-six dollars.

Entrepreneurial skills can be used in many ways. Some members of the immigrant generation took risks not in their primary businesses but in pursuit of profits from real estate. With the money they had saved from their salaries, they bought perhaps a multiple dwelling that had an apartment for themselves, then another—perhaps with a store underneath; then yet another, all the while continuing to work as painters or carpenters or managers of hardware stores. Other people, committed to the labor movement, used their skills as organizers and leaders, serving as presidents and secretaries, all the while continuing to work as, let us say, pressers or cutters. George Mandelbaum, for example, was committed not only to the labor movement but also to the Communist

229

party; his account of organizing for the party is filled with *Yiddishkeit*: he loved traveling around to organize in the same way that Harry Git-litz and Aaron Katz loved traveling around to sell their wares. Mandel-baum was born in Pinsk in 1908 but emigrated to Chicago with his parents when he was small. He joined the party, he says, in 1923, when he was fifteen years old, then quit high school in his junior year and went to work in a factory. A few years later, he was sent as a party organizer to the coal fields of Pennsylvania, trying to infiltrate the United Mine Workers, so as—eventually—to remove the union's head, John L. Lewis. "I was in seventh heaven," Mandelbaum said, recalling those days. "I was organizing. I just loved the life. I was walk-ing up and down the highways, from coal camp to coal camp, and meeting people. Sometimes we went by car, sometimes we hitchhiked. Marvelous people. I stayed with coal miners, wives, families, kids— very great, great people."

And as Mandelbaum enjoyed organizing, other Jewish immigrants enjoyed participating in what may be the greatest entrepreneurial ven-ture of them all—the creation of the State of Israel. Sol Meyrowitz, for example, spent most of his life (after finally conquering tuberculosis) as a tie salesman—but the great drama, the memorable risk, of his working life is connected to guns, not ties:

My father had a lanzman *in ties, and he asked him to take me in. I started to work there, and my first job was with the broom, and little by little I started to learn the trade, and that is what I wanted to do. I said to myself, "This is where I remain. There is nothing else I can do, I have to learn a trade." So little by little they let me work at the table, and first I became a spreader [who folds and smooths fabric prior to cutting], and after a couple of years they gave me a break and let me cut. Little by little I work myself up. I became a salesman. And when I was a salesman, I kept on getting raises, and times were changing. I remember when I was married I was earning thirty-seven dollars a week, but, believe me, it didn't come so easy for me.*

After the war [the Second World War], the word got out, I let it get out, that I was collecting. The boys that came home from the war, they brought a lot of souvenirs. From mouth to mouth came word that I am collecting. We had an organization that was collecting and shipping. You know, there was a linoleum and tile place, and that is where we

230

used to bring it down. We used to bring the guns and ship it from there, with tiles on the top and the arms inside, and mark it "TILES" and ship it to Haifa.

One time a detective passes by, the owner knew him, and here we are pushing it straight up the platform. At that time they didn't have those automatic lifts, and we were pushing that case onto the truck. And the detective passes by and he says, "Such a heavy case! What are you shipping? Ammunition to Palestine?"

At first Meyrowitz was somewhat daunted by the risks he was taking, but his commitment to the Zionist cause (and practice) eventually quelled his fears:

I used to get calls and my wife would take down the names and addresses where I should go to pick up. I remember the first time I went to pick up a German Luger—you know, I was shaking I was so scared. I saw a policeman a block away. I turned around and went the other way, he shouldn't notice me. That is how scared I was. But, you know, I said to myself, "How do crooks become crooks? Robbers. It doesn't mean anything to them." After a while I used to carry a rifle wrapped around in a burlap bag—the Japanese rifles were short rifles—and I used to walk in the street, and the police didn't even turn around to look at me. Machineguns I had. I had everything.

We had about eight people working. I used to advertise that I was looking for guns, by word of mouth, and every day people used to come to my place and leave it with me. Ammunition. I had a desk with a double drawer, and I used to put the ammunition in the bottom drawer. I would put just the pistols in there. One day my boss was looking for something, and he opens the bottom drawer and he sees all that. "What is this?" I said, "I am collecting things." And I told him, "We are sending this to Israel." He was a Zionist and a Jew, and after a while he used to send me people to collect from. He said, "Do you know what could happen?" And I said, "Don't worry. Tonight that drawer will be emptied out."

I used to bring it home and put it into my closet. And one day my little boychickl [his son], one day he opens up the closet and pulls some pistols out of there. Oy ve! I told him, "This is going to Israel. This is for the Jewish people to defend themselves. Don't ever mention a word

231

to anybody. To none of your friends, to nobody. You never saw any-thing in there." He kept his word.

These immigrant Jews who helped to create successful ventures—whether the goal was guns for Israel or profits for the bank account—were not highly educated; many had not even completed high school. Sol Meyrowitz went to work when he was sixteen; Aaron Katz and Morris Hochstadt, when they were fifteen; Irving Farber never at-tended a secular school at all. They had no formal training in manage-ment or in cost-benefit analysis or accounting, or, for that matter, in covert operations. What they learned they had learned on the job and, most crucially, at their mother's and father's knees. In each of these cases, and thousands of others, one or several aspects of the culture called *Yiddishkeit*—a desire to be self-employed, a willingness to take financial risks, a nose for a good deal, a special alertness to the messages of the market, a willingness to maneuver on the very fringes of what is legal, a familiarity with the world of banking—sped them along the road to success in America.

A Good Job for a Jewish Boy: The Professional Road to Success

For another group of immigrants, education became part of an entre-preneurial strategy, part (as we have seen in chapter 3) of what was needed to "get ahead in the world." The group of immigrant youth who chose this strategy (or had it chosen for them by their parents) speaks in a different voice: the Yiddish intonation is weaker or al-together absent. These are the immigrants and children of immigrants who became doctors, lawyers, accountants, and teachers rather than upholsterers, salesmen, pressers, jobbers, and manufacturers. *Yiddish-keit* was part of their lives but, as a result of education, in a different, subtler way.

Some members of this second group—Max Hirsch, for example—acquired at least some of their secondary education abroad. Almost all men, they were lucky enough to have filled some of the "Jewish

"I sold newspapers—afternoons, mornings—books. . . . I gave
my mother some money, but not all."
A very young newsboy, early twentieth century.

places" in *gymnasia* just before the outbreak of the First World War. These are an early group of educated émigrés, driven out of Eastern Europe not by Hitler but by the Ukrainian pogroms or the disruptions of the Russian Revolution or by the lack of jobs for Jews. Hirsch, for example, began medical school in Vienna in 1917 but was then drafted into the Austrian army; he emigrated as soon as he could after the war was over, and continued his medical studies in the United States. His travails in medical school are similar to those of other immigrant young men attempting to support themselves while undertaking a grueling course of study; his subsequent devotion to his profession—at whatever cost—is also similar to that of many professional people we interviewed.

MAX HIRSCH: *In Vienna, when the war was on, in 1917, I was at the University of Vienna and then, later, I matriculated as a student of medicine. I got called to the army, so I had to appear before a committee. The doctor listens to my chest and he says, "You have a heart condition." Little did he know that before I went to be examined by them I was given pills to affect my heart. There was a lady in charge of the students' home. She was the one who took me to a doctor who gave me those pills. "I don't want you to die for dear old Austria," she said.*

In 1922, I applied to medical school admission here in the United States to finish my studies. I studied during the day and worked during the night. I worked in the post office until eleven o'clock at night. At eleven P.M., I came home, studied until three o'clock or four o'clock in the morning, got up at eight o'clock, and walked to medical school. When you are young, it doesn't mean a thing. I also got a scholarship through the Joint Distribution Committee [a charitable organization intended to assist overseas Jews in need]. I was living with my uncle and making twenty dollars a week.

My parents were both dead by then. As soon as I could, I opened a practice. I finished my residency and I needed some money to start an office. These people had a business next door to a bank and I went to the bank for a loan and the bank asked for a co-signer, so I went to Mr. Blum [a man whom Hirsch had once treated without charge], and told him I was applying for a loan of five hundred dollars, and he said, "Let me have the paper," tore it to shreds, and let me have the five hundred dollars. *"When you have, you will give it back to me."*

The best thing in my life was to finish my medical school, to practice the way I did, to devote my life to my patients—my wife says my patients always came first—and to my family. My medical practice came ahead of Sarah [his wife], everything came ahead of Sarah. I am sorry to say it now—yes, I am sorry to say it now. I would do it exactly the same all over again. I wasn't a very good father because I was busy practicing medicine. I used to come down and sit at the table, with a spoon in my mouth. The telephone would ring: "Mrs. Brown is three fingers dilated." You drop everything and grab your bag and go to the hospital and deliver the baby and come home. It was very difficult, not like today: "Let the intern deliver the child." In those days we were anxious, we wanted to do the right thing. How can you pay attention to your family when you get up at three A.M. one day, then five A.M. the next, then eight A.M., and you are busy all day with *tsurris* [trouble]. You can't be a good father. Either you are a good doctor or a good father, you can't be both. Nowadays it is different—five days a week, eight hours a day, tremendous fees—but I would do it exactly the same all over again. Exactly the same.

Night calls, day calls, Yom Kippur calls, Rosh Hashonah calls. There was no such thing as a doctor not making a call. Some of the patients pay, some don't. I charged three dollars for an office visit, five dollars for home. My job, day and night, was in the office. I loved it. The work, the excitement, the tragedies, the heartbreaks. It never got routine.

I treated everybody. In 1930 or 1931, I was called at night, a woman called me up. She is a Catholic woman. "My daughter is very, very sick. She is bleeding profusely. She is having a very bad period. Please come to see her right away." So I took my car about two A.M. There is a girl about seventeen or eighteen years old; she is bleeding profusely and she has had a miscarriage. The brother of this girl is a priest. We have to save the honor of these people. So I take the mother into the kitchen and give her some instruments and tell her to boil these instruments and put in a pinch of salt every five minutes. I write a prescription and send the father out to get a prescription. The medicine doesn't exist; he is still probably looking for it today.

In the meantime I deliver the baby, about the size of my wrist. And

235

I took the fetus and put it on a towel, wrapped it up, and put it into my bag. And I went in to the mother and told her to stop boiling the instruments, everything was fine, she didn't have to boil the instruments. The bleeding stopped and everything was going to be all right.

I go into my car and I drive home. On the way home a cop stops me. "Where are you going?" "I am a physician." "Oh, I am sorry, I am sorry," and he let me go. I came home, open the towel, put the fetus into the toilet, and flushed the toilet, and that was that. The fee for that delivery was five dollars, a house call.

To this very day, I get a Christmas card every single year for the past fifty-five years from the family, because I saved the honor of the family.

When my son stopped medical school, it was painful, very painful. It was the most painful thing, that was the most painful thing in my life. I died a thousand deaths every day when I heard that he would not make medical school, that he will not follow in my steps. I was devastated.

Far more numerous than the educated émigrés were the sons and daughters of immigrants, either born here or brought here before entering school, who received all of their education in America. Many of these children came to maturity after the most stringent of the child labor laws went into effect in 1916, and after their families had passed through the first, and the worst, phases of American poverty. As a result, few began their employment careers in a factory. Although none of the men and only a few of the women were expected to leave school in order to contribute to the family finances, many boys were expected to earn something to help make ends meet. Newspapers, for example, provided a host of part-time jobs (there were many more newspapers then than now), such as those held by Charlie Moses, who later became a physician, and Max Weiner, who later became a radio announcer.

CHARLIE MOSES: *The first real job I got when I was thirteen years old I got at the local newspaper, after school. I had a job of taking the newspapers off the press. I had to take twenty-five newspapers at a time in a stack. I got to where I could walk all around the building and automatically the click, click, click of that machine going back and forth over the papers I knew when the twenty-fifth paper was there to fall out, and I was back there to pick those papers up.*

236

MAX WEINER: *After school, when I got older, I worked for a news company. I used to take care of their newsstand, a big newsstand in Union Station. I was behind the counter there. I sold newspapers— afternoons, mornings—books, the Tribune, Sun-Times, Daily News, the American. The papers sold for a penny apiece. I used to make twelve dollars a week at that time.*

I gave my mother some money, but not all. I gave them my twelve dollars. But I made a lot of tips, and the tips ran up to about twenty-five dollars a week, so I kept the tips. I gave her my salary. I got a lot of tips.

I made money on the side, maybe stole a few dollars every once in a while, I don't remember. I used to give her twelve dollars a week, and the tips I made I used to keep. Maybe I stole some money, I don't know. I wasn't taking any bets on the horses—but, look, I handled a lot of cash, and maybe I took some. Who knows?

In those days you took whatever you could get; you didn't get paid too much, so you helped yourself. I guess I am making this a confession. I worked there six evenings and Sunday mornings. I had to be at the stand at six in the mornings.

Sam Smilowitz, who subsequently became both a teacher and an attorney, earned extra spending money when he was a teenager in a classically mischievous fashion:

I'll tell you something about what we did when we were kids. At the corner of Walnut Street [in Philadelphia], there was a post office, and come a Saturday or a Sunday—I don't remember, I think it was a Sunday—all of the immigrants would go into the post office to mail letters across, and they never could use the ink because we kids put blotters into the ink and broke the pens. So we would walk into the post office, and we had a bottle of ink in one hand and a pen in the other. Two cents, three cents.

I never felt guilty about it because I always blamed my brother. On a good day we could make fifty cents. It was a lot of money—the equivalent of three fifty a week.

However much money they may have earned in this fashion, this group of immigrant youths were encouraged to stay in school and out of the factories. Many of the girls went to commercial high school or attended business school for a year after graduating from high school. They entered the labor market a "step up," as white-collar workers—secretaries, stenographers, bookkeepers, and retail clerks.

Lillian Winograd, disabled by polio, very clearly remembers the career encouragement she received from her mother:

My mother instilled the independence spirit in me. And I used to hear her, conversations without the kids being around. I can still hear her. I can hear her to this day say to my father, "Bennie, Lillian must learn a profession because we don't know if she will ever get married. And she must be able to take care of herself." And she instilled a feeling in me that I could do everything.

If she lived, I probably would have followed [her advice]. I was either going to be a pharmacist where I could have a chair back of the counter and make the prescriptions sitting down, or I was going to be a lawyer, but not the lawyer who appeared in court. I was going to be the brains, she used to tell my father, and write all the briefs. So she made me feel like I could do anything.

My father said whatever my mother said. She was right when it came to the children. My mother knew. She was determined that I would be an independent woman.

Rebecca Green and Jennie Grossman, like many other women, remember loving their work: the freedom they acquired, the people they met, the daily challenges, the sense that they were having an adventure in an unfamiliar world, the extra money with which to buy nice things for themselves. Many also reported, with considerable regret, that they felt obligated to choose between work and marriage, leaving their jobs either when they married or when they became pregnant.

REBECCA GREEN: *My first job was with a legal publishing company, doing bookkeeping. I think I stayed there a very long time, from 1920, when I came out of high school—it was a commercial high school. In those days you answered an ad in the papers—they never were permitted to say "Jewish or Gentile"—and I went down to this place and they hired me, never asking me whether I was Jewish or not. And the holidays came along, Rosh Hashonah, and I went to the boss and said,*

"You know, I won't be in tomorrow," and he said, "What's tomorrow?" I said, "A Jewish holiday," and he said to me, "I suppose you will take St. Patrick's Day, too." I said, "Yes, if you would give it to me!" And there was no further discussion about it.

I liked working very much. I loved the law, and I had a very retentive memory. And a lot of law firms would call up and say, "What is a good book on wills, on leases?"—you know, the different categories. I would have it on the tip of my fingers. As a matter of fact, one of the biggest law firms would call and offer me a job as a librarian, and I was never trained for a librarian. It was one of the biggest firms, so then I worked for them, and then the Depression came along, and the president of the firm sent me a note saying, "We are cutting everybody's salary, but not yours"—I was earning twenty-five dollars a week in those days—"but do not mention it to anybody." I stayed with them until I got married.

JENNIE GROSSMAN: *Working was very good. I was lucky there. I liked every minute of it. If I had continued to work there [a department store] I would have been one of their top executives. I was in charge of girdles; I had eight people working under me. I was responsible for making a schedule for their working hours. I was responsible for giving the buyer information as to what she was to order. I did everything.*

After a few years I was considered a junior executive and I decided to go to Florida for a vacation with another girl from the store. The buyers loaned us clothes to go to Florida with; they were very encouraging. We got on a train, paid our own money. We ran out of money and had to wire home, but that is how we had a vacation.

I didn't stay there because I got married, became pregnant, and was trying to stay home and take care of the baby, which I hated.

Some of the men, like Sol Meyrowitz, went directly into the white-collar job market after high school, but by far the larger number went on to college. Some went to public colleges like City College in New York, but many of the men—often on scholarship—went to private universities: Harvard, Columbia, Cornell, the universities of Chicago and Pennsylvania. Going to college usually meant rapid assimilation, but it did not necessarily eradicate the essential traces of *Yiddishkeit.*

Phillip Kohn, for example, who graduated from Yale in 1913 (see chapter 3), met the scions of several wealthy German Jewish families during his undergraduate years, and the father of one of them set him up in business (the two Yale graduates were partners) as an investment banker: they bought and sold companies in much the same manner as Kohn's ancestors in Eastern Europe might once have bought and sold goosefeathers:

What we really wanted to do is buy companies. The first thing we did was to buy a company that made an oil that could withstand sea water better than linseed oil, because it was made out of menhaden fish. The menhaden fish are fish the humans can't eat because there is too much fat and they smell terrible. But since the fish live in the water, some German scientist in the First World War discovered that you could make a paint out of this for ocean vessels that is much better than linseed oil. And so he interested some people here, who were very rich people, in starting this company, and in the First World War they made a tremendous amount of money selling this oil. When the First World War was over we bought the company for very little money [the capital came from his partner's father]. When the war was over, nobody needed it [the oil] for oceangoing things, and it was no good because it had smelled so terribly. And it [the smell] lasted forever, and you could never use it for indoor paint; on the ocean it didn't make any difference but you couldn't use it on houses or outdoor buildings, you couldn't use it at all. So we bought it from them. We bought the whole company. We bought it for a very small amount of money—all cash. You had to buy for cash in those days.

I never kidded Phillip Kohn. Phillip Kohn wasn't making money. Money was making money. I never kidded Phillip Kohn. I didn't know a goddamned thing about the banking business or any of the other businesses. I took long shots—things that seemingly looked sensible to me. I had never taken a course in accounting, nor had any of my competitors. I did all right.

There were, of course, some immigrant youths who—no matter how imbued with the culture of their parents—simply were not risk takers, either because they were trying as hard as possible to reject *Yiddishkeit*, or because by nature they needed more security than the entrepreneurial life could provide, or because the experience of the Depression had been traumatic. For these, if they were educated, teaching was the perfect profession. Few of the men who taught seem to have been passionately attached to their work. For them teaching simply had the multiple advantages, in those days, of being culturally acceptable (a good job for a Jewish boy), relatively secure (because your employer was a government, not a business, almost all Jewish teachers found a niche in the public school systems), and available. Sol Levine, for example, upon finishing college, got a job as a teacher ("the only thing a Jewish boy could do") and went to law school at night: "It was no picnic and no way to study law. In the end I dropped it." He continued in teaching:

I took courses to qualify for the high school exam and passed, but before I was able to get a regular appointment, I had to start in the lowest category—a teacher in training. You observed part of the time and taught part of the time and earned four fifty a day. No pay for summer, and no pay for holidays. No pension rights, no nothing—pretty tough. Then I became a sub [a substitute teacher] and finally, a couple of years later, a regular teacher.

I was always ambivalent about it [teaching]. I liked the security. I liked the salary. Fortunately I became a supervisor. Actually, by my temperament I am not a speculator. I am a fearful person about taking chances. So the security of the job is important to me. Maybe I have always been fearful. My father lost many businesses; my mother saved him, but he lost them anyway.

For the women, however, it was a somewhat different matter. Once having been to college, teaching was the only profession considered suitable for them; and many, like Rose Janofsky, who was trained at Simmons College in Boston in the late 1920s, thoroughly enjoyed the work itself as well as the opportunities it provided:

I had taken the elementary exam for elementary schools, and a job was open in one of the elementary schools. I was loath to accept an appointment because I wanted to teach in the high school. The woman at Simmons told me to take it because the years of working there would count toward my retirement. I took the appointment, and I was misera-

241

ble. *I hated teaching elementary school. The first few months I hated it with a deep hate. I used to come home and cry, wept—just didn't like teaching elementary school. I used to get up in the morning and go into the toilet and sit on the seat and say to myself, "What do I need this for? What in the world do I need this for?" I didn't like the people. They were petty, narrow, ignorant. The principal made me take a special course in Palmer penmanship, a special style of writing they have to fit into. And I couldn't write Palmer penmanship; I wrote a backhand. I became friendly with somebody at school, and she did all the exercises for me; she cheated for me. I got the certificate and wrote backhand on the blackboard anyway.*

When I was appointed to the high school, I was ecstatic. I took the exam, the written; it scared me to death. I had to take an oral exam and that scared me to death. I spoke well enough. They were looking for people who did not have an "ng" problem [a speech defect] or a dental problem, they wanted people who spoke English well, without any trace of an accent. It was a very strict exam. The classroom test scared me to death. To have someone in the back of the classroom criticizing every word you utter, the way you stood, the way you wrote on a blackboard, the wording in your lesson plans. They [the gentile teachers] were very severe in their criticisms.

One of my sisters coached me quite a bit, about the classroom test. She was teaching. And then she said she was going to come up to the school and observe me, and I said, "If you do that, you will walk in one door and I will walk out the other. Don't you dare come into my classroom and observe me!" The one person I didn't want to observe me was my sister. Why? Because she was a very superior teacher, and I felt I would never come near her as a teacher. I didn't want her to see me as not a very good teacher. She was too devoted to her school, her classroom, her students. Nobody appreciated that kind of devotion.

I got a notice that I had passed everything. I got the license. One thing I knew: I didn't want to teach where my sister was teaching. I was not going to be competitive with her. I went to another school. I didn't want people to say to me that you are not as good as your sister. I wasn't going to give my life to the classroom, the way my sister did. I was a good teacher. I had enthusiasm, and I think I transferred it to the kids, but I wasn't going to give my life to the classroom.

I loved teaching in a high school. We were considered rich because the high school teachers were making seven fifty a day. After school, crowds standing around talking at the clock, arguing. It was a very exciting time. We had very bright people on the faculty in those days. The brightest people became teachers.

Among those who loved teaching were the women, like Janet Sommers and Sadie Rehstock, who went back to it or started it after their children were grown. A few, like Rebecca Green, had to go back to school to get a bachelor's degree before they could begin teaching. These women were acutely aware of the status considerations: for them teaching was, at one and the same time, more interesting than housework, more profitable, and also more self-enhancing.

SADIE REHSTOCK: *I didn't become a teacher until I was thirty-eight. I was thrilled. I went back to school after my children were born. I went at night. My father was dying of cancer when I passed my teacher's exam, and I went into the room and told him that I would be earning about seventy-five dollars a week. He couldn't believe it. That his daughter was going to be earning it, he couldn't believe it! My father thought it ridiculous. All of his pals had daughters, and they didn't go to college. They went out and got jobs.*

I got the first grade, the youngest first grade, the ones who hadn't been to kindergarten. But it was just wonderful. I loved it. True, I had very little time for myself, but I loved going to school and the other teachers. I loved experiencing success because I felt that I was good. It was wonderful for me. I became a new lady. I just felt equally as important as my husband. I felt that I had something important. I was out among professionals. I felt that I might have become a very different kind of wife if I had not worked. I would have grown jealous of him if I had not done this. He was an important person in his field.

Among all the educated immigrant youth we interviewed, there was only one, Max Weiner, who pursued a career to which his parents were unalterably opposed. Weiner attended Northwestern University in the early 1930s, but instead of becoming the doctor or the dentist that his father wished him to be, he developed an interest in the theater, which his parents considered inappropriate:

When I got into Northwestern, I met a guy and we had lunch together and we started talking about theater and I was crazy about acting and he said, "Why don't you come over to the theater? We are doing a new play, and you have good speech. Read for the part." I went over and read and got the lead part.

I needed a part-time job, so I went over to the Goodman Theatre in Chicago and said, "I need a job." They said, "What can you do?" I said, "I am an actor. I can paint sets. I can do this. I can do that," and they said, "Fine. We will pay you thirty-five dollars a week, and you will have some parts, and you will also be an assistant to the scene designers." What I did for them was all the hard work—painting the scenes, the flats. Well, I really loved the place. I never got really more money than that.

I was in Northwestern about two years when I left because I wanted the theater. I never told my father. I just left and went to the Goodman Theatre and got a full-time job. And I had a girlfriend and stayed with her not too far away.

My father got angry. It was the first time he really got nasty and angry with me. "I don't want to see him! He is not to come here! You are not to let him come into this house!" He said this to my mother. "You are not to give him any money! Stay away! He is to make his own life!"

The first Sunday night I was there [at the theatre], and there was a check for twenty-five bucks! I almost fell down after the show. Twenty-five dollars! Men would work a whole week for that. I used to study for an exam I would take that afternoon, and I remember getting off the train, putting it away, going in there, getting my script, rehearsing it, putting it on the air, get back on the train, study all the way back and take my exam.

Weiner eventually went into radio work ("I hated radio, but the money was great"), first as an announcer, then as an actor, later as a script writer. During the Second World War, John Houseman asked him to work in the Office of War Information, which had been created by President Franklin D. Roosevelt to develop propaganda for the U.S. war effort; serving in O.W.I. was equivalent to being a member of the armed forces and thus exempted one from the military draft. ("And I said [to Houseman], 'How much does it pay?' And he said, 'How do you look in khaki?' And I said, 'Lousy.' And he said, 'Just shut up and take this job!' "). Although not quite the artistic triumph he had dreamed of, Weiner now assesses his career as "a good life"; his father, of course, was never quite reconciled to it:

When I was making a hundred fifty dollars a week [in the 1930s], my father used to call me up, and he used to say, "I am managing eight furniture stores and writing the copy for the advertising. I am busy eight days a week. You know what I am getting? One hundred dollars!" Here I was, making one hundred fifty dollars and hardly paying any attention to it, to the job. Sometimes, in the afternoons, I would call him and he would say, "Where are you? Aren't you working? It is in the middle of the afternoon!" And I would say, "I am not called until six o'clock." He would say, "Oh, yeah!" He got so mad! He was going crazy, and he had ulcers, and this is what killed him.

Sam Reiss, on the other hand, of all those we interviewed was the only one who had pursued the kind of career that might have been considered appropriate for an educated boy from the shtetl: he was a cantor. Reiss had immigrated when he was nine or ten years old; his family had settled in Providence, Rhode Island, where his father, who had been a *shochet*—a ritual slaughterer—became a successful restaurant owner. But Reiss had other ideas. After graduating from college, he decided to become a cantor, although his father, true to the famous joke ("My son become a rabbi! What kind of job is that for a Jewish boy?"), was not initially enthusiastic: "My father agreed to let me try it for six months, and if it doesn't work out, I would come home without prejudice and take over the business."

But it worked out. Reiss attended the Jewish Theological Seminary in New York and was hired, as soon as he was ordained in 1939, by a large Conservative congregation in New England:

Before I conducted my first service, I used to have nightmares that I was standing at the pulpit, my music open to begin the service. Suddenly the pulpit started moving away from me. Now I am standing and I don't know where to begin, for I never memorized the music. I remember that nightmare, it was a frightful experience. I have never gone out on the pulpit where I didn't have a nervous feeling: I

*shouldn't fall on my face or disgrace myself or do something that will
embarrass the congregation. When you stand, the average service is
three hours, and many things can happen, and your success is dependent upon so many factors which you do not control—the organist,
the choir. There are many factors that any one of which, if it goes
wrong, destroys a program and I end up with egg on my face. We [the
choir and cantor] depended on each other being well enough rehearsed
to know and remember the dynamics, the rhythm, every night and
every Shabbos. Every service. I am the only one facing the congregation; the others are hidden behind a curtain. I used to tell that to my
choir: "Sure, you don't care. You don't worry. I worry!"*

Reiss, not surprisingly, has strong positive feelings about the value
of Judaic tradition, not just the religious tradition (*halakha*) but also the
cultural tradition (*Yiddishkeit*). One memorable experience in his career
exemplifies those feelings:

*One event that is very special in my memory is the time we performed
[Ernest] Bloch's Sacred Service with the composer in attendance.* This
was to be done in my synagogue on a Friday night, as part of the service, with responsive readings and everything; until then it had always
been done in concert. It is a very difficult service. It is not an easy piece
of work to study and learn.*

*I rehearsed with him for three days. I was awed by him. It is almost
a frightening experience to stand in front of a man who has written
this type of music. I studied it with him. I did take the liberty, after
apologizing to him, to ask his permission to change certain things that
he had written. I explained why: the way you wrote this, to fit the
continuity of the prayer book. He had written it for the Reform prayer
book; we didn't use the Reform prayer book. He said, "Whatever you
want to do, you do. Feel free to do." He trusted me. I said, "When the
part of the mourners' Kaddish [prayer for the dead] comes in, I would
like to use part of your music as background for the recitation of the
Kaddish, rather than as an out-and-out composition." The important
part of that section of the service is the saying of the Kaddish; it needs
no follow up with music. However, as background music it would set*

---

* Ernest Bloch (1880–1959), a Swiss composer. *Avodath Hakodesh* (*Sacred Service*) was written
in Switzerland in 1930–33.

246

up and make it more important and impressive and meaningful. He agreed.

Bloch came to a rehearsal. I sang his parts of the music, of course, all of it for him, and one of the first criticisms, when I did the "Boruch hu," which is preceded by the equivalent of a trumpet call, he said, "You don't enter the service apologetically! Enter with shoulders back, head high! Boruch hu et Adonai hamvorach! [Blessed is the Lord, the one who is blessed!] It's a call to prayer, that's where the percussion comes in!"

Bloch has given me a philosophy for the pulpit which I have tried to follow. Having come from Poland where I had to bow my head, I didn't want to ever bow my head again. This was, to me, a true expression of what I felt, presenting the Jew standing on his feet, standing up and taking care of himself.

"Taking care of themselves" was something the immigrant generations of Jews managed to do, most of them, exceedingly well. Whether they followed the path from cloak maker to manufacturer, or from high school to higher education, the vast majority managed to realize their parents' dreams, to achieve the goal of affluence, in the comparatively brief span of their own lifetimes.

They were fortunate in having arrived in a country that needed the skills—the cultural skills—they possessed. But they were also fortunate in having descended from a tradition that instilled those skills in the first place. Some students of Jewish American history bewail what they call "bagel Judaism": the affection many Jews have for a particular ethnic way of life, even when stripped entirely of its religious or sacerdotal content. George Mandelbaum, member of the Communist party, child of party members, describes "bagel Judaism" aptly:

My parents were radical; they were not Orthodox. My mother used to call us "traditional." You knew you were Jewish because you had grown up in a neighborhood that was largely Scandinavian, Lutheran churches everywhere. You knew your food was different. You knew there were different holidays—Jewish holidays—and you honored them, not because you went to synagogue or anything, because it was a day off from school. It was a holiday and you were Jewish. But my mother did not light candles on Friday night, and there was no religious atmosphere around the house.

Adherents of this kind of Judaism, like the Mandelbaums, may have more than an idle attachment, for it was *Yiddishkeit*, the special culture that derived not from Torah but from the historical experience of the Jews of Eastern Europe—the bagels and the borscht, the impulse to wander, the mordant sense of humor, the risk taking, the hand gestures, the desire to be self-employed, the occasional willingness to break the law slightly—that helped this generation of immigrant youth to assimilate into America as full and prosperous citizens.

8

"IT'S A FREE COUNTRY": REMAINING JEWISH IN AMERICA

JUDAISM, like all religions, requires obedience of its followers; but over the many centuries of its existence, no one has ever been able to settle the much-debated question: "Obedience to what?" To the belief system and the ritual system together? To one or the other of them, separated? To some defined portion of each? Are you a good Jew if you observe the Sabbath scrupulously, give generously to charity, but don't believe in God? Are you a good Jew if you believe in God, take each of the Ten Commandments seriously, but hate all organized religious institutions? Are you a good Jew if you eat bagels and lox on Sunday morning, donate half your estate to an Orthodox *yeshiva*, but can't understand a word of Hebrew and haven't been inside a synagogue since your son's *bar mitzvah*?

Such questions no doubt plague all religions, but for Jews they have been particularly vexing. The Jews have been a traveling people for at least two millennia, going sometimes here, sometimes there. Always emigrating and immigrating; always having to accommodate to some-one else's culture; always affected, for good or ill, by strangers. Since Judaism lacks a hierarchical structure, there is no ultimate authority who can resolve disputes either about belief or about ritual. Arguments about "who is a Jew" and "what is right for a Jew to do" have been going on for centuries. Furthermore, since Judaism is a religion of the mundane, it is—at one and the same time—both powerful and fragile: powerful, because it governs every aspect of life—"from when thou risest up until when thou liest down"; fragile, because, being all inclu-sive, it is that much more susceptible to the myriad forces of change. Jewish law does not start with the Ten Commandments, and Jewish ritual does not begin at the synagogue door: Jewish rules and beliefs cover what to eat and what to charge a customer, how to dress and how to care for the dying, when to complain and when to accept abuse in silence. Jewish law is all inclusive: seven days a week, fifty-two weeks a year. Thus, in Judaism even an apparently inconsequential act can be significant: God kept Moses out of the Promised Land, after forty years of leading his quarrelsome people through the desert, be-cause—in a moment of irritation—he disobeyed God's command-ment, and struck a rock with his staff instead of speaking to it. To members of our parents' generation, one bite of bacon, one Saturday baseball game, could have transformative power.

Still, in the shtetls of Eastern Europe it was relatively easy to keep Jewish practice from changing very quickly. Although there was no supreme authority, each local rabbi was, in his own community, sher-iff, judge, and jury: the sole arbiter, the most respected member of the community, more authoritative than any official of the state. Judaism was, literally, the established religion of the shtetl. Everything—from the hours of business activity to the location of the cemetery—could be, and usually was, governed by Jewish law.

In the cities of Eastern Europe, and subsequently in the cities of America, that sitution did not pertain. By the middle of the nineteenth century, *haskalah* (enlightenment) was already in the air. Young Jews were courting divergent points of view—socialism, Zionism, atheism, Darwinism—and were leaving the shtetls for the cities, where they would be freer to act according to new rules. But even for those who were traditional, the cities posed a dilemma; in the cities (and this was particularly true in the cities of the New World) Jews sometimes found either that they had to violate the dictates of Orthodoxy in order to survive, or that they could violate those dictates without punishment. The rabbis could not run Warsaw—and could not even have dreamed of running Chicago. Orthodoxy is only easy to practice in small, well-organized communities: the synagogue must be walking distance from the home; the kosher butcher must be down the street; the neighbors must all follow the same ritual; the rabbi must be kept informed. In the shtetl, successful businessmen could close their businesses on Saturday without a worry, but not in Boston—and in Boston there were no penalities that could be exacted against the man—or the woman—who broke the Sabbath. In the shtetl of Stary Sambor, or even in Minsk, a housewife could walk to a kosher butcher, but she may not even have been able to find one in Kansas City—and her family still had to eat.

As a result of these pressures, the boundaries of proper Jewish belief and behavior had already begun to stretch even in our grandparents' day, even before emigration had reached its peak. Many "boundary stretchers" immigrated; although hard statistics cannot ever be compiled on the subject, it seems reasonable to assume that those who emigrated from the shtetls were those most willing to put some distance between themselves and traditional Judaism. Although millions of Jews experienced poverty and pogroms in Eastern Europe, only some portion of those millions decided to emigrate. Many of the rabbis of Eastern Europe counseled patience in the face of adversity—an unremarkable clerical position. America, they argued, was not the *goldene medina* (the golden land), but rather the *trayf medina* (the impure land). Better to stay in Poland and Russia, waiting for the Messiah to lead us back to the land of Israel, they thought, than to follow the false messiahs of political liberty and financial success.

The immigrants must have been precisely those Jews who did not agree with the rabbis. Many of our parents recall hearing their own parents disparage the Judaism they had left behind in Eastern Europe:

ESTHER GINSBURG: *My father belonged to one of those organizations, a landsmanshaftn, and they used to have heated discussions, the landslayt, about davenen [praying]. Some of the landslayt davn, but not all, not all. The ones who wouldn't davn, they said they wanted to be free. They always said they were so strict in Europe, very religious, just like the Lubavitchers [a group of Chasidic Jews, prominent now in New York* and in Israel], something like it. Very strict, you know. You were not allowed to comb your hair or you had to wash your hands when you went from *milkhik* [dairy products] to *fleyshik* [meat products], and you were not allowed to make a light on *Shabbos*, you had to leave the light all night or have a gentile woman come in the morning to make a light. So strict. And people said when they came here, it's a free country. First of all, it's free so that you can make a living, make a dollar. I don't have to be strict, they said; it's a free country. And a lot of people changed.

HANNAH TOPEROFF: *My father had also been an innkeeper and a bootlegger in Russia, and he used to tell me all the time how he hated the rabbis. They would buy liquor from him and never pay for it—just assumed they were entitled to it. Some of them, he said, were drunkards, but everyone pretended not to notice. He said that he hated the rabbis, and once he got here, he never stepped inside a synagogue again. Not until he was an old man, anyway—and then, even then, he really went more for the* shnaps *[liquor, served after the services] than for the services.*

If our grandparents had ambivalent feelings about the tradition they had left behind, our parents had even more, for our parents—many of whom were born in America, all of whom spent their youth here—wanted to become Americans, wanted to assimilate. Virtually all of the people we interviewed wanted to remain Jews in some way, but which way would it be? Assimilation to a Christian ethic and an English-speaking culture surely meant that both belief and behavior—both ritual behavior and mundane behavior—would have to change. But how much? In America the range of choice was vast; what kind of Jew would our parents choose to be? What kind of American?

The Range of Choice:
Orthodox, Conservative, or Reform

As our parents grew to maturity, as they married and created their own families, most had to decide what form of religious observance to follow. Many chose no observance at all; but for those who wished to retain some liturgical connection to Judaism, there were, in interwar America, three possible choices: Orthodox, Conservative, or Reform.

Ashkenazic Orthodoxy had a difficult time establishing itself on these shores. The Orthodox congregations our grandparents found here when they immigrated were Sephardic: old congregations, established many years before by the descendants of Spanish and Portuguese Jews who had arrived in America in the seventeenth and eighteenth centuries. Sephardic custom is very different from Ashkenazic—not only in liturgy but even in the decoration of synagogues and the pronunciation of Hebrew. In America at the end of the nineteenth century, most still-observant Sephardic Jews were comfortably middle-class; most of the Eastern European immigrants were poor. As a result, the rare attempts to absorb Ashkenazic Jews into Sephardic congregations usually ended in failure, in a polite (or not so polite) agreement that the two groups would go their separate ways.

Since few Ashkenazic rabbis emigrated, immigrant Orthodox congregations were not easily established. The *landslayt* might rent a basement room in which to hold services (there were so many of these in the New World that a special word was created—*shtibl*—to designate them); but it might be years, even decades, before a learned man was hired to lead the congregation, to turn the *shtibl* into a *shul*. Indeed, in the early years of the century—when our grandparents were making liturgical choices—there was no *yeshiva* in the United States that could train an Ashkenazic rabbi, nor any authority here that could have ordained one.

The difficult times were, however, over by 1920. American Ashkenazic Orthodoxy was beginning to stabilize; a professional association of Orthodox rabbis had been created (the Rabbinical Council of America), and a loose association of congregations (the Union of Orthodox

Congregations of America and Canada) was forming. Those of our parents who decided to adhere closely to the traditions of their parents and grandparents could easily have found congregations with which to affiliate, as long as they did not leave the major (and some minor) metropolitan regions of the country.

Reform Judaism was another available option. Reform Judaism had its roots in the Ashkenazic tradition rather than the Sephardic; the movement, which began in Germany early in the nineteenth century, came to full fruition in the United States in the years just before and after the Civil War, when many Jews were immigrating from Germany.

Reformers had wanted many things: to restructure the liturgy—especially by introducing vernacular languages—so that congregants could make sense out of their own prayers (hitherto always recited in Hebrew); to eliminate many of the rules governing daily life so that Jews would not be obviously different from their Christian neighbors (no *payess* for men, no wigs for married women, no *yarmulkes*, no food restrictions); in general, as they put it, to modernize an ancient faith and make it more attractive. Reforming Jews wanted to remain Jews; they wanted to isolate the theological core of Judaism and separate it from the liturgical and behavioral sediment deposited by four thousand years of Jewish history. "We wish to know what in our law is God's command," wrote Max Lilienthal, one the early reforming rabbis, "and what is the transient work of mortal man."[1] In both Germany and America, they wanted to graft elements of Christian (particularly Protestant) practice (a responsive relation between leader and congregation; musical interludes) onto Jewish ritual. "We wish to worship God," Gustav Poznanski, another reformer, asserted in 1841, "not as slaves, but as enlightened descendants of that chosen race whose blessings have been scattered throughout the land of Abraham, Isaac and Jacob."[2]

Even by the time our grandparents arrived, and certainly by the time our parents were making choices, there were several Reform congregations in all the major cities of the United States. The Reform liturgy had taken a definitive form, and a Reform seminary (significantly, it was never called a *yeshiva*), Hebrew Union College, had been organized in Cincinnati. In Reform synagogues, the liturgy was almost entirely in English; the congregation stood still or sat while the rabbi

*"Today we accept as binding only the moral laws and maintain only
such ceremonies as elevate and sanctify our lives, but reject all
such as are not adapted to the views and habits of modern civilization."
Services at the Plum Street (Reform) Synagogue, Cincinnati,
date unknown.*

read the prayers and the cantor sang; men sat next to their wives and daughters; no one's head was covered, and no one *shokled* [rocked rhythmically while praying].

Today we accept as binding only the moral laws and maintain only such ceremonies as elevate and sanctify our lives, but reject all such as are not adapted to the views and habits of modern civilization. We hold that all such Mosaic and Rabbinical laws as regulate diet, priestly purity and dress originated in ages and under influence of ideas altogether foreign to our present mental and spiritual state. They fail to impress the modern Jew with a spirit of priestly holiness; their observance in our days is apt rather to obstruct than to further modern spiritual elevation.[3]

Virtually everything that Eastern European Jews could regard as comfortable, familiar, and traditional had been extirpated—deliberately—from Reform Judaism. To many of our grandparents, joining a Reform congregation was tantamount to conversion. Even many of our parents, desirous of leaving Orthodoxy, were not willing to leave it quite so far behind.

The American Conservative movement was created in order to fill this breach, to be sort of a compromise between what some thought to be the obscurantism of Orthodoxy and the Protestantism of Reform. In the middle decades of the nineteenth century, some rabbis wished to loosen the iron chains of Orthodoxy without discarding them entirely: to allow mixed seating in the synagogue while still withholding from women the right to read from the Torah; to sermonize in vernacular languages, but retain Hebrew predominantly for the liturgy; to shorten services, but not eliminate them—retaining, for example, the daily morning service and the second day of Rosh Hashonah.

Conservative Judaism did not have an organizational structure, however, until 1886 in the aftermath of the famous (at least to historians) *trayf* banquet, which celebrated the first graduating class of the (Reform) Hebrew Union College in Cincinnati. Many of the invited guests were rabbis who continued to observe *kashrut*; the organizers of the banquet deliberately served Little Neck clams as the first course—clams being, of course, not kosher. The banquet broke up in confusion and rage—and out of the confusion was born the Jewish Theological Seminary and the Conservative movement.

At first, the movement floundered, since the Jews who had attained sufficient wealth to be its benefactors were all adherents of Reform. But just at the turn of the century, when the first president of the seminary, Sabato Morais, had died, and the institution was on the verge of bankruptcy (also just when waves of Eastern European immigrants were arriving on these shores), Cyrus Adler (then professor of semitics at Johns Hopkins University and a Conservative) proposed to Jacob Schiff (one of the wealthy German Jewish leaders of New York) that Conservatism, if reinvigorated, might appeal to the new immigrants, keep their children within the fold, and draw all of them, parents and children, away from the Yiddish medievalisms that were an embarrassment to already-assimilated Jews. Adler's tactic worked; Schiff led a successful campaign for funds (although he himself remained within the Reform fold); and Solomon Schecter (then a professor at Cambridge University, in England) was recruited to lead a revitalized Conservatism.

Adler turned out to be right about our parents' generation of immigrants; a goodly number did decide to join the Conservative movement, thus creating a bridge between European traditions and American inclinations.

Statistics about how many Jews made which particular liturgical choices in the interwar years are impossible to obtain. The various branches of Judaism were not organized enough to collect them; and many Jews, remembering the difficulties of life in Eastern Europe, were unwilling to tell bureaucrats precisely what their affiliation was. Suffice it to say, as a rough guide, that a few members of our parents' generation chose conversion (my parents were Jewish, but I am something else); another, much larger group, chose secularization (my parents were Jewish, but I have no religion and you won't catch me in or near a synagogue). Among those who chose to affiliate, a small number chose Orthodoxy, a larger but still small number chose Reform, and by far the larger group—compromisers—settled into Conservative congregations. Zionism was also an option in this generation, an option that had no particular theological or liturgical connotation: one could believe in the need to create a special nation-state for the Jews whether one was a secularist, a convert, or an affiliated Jew of any denomination.

The Orthodox

Some of our parents chose Orthodoxy, not allowing either modernization or Americanization to divert them from the traditional way of life.
Orthodoxy was not easy to sustain in America, what with the need to
refrain from work on Saturday (earlier in the century, the standard
work week was six days, not five), and to live within walking distance
of a synagogue (often making a move to a new, pleasanter neighborhood impossible), and to be near sources of kosher meat (often, because
it required special handling at the slaughterhouse, considerably more
expensive than nonkosher meat). Yet those, like Etta and Sol Levine,
who chose Orthodoxy remember the choice as an easy one: they simply continued to do what they had been trained to do, making no
waves, causing no arguments.

ETTA LEVINE: *You have to remember you have to do certain things if
you wanted things to continue. When I was five years old, already my
aunt was teaching us. "It isn't suitable for a little Jewish girl—es past
nisht far a yiddish meydl."*

*We were not excused, we were not allowed to think. My mother's
sister married my father's brother, and that was my aunt. And we always lived together; we lived together from 1919 to 1973. If we didn't
live in the same apartment, we lived in the same building. My mother
lived in the next apartment over until the day she died, and so did my
father. It was never in our family yours or mine but ours, us. And we
never argued—no, never.*

*It guaranteed the tradition. This is how we were disciplined. What-
ever those regulations were, are—they are not were, they are. And then
we do it this way, and I'll tell you something: it is a custom, and I was
brought up to do it that way, and I don't find it difficult, and there
is no way that it hinders me in anything that I want to do, so I just
continue.*

Etta Levine did not chafe about remaining Orthodox; so, too, she
does not chafe at the various ways Orthodoxy constrains her daily life,
because they are important to her sense of being Jewish:

258

*"You have to remember you have to do certain things
if you wanted things to continue."*
*Simchas Torah service in an Orthodox congregation,
New York City, 1935.*

*You have to know whether the man observed the Sabbath. To this day
I wouldn't go into just any butcher store. The fact that it says "kosher"
on the outside doesn't matter. You have to trust the person because
sometimes you may get something—a driver can deliver a piece of
meat that is not kosher—and you have to know, you have to recognize.
There are certain things that you have to pull out, you have to cut out,
you have to trim it, you have to know which fat to take off, and so on.*

*When my father gave up the store [he was a kosher butcher], it was
very difficult for me. I went to the man who bought it from him, and
when he gave up the store about six years ago, I had a hard time. I have
to travel now, a long way, to get my meat. There's a kosher butcher
nearby, but I don't trust him.*

Modern technology constantly creates new problems for Orthodox
women. Since *halakha*, the rules of observance, touch on every aspect
of daily life, each new household machine requires a new set of rules,
another set of decisions. *Kashrut*, for example, requires the complete
separation of the dishes used for meat meals and the dishes used for
dairy meals. How, then, to manage a dishwasher? Certain machines,
like refrigerators, have automatic features, but some of the things that
they do automatically are forbidden on the Sabbath. Can they be used?
If so, how? Cooking used to be forbidden on the Sabbath because it
was, justifiably, considered hard work. But is it hard work when all
you have to do is turn a knob?

ETTA LEVINE: *I have a cabinet for the meat, and I have the other side
for the dairy, and I don't put dishes in the sink, I wash them in my
hands. No, they never get stacked in the sink, no—on the side but
never in. My sink has two sides, a double sink, but you can never tell,
some of the water might run over to the other side.*

*I wouldn't have any dishwasher, but if you have a dishwasher, you
have to have different racks, and you run the cycle through. You could
have two different dishwashers; that is what some of the rabbis say you
should do. But if you don't have two dishwashers, then you run the
cycle through. First you wash dairy dishes, then you wait. Later on,
maybe a day or two later, you want to wash meat dishes, you run the
cycle through, without anything in it, and then its O.K. because the
water is so hot.*

There's an automatic switch in the refrigerator, turns the light on, but we keep it off all the time. It is like turning on the switch, an automatic switch, therefore we can't use it on *Shabbos*. Well, you may forget on Friday to turn it off and then . . . so we decided we can do without it. I can see what's doing in the refrigerator anyway, so I don't use the light. Never had a [refrigerator] light on. No, not even in my mother's house; we turned it off. My cousin turned it off and on, and on Friday she would remember to turn it off, but I was always afraid I might forget, so I don't do it. We do without it.

Well, you care; you have a certain reputation to maintain. There are certain people whom we call the "holier than thou," they wouldn't eat in *our* house. I used to have a Bible class come on Saturday, and I used to serve tea and cake, and I bought the cake in a certain bakery. I wouldn't buy any cake but in a certain bakery, a Sabbath-observant bakery. We had a tremendous gas range in the other house, six burners, and I had two covers for them, but I kept two lights on, because I had to have kettles with water. I prepared—you know, you have to prepare the tea—the essence of the tea before, because you can't put the tea bag into the water [on *Shabbos*], you have to do it before. These women came for about three weeks, maybe four weeks, they never would touch, the only thing they would eat was the bread, none of the fruit. I don't know why they didn't eat the fruit, they certainly didn't take the cake, and they didn't take the tea. They would buy the meat in my father's store, that was all right [she was shouting], but they wouldn't touch the tea!

One day one of them walked into my kitchen. "Oh, you have *blacha* [the burner cover] on the stove. You cover all your burners?" I said, "Of course." She said, "I'll have a cup of tea."

Women focus their Orthodoxy on their homes; men, on the synagogue and the rabbi.

SOL LEVINE: *I lived with my parents until they died and then I lived with one of my married brothers. Where I came from I had a shul, but my wife insisted that we had to live near her parents and her brother, and I was worried about where I would find a shul in my new neighborhood. When I found out there was a shul, then I felt better. Oh! I could go to shul.*

I went to that shul many years. The rabbi died about ten years ago. I miss the rabbi every second. You understand what I mean: I miss him every second, even today. He opened up my mind.

He was sincere. The other rabbis were not as strict as he was; they were Orthodox, but he was a strict Orthodox. You follow a good example. In life choose a better example; in life follow a good example. Don't go after the rapists, thieves, murderers. It says that in Gemara [part of the Talmud]: fifteen hundred years ago we were taught to choose a better example in life.

Rabbi Taleisnik was his name. He taught me to be more and more Orthodox, strict. His conduct was wonderful. May I give you a couple of examples? A couple of years ago there was small-town doctor, and this doctor [a gentile] came to Rabbi and said he wants to be a convert because he met a Jewish girl. So the rabbi said there were certain conditions. He said to him, "You have to do this, this, this." But he [the doctor] didn't want to do this. So he offered to give the rabbi two hundred dollars, and Rabbi said, "No, you have to live up to certain conditions." So he [the doctor] went to another rabbi and gave him seventy-five dollars and converted.

Although Sol Levine is a college graduate, he regards his religious education as considerabley more meaningful:

He was a strict Orthodox rabbi. He was perfect. He practiced what he preached. He preached what he practiced. He didn't bow down to anybody. I saw it. This I saw. I graduated from the kindergarten under Rabbi and then the second grade and I was in my forties. I really became a student. Under Rabbi, I became a real student of Judaism. Everybody else was just amateurs. I was very close to him. I loved him. I am telling you, I miss it every second. I was close to him. He was so sincere. I never had dinner in his home.

Orthodox rabbis provide counsel as well as education, as Etta Levine illustrates by her courtship story:

My husband was the brother of a friend of my sister-in-law. A blind date. I was in my late thirties. He was Orthodox, and I liked him immediately. I never would have gone out with him if I had known that he would be bald. I went to this party and there was this guy with gor-

geous hair: he had a nice head of hair. This had to be a certain physical attraction. So I had started to go out with Sol, and he was teaching. He lived with his brother. He was family oriented. I thought he was very fine and handsome and suitable, and he was Orthodox. I avoided non-Orthodox people—fine to go out, yes, but never close.

I think that what happened was that he took me to his family, and then it was all taken for granted. If you were taken to meet the family, it was a foregone conclusion. He spoke to my father, and my father asked him a few things: What synagogue he went to. Then my father went to his synagogue and investigated and asked. That is the custom and the proper thing: you investigate. He talked to the rabbi. So my father talked to the rabbi, and he told him what's what. My father wanted to know: Is he really sincere about his religion? The rabbi would know.

And the rabbi said to him, "If I had a daughter, I would be very happy to have him in my family." And then we decided to set the date.

Those of our parents who accepted Orthodoxy did so with the conscious realization that they were also accepting a less affluent way of life. American society opened new paths to Jewish youth in the interwar years, but the most affluent and prestigious paths were still closed—because of the work pattern that they required—to those who wished to remain Orthodox.

SOL LEVINE: *At one time I wanted to become a lawyer or a doctor, but because of Shabbos I became a schoolteacher. I didn't want to have to work on Saturdays. Teaching salaries were comparatively good, if you got your appointment. The leisure was good; you only had to work until three o'clock—that was good. As far as I was concerned, you had civil service status: that was good, as far as I was concerned.*

Being a teacher, you had status. Of course being a doctor, you had more status. A doctor had more status than a lawyer, than a teacher. Being a lawyer—I couldn't do that either; they have to work on Saturdays. When a thing is impossible, you have to be practical. I knew it couldn't be done.

Yet despite all the restrictions, those who chose to remain Orthodox, who chose to live as a community somewhat apart, who chose not to Americanize as thoroughly as their peers, are convinced that they made the right choice.

SOL LEVINE: *We are glad. We are happy. A Jew is a Jew. Accept no substitutes. If I have the original, then I should quit worrying around.*

Kashrut is a spiritual acceptance. Now there are certain statutes in the Bible that tell you the animals that you can use in the home; they tell you the names of the animals that you cannot use in the home. There are so many kosher animals, why do you have to bother with anything else? Did you ever hear of the expression "Birds of a feather flock together?" I heard that expression years ago. Where do you find it? In the Gemara. The Hebrew scholars wrote that in the Gemara. They said that at sundown birds would come flock together near the water. They found on one side the birds that were kosher and the nonkosher birds would get together on the other side. This is in the Gemara. Birds of a feather flock together. I am telling you. I observe.

Jews learn from everybody. I try to learn from everybody. The time that I have I give to my Hebrew learning, which is why I don't read books by non-Jews. There is nothing in the learning of the peoples of the world that Hebrew scholars, that we do not have. Judaism is complete. It encompasses all of the history, philosophy, and learning of the other religions. If you sit down at the Gemara, you'll find our scholars knew about human life. The Gemara contains everything; everything is in the Gemara. It is amazing how Hebrew scholars knew about life. I never questioned any aspect of Judaism.

If you obey the law, the law will protect you, but if you don't obey the law, you will not be protected. There is a punishment, there is a reason that the punishment came. The Jews in Germany, what did they say? "I am not a Jew. I am reformed. Or, I am not a Jew. I am a Pole." And you see what the Nazis did.

Disenchantment with Judaism: The Converted

At the opposite extreme from those who chose Orthodoxy were those who chose to convert out of Judaism entirely. No one really knows how many of our parents took this way of resolving the conflict between being Jewish and being American. All that is clear, however, is that among those who did so a considerable number chose either Unitarianism, a form of Protestantism that has the distinct advantage of denying Jesus a seat alongside God; or Ethical Culture, which advocates a moral system virtually identical to the Judeo-Christian ethic, but refuses either to accept a deity or to create a ritual addressed to one.

Thus, among those Eastern European Jews who converted, only a minuscule number chose the path that had been pioneered a century earlier by the likes of Heinrich Heine, the German poet, who converted to an established religion because he believed "the baptismal certificate to be a ticket of admission to European culture."[4] Either because there was no established religion in the United States, or because Eastern European Jews had a more lasting (if attenuated) emotional tie to their religion, few second-generation Eastern European Jewish Americans chose to convert to a traditional form of Christianity. Those few who did almost invariably chose one of the branches of Christianity that would confer social status along with a new religious identity. Catholicism, for example, was not a frequent choice, since, whatever its virtues, it was also an immigrant religion and lacked the prestige of the established Protestant denominations.

The voices of those few Jews who converted to the mainline Protestant churches reverberate with the many personal and social difficulties our parents faced as they tried to grow up both Jewish and American. George Isaacs's mother was Hungarian. Both of her parents died when she was seven years old. She emigrated with an older brother, twenty years her senior; and, once in this country, he placed her in a convent for lack of any other means of caring for her. She was baptized in that convent. When she emerged, her brother sought a man for her to marry and settled on Isaacs's father, who was Jewish, but not enthusiastically so:

GEORGE ISAACS: *My father was never a very good Jew, he never did follow up much on his religion. He did not practice his religion; he*

265

was very embittered. In the course of his travels, he was in a small town in the Midwest on a Jewish holiday and thought he had to go to a synagogue. Well, he went, and when he got to the door, somebody stopped him and asked him if he had a ticket. "Well, no," he said. I'd say he was in his late twenties or perhaps early thirties. Well, you had to pay to come in. They wouldn't let him in. And he explained that he was a traveling man and all alone and knew nobody, and they were firm about it. He became embittered. He never renounced his own religion, but a lot of people I knew subsequently called him a Jewish Nazi because he was so embittered.

Like many members of his generation, Isaacs's feelings about Judaism are intimately connected to his feelings about his parents:

My mother was so beautiful that people stopped to gaze at her. I used to say, after looking at a picture of her, that she was a typical Gibson girl—clean skin and jet-black hair and beautiful features. She was a simple person. She died at the age of going on ninety-one. I was very fond of my mother, which is not a remarkable statement. I became close to her. I never heard my mother raise a voice, heard her curse, say "dammit" or "hell." I just think she is probably close to being the ideal woman, outside of being beautiful. I never met anybody who just didn't fall in love with her.

My father was the most successful businessman I ever knew. I didn't have too much in common with my father. My father's horrible attitude toward my mother alienated me. So my father and I took opposite paths. I would suppose he alienated me. My father lived on hate; if he didn't hate my mother, he hated my brother. Me, no—I was the apple of his eye. But subsequently I let him have it.

I was about fifteen or sixteen years old and told him one night, I told him that I was fed up, I was going to leave the family and take my mother with me, because I couldn't stand his hypocritical way, and his hate and condemnation of people. He condemned all he knew, no matter what they did to him. Everybody. Everybody. In 1929, I pleaded with my mother to get a divorce, but she was brought up in another world. I took an oath at the time that I would defend my mother in getting even with my father. But I never got even with him, but I did

266

tell him off and that broke our close relationship, I told him that I thought he was a horrible creature with a vicious tongue, and he was made of hate and that God would punish him.

In the ethnically mixed neighborhoods into which Jewish families moved as they prospered, Jewish children could, if they wanted to—and children like George Isaacs apparently very much wanted to—experience other forms of religious observance at close hand:

Even at an early age I had definite feelings and when my friends were bar mitzvahed, I refused. Of course, I had the opportunity. My father wouldn't consider me going to church, but he probably asked me or suggested that I be bar mitzvahed the way my brother was. And I absolutely refused to. And he sent me to Sunday school, too, but after the second time I turned around and refused to go. I didn't want any part of it. I rejected it. Totally. I rejected Judaism, because I said that I had heard about Jesus Christ and I wanted to follow Jesus Christ. Judaism offered faith and hope but it didn't offer inspiration and Christ offered me inspiration. And that motivated my thinking for the rest of my life.

My mother, as an adult, never went to anything. She looked upon religion as something man-made, and she figured she would make her own religion. It was in her heart.

I, in turn, often pleaded and went with my neighbors who were Catholic. On Sunday morning when I saw them go to church, I was very envious. When I went to camp, on Sunday I saw Christian boys— eighty or ninety boys got into station wagons or cars—go to church. I had a great yen to go to church.

But as a young preteen lad, you couldn't make the decisions, but sometimes my father would let me go. But I didn't like it because there was nothing beautiful about it. It was one of those little local churches that offered very little beauty to the eye. I could see the quality, the soberness about it, but I didn't like it.

Subsequently, I went to the Christian Science Church, too, in my effort to find a new faith. Sometimes my mother went with me.

To young Jews in these neighborhoods, the families of gentiles often seemed—as they did to Isaacs—more appealing than their own:

There was a man in my neighborhood who called his kids by blowing this horn; the women would call out the window, but he wouldn't, he would blow this horn. He wasn't home all the time, and he had a sister—such a symbol of femininity, so soft and sweet, beautiful and soft-spoken and sweet. And I used to go visit them and love it. The mother was Episcopalian, and the father was Jewish. Their son was brought up an Episcopalian. And I was so envious of this. He had a certain gentility about him in contrast with the other boys—let us say, from a different environment. I didn't know what it was; I wouldn't equate it with a religion. All I know is when I left his apartment I always wanted to go back.

In the end, Isaacs converted:

I was disenchanted about Judaism. Early in my life, having been exposed in a very, very small way, a limited way, to Christianity, I was exposed to the teachings of Christ, and I thought they were—I did my own questionings, and I am using retrospect, it must have been intuitive on my part, I felt—I sensed that what Jesus Christ stood for was good and inspiring.

To me the Jewish faith, as I saw it through the eyes of my friends, was a faith of one dimension: you were always doing something wrong. Apparently nothing that they did met the approval of their rabbi: they mustn't do this, and they mustn't do that, and they mustn't do the next thing. It seemed to me, as a child, that Jews didn't enjoy themselves. I must have analyzed it without knowing that I was analyzing it, and sensed that there was nothing inspirational. They had dedication and belief and consecration, on fulfilling certain requirements, and it was a wonderful training, but it was nothing inspirational.

I can remember that as a seven-year-old on the High Holy Days my friends were going to davn. It bothered me that these kids were walking around and talking about their high holiness and how they fasted, and they were little bastards most of them. They did a lot of things that I didn't think was right. And all of a sudden they were holy.

Thirty or forty years, twenty-five years, I was being forced to live different from what I desired; I was frustrated. Most of the time in my Jewish life I never observed the holidays. My parents didn't, and when

268

I went to college, I didn't. When I was married I still considered myself Jewish. But eventually I went to a doctor [a therapist], and I learned that I really wanted to be a Christian, and finally—at the age of fifty-four—I became a Presbyterian. I was baptized by my closest friend. I became very devout—an alderman and president of the men's club.

My mother used to say that everybody was out of step but her son. I discovered suddenly that my children were important. I had never exposed myself to them until then. I was a purist in a nonpurist world. I even thought of becoming a minister myself.

"No More Kosher Meat": Becoming Emancipated

On the continuum of Jewish belief that begins with Orthodoxy and ends with conversion, most Jews of our parents' generation fell somewhere in between. Defining precisely where they fell, however, can prove difficult. Our parents sometimes traversed several categories during a lifetime: rebellious, for example, early in life, conformist later on. Indeed, some can traverse categories in the space of just one year: Orthodox during the High Holy Days in September and indifferent by Hannukah in December. Some were *halakhic* when self-employed but Reform when they worked for a non-Jewish employer. Each Jew, it is sometimes said, practices his or her own brand of Judaism; some practice several different brands simultaneously.

A few generalizations are, however, possible. Many of our parents who were the children of Orthodox parents began to drift away from the law when they were very young—sometimes, as with George Isaacs, out of dislike for one of their parents, often the father.

MORRIS HOCHSTADT: *My father was a laconic person who never sat down and spoke to us or explained anything to us. He probably didn't know enough about it to explain it. He told us how smart his father was. He use to revel in stories of how brilliant his father was, but never revealed anything to us.*

One Saturday morning, I got up to polish my shoes to go to shul, and he came out and saw me and gave me such a sock in the face, my mother almost killed him. [She said,] "What right did you have to do

269

*that? I am teaching him Yiddishkeit, not you. You think you are hold-
ing God by both legs!" And my grandfather is saying to my father,
"The shine will leave the shoes, but what is in the brain will always
stay there."*

*That's how my father was. The only time I almost wept in this con-
versation is when I told you about my father, 'cause I felt sorry for him,
I felt sorry for him because he was a person who went through life
without ever having lived.*

Other young Jews, the first in their families to attend public schools,
were keenly aware of the flaws in their religious education. In the
United States, those children who were sent to *cheder* were sent after
regular school hours; the *cheders* were badly maintained (the parents
were, after all, poor), and the *melameds* (just as in Europe) poorly paid.
Charlie Moses, who later became a physician, was a good student in
cheder, but that does not make his memories of the atmosphere or the
pedagogy any fonder:

*Every three years there was another teacher, and the cheder was always
next to the toilet in the basement and smelled from urine. In the basement of the shul. The plumbing, they never took care of it; we were
on the bottom rung of the community.*

*Each class must have had twenty-five or thirty kids. It was a rowdy
place, and it was just like a Harlem school today—Jewish kids who
didn't want to go to Hebrew school.*

*It might have been better with me, but I was taught whatever Jew-
ishness I was taught without explaining what it meant. The chumash
[Torah and Haftorah readings arranged by weekly portions] that I read,
I could interpret it but I never knew what it meant. No attempt was
made to bring any sort of relationship between what was going on then
and what was going on now. In other words, I read it as though it was
foreign history, not as though it was part of my history.*

*My parents followed the dogma of Judaism without asking ques-
tions. When I went to Hebrew school, I was the best student in the
school. The rabbi told my mother, "Yussel is a very smart boy. He
should become a rabbi. The only thing is, he is a groyser [great] anti-
Semite." I rebelled against his teaching on occasion. I hadn't done what*

he said. To him my questions meant insubordination. I never became a rabbi.

Occasionally, in discussing their retreat from Orthodox Judaism, some of our parents refer to various attractive aspects of Christianity, especially as they were made manifest in public schools. Rose Janofsky, for example, was one of several women we interviewed who were much influenced by the attitudes and the behavior of their teachers. She is now aware that that influence pulled her away from her parents' traditions:

In the goyishe schools, they can hurt you, they can do damage to you. In high school they made a big to-do over Christmas. It was a very festive occasion—the last day before the holidays, before the schools closed. I was very conscious of being Jewish. The school was predominantly Christian, Catholic, Italian.

Christianity seemed more festive; they had more fun. They went to church and had boyfriends at church—the dating, going to church, dating with the boys that went to church. Very different from the life we led. We didn't have the socializing; we had family, relatives. You were very conscious that you were different.

We sang all the Christmas songs in the assembly, and there were Jewish girls who didn't sing. The really religious girls didn't sing. The ones who went to Hebrew school, they didn't sing. The Christmas songs are really very Christian. I remember all the songs. I think they are beautiful.

All those Christmas carols and repetitions of the Lord's Prayer, each probably insignificant in itself, had a cumulative effect. Some of our parents came to see their own religion as somehow less important, less acceptable, less commanding, less beautiful than Christianity.

For those who attended college, this impression was augmented, first by the anticlerical, Darwinist attitudes of many of the faculty and their fellow students, and second—perhaps most crucially—by the discovery that one could break the rules, violate *halakha*, without untoward consequences. Sam Smilowitz had come, for example, from a traditional household; his mother "kept kosher"; his father went to morning services every day. Sam's older brothers had begun to drift away

271

from Orthodoxy (they stopped *leygn tefillin* every morning—that is, stopped strapping phylacteries to their body and praying), but Sam remained very much within the fold until he went to college: "When I went off to school, that stopped it. There was no place for services [at the University of Illinois]. There was no community. I didn't miss services." Charlie Moses describes a similar experience, at Cornell, in more detail:

My parents were Orthodox. In fact, I was Orthodox, too, until my adolescence. I put on tefillin every day, went to synagogue most every day—morning, afternoon. I was real nuts. It was a little too much.

When I went up to college, I had never—but never—been away from home. In the summer, for a couple of weeks, I had visited an uncle of mine who had a farm, but that is not the same thing; my sister was with me. I had never—but never!—eaten out in a restaurant. Furthermore, I had always eaten kosher, naturally, at home. And the nonkosher was like poison to me—psychologically, I mean. So here I am. I don't know how I had the nerve for it. Fortunately a close friend of mine was in the same boat.

He was in the same boat, so what we did, I had a dumpy basement apartment, along with a couple of other guys, and there was some kind of makeshift kitchen facilities. So for three months we brought in food: vegetables, fruit, whatever else doesn't need to be kosher. And we ate—for three months.

Gradually, though, we went out to cafeterias and bought likewise nonkosher meats and so on. And one sin leads to another, and that is how I became emancipated. And since no synagogue was available anywhere nearby, that was it. Passover was the one remnant of religion that I had while I was in college.

Other young Jews, rebellious but not able to attend college out of town, deliberately challenged their parents by flouting *halakha* close to home. Yom Kippur, the holiest and most solemn day of the year—a day of fasting—was often the occasion for such rebellion. Janet Sommers recalls that her brother, Ben, attended a radical political meeting deliberately scheduled for the evening of Yom Kippur: "My mother never forgave him for that. She was always hurt by that." An anarchist organization published an announcement for its Yom Kippur "ball" in a New York newspaper in 1890; the text provides some sense to the deliberate antagonism that was intended:

Grand Yom Kippur Ball.
With theatre.
Arranged with the consent of all new rabbis of Liberty.
Koll Nydre Night and Day.
In the year 5651, after the invention of the Jewish idols,
and 1890, after the birth of the false Messiah. . . .
The Koll Nydre will be offered by John Most.
Music, dancing, buffet, "Marseillaise," and other hymns
against Satan.[5]

Sol Meyrowitz also recalls violating the sanctity of Yom Kippur, although he now tells the story with a bit of ambivalence in his voice:

Every Yom Kippur we would meet outside somebody's house and "go for a walk." Going for a walk means a couple of guys going to the German bakery and getting coffee and buns. During the night, in the evening, at the end of Kol Nidre, we would all walk to the German bakery. If our parents had known this, oy!

I think we did this not as protest but as ignorance. We did not realize what this stands for, Yom Kippur is the Day of Atonement. We only knew that we were Jewish—nothing more. We knew it was wrong, and that is why we would go for a walk in another neighborhood to get the buns. We lived in a solid Jewish neighborhood.

In our parents' generation, such deliberate efforts to flout tradition were frequent. Sam Reiss recalls an incident during the first year of his first job as a cantor. A young woman in the congregation (Conservative), roughly his own age, granddaughter of the chairman of the board, was about to get married, and came to see him in his office. She had a request to make about the music for her wedding ceremony.

SAM REISS: *"When we come down the aisle," she said, "I would like the organ not to play, just chime." Well, that is interesting. "What would you like them to play for you?" "I want the chimes to play 'Hi, ho! Hi, ho! It's Off to Work We Go.'"*

273

I didn't laugh. Sweat came over my face. Here I am. I see my job flying out the window. I am there on the job two, three weeks—this bombshell! My eyes popped out of my head. "You must have a good reason for asking this. You must have a very good reason for requesting this." She said, "Yes, when my fiancé proposed to me, we were in the movies, and this was on the screen, this song." I said, "And for this you want me to lose my job?" I said I would be laughed out of the congregation. "Don't you realize that?" She said, "It's my wedding and that is what I want." I said, "But that is not what you are going to get. I would rather give you Wagner [the wedding march used in churches] than this."

I didn't know at the time that she was the granddaughter of the chairman of the board of the congregation. In the next two or three days, I get a memo requesting me to appear before the board of the congregation. I still didn't know why. I came down and I was welcomed very cordially. "You are a young man, and as a young man you are going to grow with us. But as a young man why don't you encourage young people to come to the congregation? Get to know them." I said, "You must have more of a specific reason for having called me down." They said, "Yes, we received a letter of complaint" that I refused to have the organ play certain music during a wedding. I said, "All right, it will take me two minutes to tell you my side, which I think you want to hear."

And when I finished, there was an uproar of laughter, everybody couldn't stop laughing. The chairman turned red and kind of slid down into his chair. They said, "Keep it up. You are doing fine. You are absolutely right." A unanimous vote of confidence.

Some immigrant youths, not as rebellious, not interested in flouting convention, nonetheless began to slip away from it as they entered the workforce. Violating the rules against various kinds of activities on the Sabbath was particularly painful for them, since the Sabbath lies at the liturgical and emotional heart of Orthodox observance. Yet the Sabbath had to be violated if one was to succeed in a country that regarded Sunday, not Saturday, as the day of rest. Sadie Rehstock's sisters had preceded her in loosening the bonds of Sabbath, but that did not much lessen the pain:

When I graduated high school, I had a job interview where I had to work on Saturday mornings. I finally took that job. But, you know, the conditioning is so strong that when I rode on the train I felt that I was violating the Sabbath. When I came into the office the first Sabbath, I was nervous because I was a new worker and I was there early. I sat and I did not put the light on. I sat in the dark until somebody else came in and turned on the light.

But to know that I had done that! I had ridden on the Sabbath. I had paid my fare! I came in, but to do the last thing of putting on the lights: it was so hard. I did not turn on the lights. But I remember it was something riding on that train!

And Jennie Grossman's husband, like many Jewish businessmen, found that, because customers expected to be able to shop on Saturdays, retail businesses had to stay open:

My husband was in business, the grocery business. He had to work Shabbos. He had to because he was in business, and he had a partner and he wanted to work Sunday and the partner should work Shabbos, and the partner said, "No, Saturday's a busy day and I don't want to be alone," so he had to work Shabbos.

The partner was Jewish but he was not religious. But he had to do it; if you wanted to make a living you had to do it. On Saturday. It bothered him, but he couldn't help it. He wanted to make a living. He wanted on account of me; he could make a living for me.

Max Hirsch remarked that, when he came to America in the 1920s, he discovered, to his surprise, that some American Jews ate on Yom Kippur, "doing the hopelessly opposite of what it should be." He thought that they violated the fast to show that they were good Americans, "to show people that they are not afraid of God's anger, they are not afraid of anything." Esther Ginsburg thought it was just plain hypocrisy; and as with other people of other faiths in other generations, the sense that others were hypocrites caused a slackening of her own observance:

When I was first married, I wanted to be kosher because my mother-in-law wanted me to be kosher and observe all the holidays. So I started off in my home to be kosher and do everything right. And I would only buy kosher meats. So I kept buying these steaks and they were inedible, because kosher steaks, the way they were cut, and I would make these steaks and throw them in the garbage. I cooked vegetables like crazy, but Mike [her husband] never ate a vegetable in his life, he never knew what they were, so I used to throw vegetables away. I was a good wife and I was a good cook. I was really a marvelous housekeeper. Money was no problem.

Anyway, one day—and I observed all the holidays, Yom Kippur to me was, like if you didn't observe Yom Kippur and not eat, forget it!— well, one day I went to my mother-in-law's house for Yom Kippur. She was supposed to be the real religious one, right? And I didn't eat a morsel of food because it was Yom Kippur. I come into the house. Guess what? All the shades are down, and they are eating up a storm. I never said anything. I came home and I said to myself, "They are lying there." And from then on, I said to myself, "No more kosher meat." A girlfriend whose father was a rabbi taught me to use nonkosher meat.

Tess Egrovsky stopped keeping her home kosher when she came to the conclusion that in America, since everything was cleaner than it had been in her native Russia, special hygienic efforts were unreasonably burdensome:

I come [in Russia] from a very Orthodox home, but here I didn't care if it was necessary to be Orthodox. I felt, you see, first of all, my husband was very ill; and, secondly, I felt that so much more was clean and everything—why should I be so foolish? Plenty of hot water. In Russia, when we had to wash dishes, we had to warm up a pot of water to wash dishes. We had to do things in Russia we didn't have to do here.

So I felt, why should I be Orthodox when everything is so clean? So I didn't think it was necessary. I used to buy kosher meat, you know. I used to cook like home, if you know what I mean. But as far as dishes was concerned, I felt the water was so clean. That's what I felt.

I didn't go to shul on Rosh Hashonah or Yom Kippur. And my husband surely didn't care. In the beginning, he thought we would have a kosher house because he wanted his people to eat. But I felt it is too much trouble to have two kinds of dishes. I bought two kinds of dishes but I never used them. I rather make it unkosher.

form, to identify
ied, authoritative
f course, chose to
. Especially when
rebellious young
e about their reli-
ther than—to use

house, and my mother-in-
father-in-law used to eat

e-born Americans, Rose
t, objected to the lack of

a home as I could.
nt to the same shul
ght away. I should
ated all the holidays
prayers are not the
w; my father didn't
w it either.
ized I could be both
d our daughter was
w Hebrew. I do not
mple I would be the
ne! The Y that we
l into the Y, and the
children. And came
uld read English. The
e prayer books in En-
read them in English

nineteen, twenty—my
o go. Whoever heard of
d in the dirty water and
the same water. The
anted money from my

e the story, I told my
married you will not
right in the house," I
r, and that's it." And
ne.

re less observant—
been. George Man-
osh Hashonah and
even that remnant
re complex. Some
e out of laziness,
But whatever the
vious. *Yarmulkes*
makers went out
ed to reveal their

hough proud of being
gation. They chose to
ommers, for example,

and science—how the
nder. I don't believe in
God? Particularly the
re. How can a God be
particularly in today's

Tradition

parents were
identity, al-
tive; perhaps

"ethnic" would be better. Most continued, in some [
themselves as Jews; but, lacking role models and unif
leadership, the forms varied all over the map. Some, c
affiliate with Conservative or Reform congregations
they became parents themselves, some previously
people decided that, however ambivalent they wer
gion, they preferred to raise their children as Jews r?
their phrase—"as nothing."

REBECCA GREEN: *In my own way I made as Jewish*
My parents were very Orthodox and my father we
his whole life here. I didn't keep a kosher home r
have. I did not make the effort, I didn't. But I celebr
all my life and I lit candles on Friday night. But m
prayers in Hebrew because I never learned Hebre
care about teaching me, and my mother didn't kno

Later on when I started to read and think, I real
American and Jewish. When we moved here ar
growing up, I said, "My daughter does not kno
know Hebrew. If only there was a Conservative t
first one to join." Lo and behold, they created
belonged to started one in a storefront. It move
minute they did have services, we yanked our tw
the holidays now there was no excuse—we all co
Conservative synagogue could provide us with tl
glish. My husband read them in Hebrew and we
and it was perfect.

But many of the people we interviewed, alt
Jewish, had never been affiliated with a congre
cultivate their Judaism in other ways. Janet S
defines herself as a Jewish atheist:

I don't believe there is a God. I believe in reality
world got to be, what makes lightning and thu
any image or any person. How can there be ?
God is only for good, to bless you, to take ca
anywhere with the terrible things going on,

278

"The Conservative synagogue could provide us
with the prayer books in English.
My husband read them in Hebrew and we read them in English
and it was perfect."
Bar mitzvah boy with his rabbi and parents, Brooklyn, 1971.

society? Every country they are killing one another. How can a God permit that?

I am a Jew, but I am not Jewish in any of the symbols. I am not religious at all. I don't believe I can identify matters of religion with the stomach. My idea of a truly religious person is at Yom Kippur, instead of members of our family going to temple to pray, they should come to visit us on Yom Kippur. That to me is religion, true religion— when you are considerate and kind to a living person who needs you. That is how I feel about it.

Rose Janofsky echoes Janet Sommers's sentiments. "I am not a religious Jew," she says, "but I am a very traditional Jew. I can't go to *shul* and pray. I don't believe in God, not when there is all this suffering in the world. If there really was a God, there shouldn't have been a Holocaust, nor the terrible epidemics, the poverty, the terrible starvation." Yet some traditional rituals continue to play a role in Mrs. Janofsky's life, and so does the State of Israel:

I love to believe in tradition. When I was rewriting a will, I arranged, I paid, to have Kaddish said for Jack [her husband]. The man asked to have it arranged for me, and I told him that I didn't believe, but he [Jack] believed, so I'm having it done for him. I don't do it because I think I will or will not get a blessing from God. It makes life very colorful to be religious. My religious friends have lives that are enriched because they are religious. If you have children, especially if you are Jewish, you have to give them the enrichment.

I'm proud I'm Jewish. I wouldn't want to be anything else. I go to Israel because I am a Jew without being religious. Kaddish is being said because it would make him [Jack] feel good even though I know he can't hear it.

I read someplace not too long ago that if you don't have God you won't have man. Maybe the average person or the great majority of people need a God. Maybe they do in order to be civilized. Right now man is somewhere between the ape and the human being. We really have not evolved to a true human being yet. And the behavior that is going on now is as barbaric as anything that has gone on in the caves.

REMAINING JEWISH IN AMERICA

Devotion to tradition has not, however, helped Rose Janofsky to resolve her ambivalence about being Jewish:

My mother did not look like a Jewish woman at all, so wherever we lived, wherever we shopped, she never denied it; it was a part of her. But I think if I had my druthers, I would have liked to be born a white Protestant. It is easier. Just for the matter of peace without having to worry, "Will somebody hate me? Will they keep my children from getting a job? Will they keep my husband from making a living because he is Jewish?" Just from matters of ease, it would have been easier to be a non-Jew.

That ambivalence arises, at least in part, from the immigrant desire simultaneously to reject that which is non-American and to cling to it, as Rebecca Green's account of her first years in New York reveals:

I was a typically American Jewish girl—American first, Jewish second. I remember the first day we were here, standing on the train there, and holding on to a rail and shaking, and I am looking around and seeing all these people and seeing everybody's mouth going up and down, and I say, "Ah! An American custom!" And I started to move my mouth up and down: they were chewing gum. Right away I started to be an American. That's all I wanted. I was so determined to become an American. I really wanted to start anything that was American.

I wanted no part of anything that was Europe. For a long time I really hated the fact that I came from Europe and I was a greenhorn. I didn't want to be associated with being Jewish. I remember also my father's father, my grandfather Itzhak. I think I was afraid of him. He was a stern man. I remember afterward we moved into our own apartment and he used to come to visit us. If I see him down the street, I would go hide behind a bench or something and let him walk by. I felt badly about that afterward. I didn't know why I did it. I think the reason was he looked so Jewish. I didn't want to be associated. He had a beard, and he looked so foreign. I wanted to be part of where I was.

The double tension, between theology on the one hand and tradition on the other, between the desire to become an American, on yet another pair of hands, and the inclination to remain Jewish, is precisely what has produced the phenomenon earlier called "bagel Judaism"—a cultural package from which the religious content has been removed, a life style rather than a set of rituals, *Yiddishkeit* without Judaism. Both Sadie Rehstock, who arrived when she was elementary school age, and Max Hirsch, who did not emigrate until his twenties, reflect different aspects of that resolution. For Hirsch it is political:

I grew up with strong religious beliefs but when I came here in 1923 I was not really a Jew. I came back to Judaism because I had two children and I didn't want them to grow up any other way but Jewish. In one form or another, Jewish was the best way.

So we joined a Reform synagogue, and by 1931, I became the president. I didn't become a religious Jew but a good Jew—working for the temple, working for the different societies.

When the Scottsboro boys case* came up—you heard about that?—I went around from door to door, ringing doorbells collecting money for the defense. That was the kind of Jewishness that I wanted. I wanted to be a Jew—feeling the sympathy, the responsibility for goodness, the desire to do goodness. And I couldn't get that in a yeshiva.

For Rehstock it is ethical:

The repetition of "glory to God" to me is meaningless; it doesn't move me. If I want spiritual uplift, I can get it from a good concert. I have heard rabbis who have left me cold. Fortunately my husband feels the same way; we have no problems. I live by a strict sense of ethics. I have come to feel this way about my kids, too, finally saying to them "If you have got to marry somebody who is not a Jew, please don't do it with somebody who is a religious something else."

---

* A famous legal battle that began in 1931 when nine black youths were charged, on insubstantial evidence, with raping two white women in Alabama. After several trials, seven were sentenced to death. In 1938, however, four were set free and three death sentences were commuted to life imprisonment. In 1976, the last surviving prisoner was given an unconditional pardon by Governor George Wallace.

282

I went to Hebrew school and went every day because I was Ortho-dox and said the Sh'ma [the central prayer of Judaism; it asserts the unity of God] every night, and then I had a Communist piano teacher. I used to go to his apartment, and we had a lesson for half an hour, and then the rest [of the time] he tried to get me to sign a petition against the Kellogg-Briand Pact.* He said if there is a God he would be in-sulted by the way human beings worship Him. I thought of that and little by little—and that plus college and a few courses—it just didn't exist any more.

But I have a predicament, and I will never be able to solve it. I love being a Jew and I love the Jewish people. I think they are absolutely fantastic. I love the fact that I come from something; that it is old and substantial. I love the fact that it has followed and always been there, and stands for something free and upright, with character. I love all of that. And if I can only believe in God, I would probably go to shul.

I don't believe in God, I don't believe in any divinity. Absolutely not. I do believe in Jews.

Anti-Semitism, in its various forms, motivated our parents not just to remember the roots but also to fertilize the plant. When he was a young man living in Philadelphia, Aaron Katz says, "I didn't have the slightest desire or need for the expression of the ritual or the obser-vances to perpetuate Judaism." But when he moved to the South, which he compares to the Negev, "the population is less than one half of one percent Jewish." There he became aware of anti-Semitism, "not at the bottom, but everywhere at the top." Katz's reaction was not to run but to stand his ground, build a firmer base:

A person has to live with a measure of self-respect, otherwise he will be looked upon with suspicion. In the years 1948 to 1958, I really studied everything about Judaism, and now I am comfortable with my-self as a Jew. My background and my education and the conditions of my life until now have led me to feel that we are different than anyone else. How we have survived, with all that persecution, it is really a mystery. But survival is important. I became active in the synagogue,

---

* The Kellogg-Briand Peace Pact, under President Calvin Coolidge and ratified by the U.S. Senate on 15 January 1929, "renounced war as an instrument of national policy" and promised to solve "all disputes or conflicts of whatever nature or of whatever origin" by "pacific means."

contributed a lot of money. And now we are building a Jewish center—for the kids.

Many of the people we interviewed have developed a unique form of Zionism as part of their reaction to anti-Semitism. Few want actually to become citizens of Israel (they don't want their children to go either: too dangerous; too faraway), and fewer still see Israel as a place where it would be more comfortable to be more observant. Theirs is a post-Holocaust Zionism: they want Israel to exist, and they want organized Jewry to exist, as a protection against persecution, as a shield for their children and their grandchildren. Max Weiner expresses these connections explicitly:

I never denied being a Jew, but I never gave it much thought either until a guy named Hitler arrived. And he made me believe, realize that I was a Jew. The Holocaust brought a lot of us back.

What do I do? Well, I give money. I just sent a check to a Senator Arlen Specter [of Pennsylvania]; he is a great Jewish protector; he speaks up in the Senate, and the Arabs are running a campaign now against him. And against Israel. So I give money to Israel, too. I buy bonds, Israel Bonds. The bonds you don't buy for investment. Most of the people who buy those bonds don't buy them for investment.

If I wanted to get a message to my grandchildren that they would remember forever, it would be: Don't wait for another holocaust to go back to your religion. I want them to come, become part of the Jewish tradition and religion, without being Orthodox. Knowing what I do now, I might have become active as a religious person. Giving my temple more than twelve hundred dollars a year is O.K., but it is not doing what I should have done years ago.

And so does Morris Hochstadt, whose dislike for his father and his father's Orthodoxy is nonetheless tempered by the reality of the ovens:

Now when we came to this country, my father used to go to shul right across the street, but my brothers and me, we tried to wiggle out and come in late. Now I realize that he was eager to have people see that he comes in with three sons to shul. So I say to myself, "You jerk! Why do you take away his pleasure?" We used to come in late, the service would be half over, he would give us dirty looks: "How come you are coming in so late?" The shul was right across the street. But we had other things to do. We used to run around, sleep late.

Later on, we regretted it. What the heck did we have to aggravate him for? If he got pleasure, let's give him the pleasure. After all, we have to thank him; otherwise, we would be a pile of ashes. When I first went into business, I used to stay open on the holidays. The feeling was that you shouldn't take the day off if you didn't believe. But when Hitler came in, then it was another story. The solidarity of Jews made the difference. Hitler was in, and he was demonstrating, and it was important to let the world know you were Jewish.

Morris Hochstadt, like many members of his generation, is thrilled to discover that his grandchildren are not troubled by the ambivalence that plagued him in his early years, that led him to hide or to deny his Jewishness when he was young: "My grandchildren carry their Hebrew book outside because their sense is so much stronger than it was in my days. I was a greenhorn. I was a Jew in a Christian milieu, and Jews in those days are not what they are today."

Precisely so. The Jews in those days were not what they are today—or, for that matter, were yesterday. Our parents' generation of Eastern European immigrants, the Jews who were born between 1895 and 1915 and became American citizens, created forms of Judaism that were historically, even personally, unique. With the exception of those few who remained Orthodox and those even fewer who converted, most American Jews of that generation practiced a Judaism that would have been incomprehensible to their ancestors—and is sometimes incomprehensible even to their neighbors, children, and friends. One will light the Sabbath candles on Friday night and then serve shrimp for dinner. Another reads extensively in Jewish history but insists that his children must not invite a rabbi to preside over his funeral. A third is an avowed atheist who has sent each of her six grandchildren to Israel to study for a year. With the exception of those who remained Orthodox, almost all of the people we interviewed are practicing some insignificant number of the 613 commandments while still calling themselves Jewish.

Each is passionately Jewish, and each, realizing the promise of a "free country," has created unique ways of celebrating, affirming, that

285

passion. "We raised ourselves," Hannah Toperoff remarked more than once during our interview, and we have come to understand that this was as true of religious observance as of other aspects of our parents' lives. They had no models, no reliable guides to depend on. Never before in history had Jews found themselves assimilating to a culture quite like America in the early decades of the twentieth century: expansive, expanding, growing more secular with every passing year. Unable to turn to their parents, because their parents—even could they have heard the questions—had no answers, they created a culture, a Jewish culture, all their own.

And, being our parents, they ought, of course, to have the last word on this subject.

SAM SMILOWITZ: *I have a picture in my head—a line or tribe of people with me standing up on my toes and looking behind me and seeing my past. I have to be on my toes because it is a long line and I am trying to see to the very end, which I can't see because of time.*

It is the most fantastic thing in the world to be an American. It is unbelievable! Pie in the sky! Streets are paved with gold! We have fallen into the most wonderful world conceivable. I am always astonished by it. I can't imagine, how lucky can I get, could I have been, to have been born at this time, to have been spared my ancestors' hardship in Europe. Living in this land of plentitude, this having the ability of making it, go out and seek it, and get it. And get it! It is available. My goodness, my goodness! Including my washing machine, my washing machine. You know, my mother's scrubbing brush is down in the basement. That is America.

It made no difference whatsoever if we didn't have a kosher home and lit candles. We make contributions to Israel because we are Jews.

Why would you want another religion when you have one that is perfectly good?

Notes

Chapter 1. "Dangerous Just to Be": Life in the Old Country

BIBLIOGRAPHICAL NOTE: In addition to the works cited below, the following have provided useful background in the preparation of this chapter: Mary Antin, *From Plotsk to Boston* (Boston, 1899); Mary Antin, *The Promised Land* (Boston, 1912); Salo W. Baron, *The Russian Jew under Tsars and Soviets* (New York, 1964); Harry E. Burrows, *Tale of a Vanished Land: Memories of a Childhood in Russia* (London, 1930); Abraham Cahan, *The Rise of David Levinsky* (New York, 1917); Bernard Horwich, *My First Eighty Years* (Chicago, 1939); Paula Hyman et al., *The Jewish Woman in Europe and America* (New York, 1974); Pamela Susan Nadell, "The Journey to America by Steam: The Jews of Eastern Europe in Transition," (Ph.D. dissertation, Ohio State University, 1982); U.S. Congress, *Reports of the Immigration Commission: On Steerage Conditions*, Senate document 753 (Washington, D.C., 1911); Bernard Rosenberg and Ernest Goldstein, *Creators and Disturbers: Reminiscences by Jewish Intellectuals of New York* (New York, 1982); Mark Zborowski and Elizabeth Herzog, *Life is with People: The Culture of the Shtetl* (New York, 1952).

1. Mark M. Warshawsky, "Oyfn Pripitshik" (originally "Dem Alef Beyz"), in Eleanor Gordon Mlotek, *"Mir Trogen a Gezangl"*: *Favorite Yiddish Songs of Our Generation* (New York, 1972, 1977, 1982).

2. Esther Ginsburg's comments are from the Union College Collection. Henceforth, those quotations not from our interviews but from either the Union College Collection or the William E. Wiener Oral History Library, American Jewish Committee, New York, will be designated as UCC and AJC, respectively.

3. AJC.

4. W. I. Thomas and Florian Znaniecki, *The Polish Peasant in Europe and America* (Chicago, 1918), vol. I, p. 503.

5. Ibid., vol. II, p. 1241.

6. Ibid., vol. II, p. 1243.

7. UCC.

8. Simon Dubnow, *History of the Jews in Russia and Poland* (Philadelphia, 1920), vol. III, pp. 22–23.

9. Thomas and Znaniecki, *Polish Peasant*, vol. II, pp. 1200–1201.

10. Ibid., vol. I, p. 472.

11. AJC.

12. Dubnow, *History of the Jews*, vol. II, p. 271.

13. As quoted in Cyrus Adler, *The Voice of America on Kishineff* (Philadelphia, 1904), p. *xii*.

14. Excerpt from a memorandum written by the Jewish Colonization Society of St. Petersburg (sometimes called the Baron de Hirsch Fund), as quoted in U.S. Congress, *Reports of the Immigration Commission: On Emigration Conditions in Europe*, Senate document 748 (Washington, D.C., 1911), p. 278.

15. This account, which derives from the transcription of an interview, is quoted in Saul Friedman, *Pogromchik* (New York, 1976), p. 18. The transcript belongs to YIVO-Institute for Jewish Research, Inc., New York.

Chapter 2. "Tempest Tossed": Learning to Live in America

BIBLIOGRAPHICAL NOTE: Background material for this chapter was derived from: Allen F. Davis, *Spearheads for Reform: The Social Settlements and the Progressive Movement, 1890–1914* (New York, 1967); Henry Feingold, *Zion in America: The Jewish Experience from Colonial Times to the Present* (New York, 1974); David Handlin, *The American Home: Architecture and Society, 1815–1915* (Boston, 1979); Oscar Handlin, *The Uprooted*, 2nd ed. (Boston, 1973); Irving Howe, *World of Our Fathers: The Journey of the East European Jews to America and the Life They Found and Made* (New York, 1976); Irving Howe and Kenneth Libo, *How We Lived: A Documentary History of Jews in America, 1880–1930* (New York, 1979); Samuel Joseph, *Jewish Immigration to the United States from 1881 to 1910* (New York, 1914); Deborah Dash Moore, *At Home in America: Second Generation New York Jews* (New York, 1981); David W. Noble, *The Progressive Mind: 1890–1917* (Chicago, 1970); Moses Rischin, *The Promised City: New York's Jews, 1870–1914* (Cambridge, Mass., 1962); Henry Roth, *Call It Sleep* (New York, 1934); Gwendolyn Wright, *Moralism and the Model Home: Domestic Architecture and Cultural Conflict in Chicago, 1873–1913* (Chicago, 1980).

1. Boris D. Bogen, "The Children of the Jewish Poor," *The Menorah* 33 (1902): 316.

2. John Ruskin, *Sesame and Lilies* (New York, 1891), pp. 136–37.

3. Robert W. DeForest and Lawrence Veiller, "The Tenement House Problem," in Robert W. DeForest and Lawrence Veiller, eds., *The Tenement House Problem* (New York, 1903), vol. I, p. 3.

4. Robert Coit Chapin, *The Standard of Living of Workingmen's Families in New York City* (New York, 1910), p. 65.

5. Lawrence Veiller, *Housing Reform* (New York, 1910), p. 33.

6. UCC.

7. Kate Hooladay Claghorn, "Immigration and the Tenement House," in DeForest and Veiller, *Tenement House Problem*, vol. II, pp. 87–88.

8. Maurice Fishberg, "Health and Sanitation of the Immigrant Jewish Population

9. UCC.

10. Frank Tucker, "Public Baths," in DeForest and Veiller, *Tenement House Problem*, vol. II, p. 54.

11. Fishberg, "Health and Sanitation," p. 74.

12. "Report of the [New York] Small Parks Committee of 1897," as quoted in Lawrence Veiller, "Playgrounds and Parks for Tenement Districts," in DeForest and Veiller, *Tenement House Problem*, vol. II, p. 7.

13. Anatole Leroy-Beaulieu, *Israel Among the Nations: A Study of the Jews and Anti-*

semitism (1895) as quoted in Maurice Fishberg, "The Homes of the Jews in the New York Ghetto," *The Menorah* 33 (1902): 43.

14. Bogen, "Children of the Jewish Poor," p. 319.

Chapter 3. Breaking Away from Torah: The Impact of American Schooling

BIBLIOGRAPHICAL NOTE: Background material for this chapter, in addition to materials already cited in previous chapters, is derived from: Morris Isaiah Berger, "The Settlement, The Immigrant and the Public School: A Study of the Influence of the Settlement Movement and the New Migration upon Public Education: 1890–1924," (Ph.D. dissertation, Columbia University, 1956); Stephen F. Brumberg, *Going to America, Going to School: The Jewish Immigrant Public School Encounter in Turn-of-the-Century New York City* (New York, 1986); Lawrence Cremin, *The Transformation of the School: Progressivism in American Education* (New York, 1961); Ellwood P. Cubberley, *History of Education: Educational Practice and Progress Considered as a Phase of the Development and Spread of Western Civilization* (Boston, 1920).

1. UCC.

2. Mark Zborowski and Elizabeth Herzog, *Life is with People: The Culture of the Shtetl* (New York, 1952), p. 90.

3. UCC.

4. UCC.

5. Zborowski and Herzog, *Life is with People*, pp. 83, 85.

6. Isaac Babel, "You Must Know Everything," in Isaac Babel, *You Must Know Everything: Stories 1915–1937*, translated by Max Hayward (New York, 1966, 1984), pp. 7–8.

7. Ibid., pp. 11–12.

8. UCC.

9. Simon Dubnow, *History of the Jews in Russia and Poland* (New York, 1920), vol. III, p. 30.

10. William H. Maxwell (superintendent of schools, City of New York), "The Personal Power of the Teacher in Public School Work," *Addresses and Proceedings of the National Education Association* (1908), p. 117.

11. K. Paulding, "Educational Influences: New York," in Charles S. Birnheimer, ed., *The Russian Jew in the United States* (New York, 1905), p. 63.

12. Richard Watson Gilder, "The Kindergarten: An Uplifting Social Influence in the Home and District," *Addresses and Proceedings of the National Education Association* (1903), p. 390.

13. Maxwell, "Personal Power of the Teacher," p. 121.

14. Extract from a lecture delivered by Dr. J. Silverman at Temple Emanu-El (New York City), 1 December 1889, as reported in *The American Hebrew* 41 (6 December 1889): 119.

15. Selection from the transcript of an untitled address given by Jane Addams, *Addresses and Proceedings of the National Education Association* (1908), p. 99.

Chapter 4. The Evil Eye, the X Ray, and the Promise of Good Health

BIBLIOGRAPHICAL NOTE: The background sources for this chapter were quite different from the three preceding. Various articles in Charles S. Bernheimer, ed., *The Russian Jews in the United States* (Philadelphia, 1905) were helpful. So also were: Charles J. Bolduan, "Diabetes—Of Special Interest to Jews," *The Hebrew Medical Journal* 1 (1941): 23–45; Michael M. Davis, Jr., *Immigrant Health and the Community* (New York, 1921); René and Jean Dubos, *The White Plague* (Boston, 1952); Maurice Fishberg, "Health and Sanitation of the Immigrant Jewish Population of New York," *The Menorah* 33 (1902); John Rodman Paul, *A History of Poliomyelitis* (New Haven, Conn., 1971); New York City Board of Health, *A Monograph on the Epidemic of Poliomyelitis in New York City in 1916* (New York, 1917); Edward O. Otis, *Tuberculosis: Its Cause, Cure, Prevention* (New York, 1914); George Rosen, *Preventive Medicine in the United States, 1900–1975* (New York, 1977); George Rosen, *A History of Public Health* (New York, 1975); and Paul Starr, *The Social Transformation of American Medicine* (New York, 1982).

1. AJC.

2. UCC.

3. Gershon Levin, M.D., *The Development of Social Hygiene and Medicine by Jews in the Twentieth Century* (Warsaw, 1939), p. 1. A copy of this pamphlet, published in Yiddish by T.O.Z. (a charitable organization devoted to improving the health of Polish Jews), can be found in the YIVO Institute, New York. It was translated for us by Dina Abramowicz and Helen Rapaport.

4. Ibid., p. 4.

5. From the short story "Schloyme," by Mendl Mocher Sforim (1836–1917), as quoted in Levin, *Development of Social Hygiene*, p. 3.

6. Levin, *Development of Social Hygiene*, p. 11.

7. New York City Board of Health, *A Monograph on the Epidemic of Poliomyelitis in New York City in 1916* (New York, 1917), p. 64.

8. Ibid., p. 59.

9. Charles F. Bolduan, "Diabetes—Of Special Interest to Jews," *Hebrew Medical Journal* 1 (1941): 24.

10. W. Gilman Thompson, M.D., *Practical Dietetics with Special Reference to Diet in Disease* (New York, 1895), p. 648.

11. These data are from George Rosen, *Preventive Medicine in the United States, 1900–1975* (New York, 1977), p. 32.

Chapter 5. "Of Course I Was a Virgin When I Married": Changing Sexual Mores

BIBLIOGRAPHIC NOTE: Aside from the works cited in the references, only a few secondary sources informed this chapter: Peter Gay, *The Bourgeois Experience, Victoria to Freud* (New York, 1982); Linda Gordon, *Woman's Body, Woman's Right: A Social History of Birth Control in America* (New York, 1976); Norman Himes, *Medical History of Contraception* (Baltimore, 1936); David M. Kennedy, *Birth Control in America: The Career of Margaret Sanger* (New Haven, 1970); James Reed, *From Private Vice to Public Virtue: The Birth Control Movement in America* (New York, 1978); and Paul Robinson,

The Modernization of Sex (New York, 1976). The remainder of our reading was in such sex manuals as: Havelock Ellis, *Little Essays of Love & Virtue* (New York, 1922); Winfield Scott Hall, *Instead of Wild Oats* (New York, 1912); E. A. King, *Clean and Strong: A Book for Young Men* (Boston, 1909); Judge Ben B. Lindsey and Wainwright Evans, *The Companionate Marriage* (Garden City, N.Y., 1929); John Rainsford, *What To Tell Your Boy* (Philadelphia, 1918); Margaret Sanger, *What Every Boy and Girl should Know* (n.p., n.d.); Marie Stopes, *Married Love: A New Contribution to the Solution of Sex Difficulties* (London, 1918); D. O. Teasley, *Where Do They Come From? Earth, Sky, Sea, Sun, Moon, Flowers, Fishes, Birds, Animals, Men* (Anderson, Ind., 1917).

1. Mark Zborowski and Elizabeth Herzog, *Life is with People: The Culture of the Shtetl* (New York, 1952), pp. 136–37.

2. Ibid., p. 136.

3. Rabbi Solomon Ganfried, ed., *The Code of Jewish Law–Kitzur Shulchan Aruk*, vol. IV (New York, 1961), p. 15.

4. Ibid., p. 13.

5. Louis M. Epstein, *Sex Laws and Customs in Judaism* (New York, 1948), p. 127.

6. Katherine Bement Davis, *Factors in the Sex Life of Twenty-Two Hundred Women* (New York, 1929), p. *v*.

7. Ibid., p. 5.

8. Della Thompson Lutes, *The Story of Life for Children* (New York, 1914), pp. 56–57.

9. Dorothy Dunbar Bromley and Florence Haxton Britten, *Youth and Sex: A Study of 100 College Students* (New York, 1938).

10. Alfred C. Kinsey et al., *Sexual Behavior in the Human Female* (Philadelphia, 1953), p. 298.

11. H. W. Long, M.D., *Sane Sex and Sane Sex Living* (Chicago, 1919), p. 3.

Chapter 6. "Trapped in the Book": Childbirth and Child Care

BIBLIOGRAPHIC NOTE: In addition to the primary sources cited in the reference notes and forty-five years of *The Ladies' Home Journal* (1900–45), we relied on the following sources for this chapter: Rima Apple, *Mothers and Medicine: A Social History of Infant Feeding* (Madison, Wis., 1987); Daniel Beekman, *The Mechanical Baby: A Popular History of the Theory and Practice of Child Rearing* (Westport, Conn., 1977); Daniel Hine and John Hamer, eds., *The History of Childhood in America* (Chicago, 1977); Janet Silver, *Raising a Baby the Government Way: Letters to the United States Children's Bureau, 1910–1940* (New Brunswick, N.J., 1986); and Dorothy and Richard Wertz, *Lying-In: A History of Childbirth in America* (Boston, 1976). We also consulted many child-rearing manuals from the first decades of this century, including: Arnold Gesell and Frances Ilg, *Infant and Child Care in the Culture of Today* (New York, 1943); Harry Lowenberg, *Care of Infants and Children* (New York, 1938); Miriam Finn Scott, *How to Know Your Child* (Boston, 1915); John B. Watson, *Psychological Care of Infant and Child* (New York, 1928)—as well as several others, cited in the reference notes.

1. U.S. Children's Bureau, *Prenatal Care* (Washington, D.C., 1930 [1913]), p. 4.

2. "At Home in Your Hospital," *Congratulations* (proprietary magazine of Beth-El Hospital, Brooklyn, New York, *c.* 1941), p. 6.

3. S. Josephine Baker, M.D., "Feeding the Baby," *Ladies' Home Journal*, September 1922, p. 23.

4. U.S. Children's Bureau, *Standards and Recommendations for the Hospital Care of Newborn Infants* (Washington, D.C., 1943), p. 6.

5. Baker, "Feeding the Baby."

6. U.S. Children's Bureau, *Standards and Recommendations*, p. 9.

7. Text of an advertisement for Nestlé's Milk Supplement, *Ladies' Home Journal*, July 1925, p. 18.

8. Text of an advertisement for the Davol Rubber Company (makers of rubber nipples) on the inside front cover of *Congratulations* (1941).

9. U.S. Children's Bureau, *Lesson Material in Child Management* (Washington, D.C., 1930). The frontispiece of this booklet explains that the manuscript was prepared by Dr. Blanche C. Will of the Children's Bureau and Dr. D. A. Thom of the Habit Clinics of Boston.

10. Emelyn Lincoln Coolidge, M.D., "The Baby's Nursery Clock," *Ladies' Home Journal*, May 1915, p. 31.

11. Beulah Francis, R.N., "Return to Routine," *Congratulations* (1941), p. 9.

12. Benjamin Spock, M.D., *The Common Sense Book of Baby and Child Care* (New York, 1946), p. 41.

13. U.S. Children's Bureau, *Infant Care* (Washington, D.C., 1935), p. 8.

14. Emmet Holt, M.D., *The Care and Feeding of Children: A Catechism for the Use of Mothers and Children's Nurses*, 14th ed. (Boston, 1929), p. 56.

Chapter 7. *Yiddishkeit*: The Key to Success in America

BIBLIOGRAPHIC NOTE: In addition to works cited in the reference notes and in earlier notes about the history of Jews in America, we have found the following helpful in the preparation of this chapter: Alice Kessler-Harris, *Out to Work: A History of Working Women in America* (New York, 1982); Melvin Dubofsky, *Industrialism and the American Worker, 1865–1920* (Arlington Heights, Ill., 1975); Benjamin Stolberg, *Tailor's Progress* (Garden City, N.Y., 1944); Elias Tcherikower, *The Early Jewish Labor Movement in the United States* (New York, 1961); and William I. Trattner, *Crusade for the Children: A History of the National Child Labor Committee and Child Labor Reform in America* (Chicago, 1970).

1. These data from Thomas Kessner, *The Golden Door: Italian and Jewish Immigrant Mobility in New York City 1880–1915* (New York, 1977), p. 33.

2. Abraham Bisno, deputy inspector of factories for the State of Illinois, as quoted in Charles S. Bernheimer, *The Russian Jew in the United States* (Philadelphia, 1905), p. 135.

3. Data from Kessner, *Golden Door*, p. 33.

4. Beryl Lieb, subsequently a founder of the Cloak Makers Union, as quoted in Melech Epstein, *Jewish Labor in the USA: An Industrial, Political, and Cultural History of the Jewish Labor Movement 1882–1914* (New York, 1969), p. 91.

5. The United States Industrial Commission, 1901, quoted in Arthur Liebman, *Jews and the Left* (New York, 1976), p. 204.

NOTES

Chapter 8. "It's a Free Country": Remaining Jewish in America

BIBLIOGRAPHIC NOTE: In composing this chapter, we profited from the insights of several authors: David Bakan, *The Duality of Human Existence: An Essay on Psychology and Religion* (Chicago, 1966); Joseph L. Blau, *Judaism in America: From Curiosity to Third Faith* (Chicago, 1976); Naomi W. Cohen, *Encounter with Emancipation* (Philadelphia, 1984); Lucy S. Dawidowics, *On Equal Terms: Jews in America* (New York, 1982); Arthur A. Goren, *The American Jews* (Cambridge, Mass., 1982); Calvin Goldschneider and Alan S. Zuckerman, *The Transformation of the Jews* (Chicago, 1984); Milton Himmelfarb, *The Jews of Modernity* (New York, 1973); Charles S. Liebman, *The Ambivalent American Jew: Politics, Religion, and Family in American Jewish Life* (Philadelphia, 1973); and Stuart E. Rosenberg, *The New Jewish Identity in America* (New York, 1985).

1. As quoted in Henry L. Feingold, *Zion in America: The Jewish Experience from Colonial Times to the Present* (New York, 1974), p. 100.

2. Ibid.

3. Henry L. Feingold, *A Midrash on American Jewish History* (Albany, N.Y., 1982), p. 65.

4. Quoted in Milton Himmelfarb, *The Jews of Modernity* (New York, 1973), p. 28.

5. Quoted in Irving Howe, *World of Our Fathers: The Journey of the East European Jews to America and the Life They Found and Made* (New York, 1976), p. 106.

Credits

Excerpts on page 81 from "You Must Know Everything" by Isaac Babel copyright © 1969 by Nathalie Babel. Reprinted by permission of Farrar, Straus & Giroux, Inc.

Frontispiece reproduced by permission of the Harvard College Library.

The photographs on pages 15 and 29 are reprinted by permission of *The Jewish Daily Forward*.

The photographs on pages 47 and 179 are reproduced from the private collection of Sylva Bulwer.

The photographs on pages 59, 215, and 233 are reproduced courtesy of the Lewis W. Hine Collection, U.S. History, Local History, and Genealogy, The New York Public Library, Astor, Lenox, and Tilden Foundations.

The photograph on page 77 is reproduced by permission of the Archives of the YIVO Institute for Jewish Research.

The photograph on page 95 is reprinted courtesy of the Museum of the City of New York.

The photograph on page 133 is reproduced from Sigard A. Knopf, *Tuberculosis* (1909).

The handbill on page 163 is reprinted courtesy of the Library of Congress.

The illustration on page 195 copyright © 1915, Meredith Corporation. All rights reserved. Reprinted from *Ladies' Home Journal* magazine.

The photograph on page 255 is reproduced by permission of the American Jewish Archives, Cincinnati Campus, Hebrew Union College, Jewish Institute of Religion.

The photograph on page 259 is reproduced by permission of the photographer, Arnold Eagle.

The photograph on page 279 has been reproduced from a private collection.

Index

295

INDEX

INDEX

Nail cutting, 58, 151, 152

Name changing, *see* Evil Eye

National Research Council, 178

Nazis, 6*n*, 9*n*, 234, 264, 284–85

Networking, 212

Newspapers, 69, 236–37; and Progressive reform, 43

New York City, 40, 45, 49–50, 63, 85, 96, 135, 178, 214, 216; polio epidemic in, in 1916, 113, 123–32

New York City Bureau of Child Hygiene, 182

New York Times, 126, 130

Nicholas II, Czar, 22–23, 27–28, 80, 84

Nursery schools, demonstration, 178

Obstetrics, 184

Odessa, 5, 60, 81, 89, 111, 112, 115

Office of War Information, 244

Old World, *see* Eastern European Jews

Orgasm, 147, 153, 172

Orientalism, 103

Overcrowding, 44–46, 86, 137, 138

"Oyfn Pripitshik" ("In the Fireplace"), 9–10

Oyfshtelbetl, defined, 45

Pale of Jewish settlement, 84

Parent-child relationships: and Americanization process, 72–73, 99, 104–5, 108; and religious observance, 266–67, 269–70; and schedules for babies, 198–209; secular education as strain on, 82, 83; and sexual ignorance, 155–56; and sexual mores, 167–69; and teachers, 89–91, 96, 98, 104–5; *see also* Child-rearing practices

Parent education, 180

Parents' Magazine, 178, 180, 193, 202

Parent-Teacher Association, 180

Parks and playgrounds, 67–68, 208

Passivity, 89–91

Passover, 12, 141, 272

Pasteur, Louis, 58, 109

Payess, 83–84, 254; defined, 82

Pedagogy, 75, 76, 78, 86–88, 270; *see also* Education

Penicillin, 134, 138

Philadelphia, 45, 63, 86, 112, 178, 214, 224, 225, 237, 283

Philanthropists, 178

Phylacteries, 83*n*, 272; *see also* Tefillin

Physical abuse: by parents, 91, 180–81; by teachers, 75, 76, 87–88, 93

Physicians, 111, 114, 263; in the age of experts, 187–94; as Jewish cultural heroes, 110; professional life of, 234–36; training of, 85, 234–35; *see also* Medical revolution

Piecework, 214, 216–17, 218, 224

Pishe, defined, 65

Plumbing, 57–64

Pneumonia, 114–15, 123, 132, 134, 137, 143

Pogroms, 53, 224, 234, 251; "blood libel" as excuse for, 13; impact of, 26–38, 85; Jewish inns as breeding place of, 22

Poland, 3, 7, 17, 18–21, 22, 28, 30, 31–32, 34, 49, 62, 78, 85, 86, 146, 149, 206, 212, 247, 251

Polio, 108, 110, 115, 143, 238; 1916 epidemic of, 113, 123–32

Political activism, 5, 282

Political bosses, 43

Pomeshov, defined, 61

Poverty: in Eastern Europe, 5, 18, 19, 21, 33, 44, 251; and the immigrant experience, 42, 45, 56, 167, 176, 210, 236

Poznanski, Bustav, 254

Pregnancy, 147, 149–50; in the age of the experts, 183–84, 185; and sexual ignorance, 156, 165; and sexual mores, 167, 170, 171; *see also* Abortion; Birth control; Childbirth

Premarital sex, *see* Sexual mores

Prenatal care, 181, 184

Pripitshik, defined, 9

301

INDEX